CREATING HEALTHY
NEIGHBORHOODS

EVIDENCE-BASED PLANNING AND DESIGN STRATEGIES

ANN FORSYTH | EMILY SALOMON | LAURA SMEAD

CREATING HEALTHY
NEIGHBORHOODS

EVIDENCE-BASED PLANNING AND DESIGN STRATEGIES

Contents

List of Figures

List of Tables

Acknowledgments

Books such as this reflect many activities and multiple collaborations. This work is one of the outputs of the Health and Places Initiative (HAPI), a project to examine how health is affected by the built environment. Interactions with Peter Rowe, Har Ye Kan, David Mah, and Leire Ascensio Villoria, who were working on companion volumes, provided extremely useful input. Katherine Crewe, Amanda Johnson Ashley, and Aly Pennucci reviewed the draft manuscript providing many helpful comments.

The three authors drafted tables, created diagrams, and developed charts. Ann Forsyth took most of the photos, including the cover images. Yannis Orfanos most ably and with good spirits converted graphics into a more consistent and engaging format, helped by Antara Tandon. Laura Smead took a lead in layout and provided the photo of a little girl at a drinking fountain on page 149. Emily Salomon took the lead in working out numerous details.

This manual also draws on research briefs synthesizing research on the connections between health and tools for health assessment, developed through HAPI and edited by the three authors in various combinations. Chuan Hao (Alex) Chen, Joyce Lee, Stephany Lin, Yvonne Mwangi, Yannis Orfanos, and Tim Czerwienski played important roles related to research assistance, writing, and reviewing of those briefs and health assessments. A wider team of terrific HAPI research assistants worked on additional aspects of these resources: Heidi Youngha Cho, Sang Cho, Nomin Jagdagdorj, Lydia Gaby, Joy Jing, Wei Li, Cara Michell, John McCartin, Weishun Xu, and Dingliang Yang.

Several others reviewed background materials or helped us test the health impact assessments including ChengHe Guan, Andreas Georgoulias, Elizabeth Hamin, Patrick Harris, María Luisa Gómez Jiménez, Kevin Krizek, YingYing Lu, Rebecca Miles, Anna Ricklin, Joyce Rosenthal, Lisa Schweitzer, Nancy Wells, and Yifan Yu.

Major funding for this research project was provided by the Charoen Pokphand Group Co. Ltd. We thank its representative Naree Phinyawatana for extremely helpful feedback. At the American Planning Association's Planners Press, Camille Fink and two reviewers provided extremely helpful comments and advice.

Introduction

In the coming decades, the world's population will grow substantially reaching around 9.6 billion by 2050.[1] Almost all of these additional people will live in towns and cities. How can the neighborhoods and districts people live, work, and socialize in be made healthier? What role can physical planning and design play?

Creating Healthy Neighborhoods: Evidence-Based Planning and Design Strategies is a guide for this practice, covering both the process and substance of making places healthier.

This book creates an evidence-based approach to both the process and substance of making healthier places.

Creating Healthy Places focuses on health because this is a fundamental aspect of human quality of life and well-being. It emphasizes the neighborhood and district scale of development because such places are where people live out their daily existence, and they are important building blocks of larger urban places.

Research, Health, Well-being, and Place

Planners, designers, civic leaders, and activists seeking to change existing neighborhoods and districts or to revise proposals to make them healthier face a complex challenge. They need to consider a variety of topics relevant to health—from air quality to social interaction—and scales—from the blocks that make up the district to the town or city the blocks are embedded in. They also need to know the limits of how much the physical neighborhood environment can affect health. How much does a place matter compared with other sources of health and healthy behaviors from biology to culture? Healthy built environments are as much about how a place is used, maintained, and priced as they are about physical

development and redevelopment. Policies matter. A beautiful play area that is too expensive to use is a visual amenity only.

This book helps planners, urban designers, activists, and public officials gain access to and assess the evidence base on healthy places, largely produced by other fields. Those in public health will be familiar with many of the ideas covered in the book. However, it provides insights into how to engage with planning, development, and redevelopment activities focused on neighborhoods and districts.

Making the leap from research to action can be tricky, however. There are three main reasons:

- In some topical areas there is a great deal of research that needs to be evaluated. Unfortunately it is often highly specific, requiring much sorting and analysis to find the big picture. This is the case even when only considering one scale, that of the neighborhood or district of a few hundred to a few thousand people or few hectares to a few hundred hectares or acres. While there may be summaries of the research, they do not necessarily specify actions.

- In addition, there will never be research on everything of importance as there is so much environmental variation. So some kind of bridge is needed between theory and practice.

- Finally, much work on the connections between health and place focuses on the substance of the connections between health and built environments.[2] To actually make change to places requires knowledge of both—process and substance. Further, the process is complex from prioritizing health issues and engaging stakeholders to finding the right tools for incorporating health into plans and programs.

This handbook bridges this gap by doing three things: synthesizing and adapting research findings, proposing how to make informed decisions in the absence of research, and embedding this in a health-informed planning process.

We use guidance based on research findings where those are available. However, because there are so many domains in which health and place are connected that have not been researched, we fill those gaps with guidance based on frameworks about how health and place are related. In addition, some aspects of making healthier places—the processes of developing proposals and implementing good ideas—are not unique to health but rather draw on a larger base of research evidence and professional experience.

This book creates an evidence-based approach to both the process and substance of making healthier places, taking a broadly international perspective. It draws on health research, conceptual frameworks about how health should matter, and the body of professional and research knowledge about the planning and design process. Overall, making healthy neighborhoods and districts is both a set of methods and products that build upon other aspects of neighborhood planning and design to create a rich and comprehensive approach to the quality of place.

This, of course, raises the issue of what is health. As we describe later, health is a topic of enduring interest that predates fields and professions, and interests

A broad view of health includes physical, mental, social, and possibly spiritual well-being.

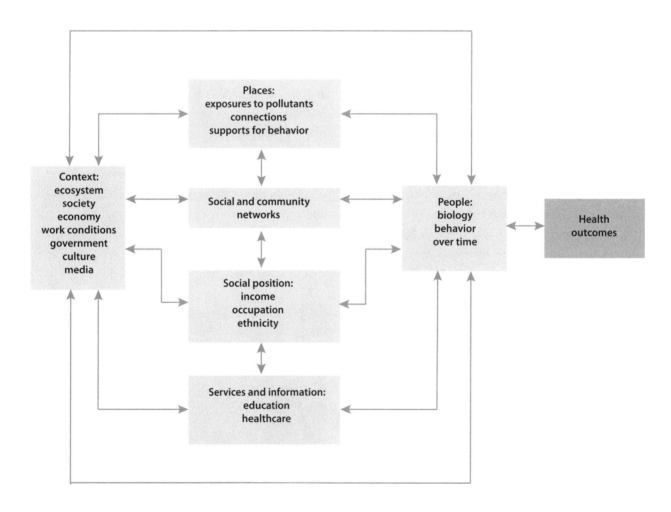

Figure 1. How health, people, places, and wider context are linked over time

Health outcomes are related to biological and behavioral factors, and the context—which includes physical spaces, wider social influences, and change over time. The arrows illustrate the complex relationship between these elements.

Source: Synthesis of materials in this book with some adaptation from UCL Institute of Health Equity 2014

most people in a way few other issues do. While it can be seen narrowly as an absence of disease, those in public health typically see it as much broader—about physical, mental, and social well-being.[3] Some would add spiritual well-being as well. As such, health deals with issues of disease, disability, and death, but it is cast in larger terms.

Health and Place over Time

Health is connected to place through a number of facets. Figure 1 shows generally how health outcomes relate to biology, behavior, and context over time. First, a person's biology (gender, heritage, and age) affects health, and these factors interact with behaviors over decades.

Beyond the individual is the larger context, of which places such as neighborhoods and districts are a part. Places—at varying scales, from the room to the region—expose the biological person to various hazards either now or over time. These include harmful contaminants and hazards (from toxic chemicals to insect-borne diseases), irritants (like pollen), and events (for example, floods). Some of these are the direct or indirect result of human activity. But others—like earthquakes—are natural. These affect a person's biology and behaviors to create health outcomes like diseases or disabilities.

The design of a local environment may support healthy behavior, making it interesting, fun, or easy. Examples include opportunities to eat well and exercise, to achieve mental health benefits from contact with nature, or to live in a safe environment. Design can also make unhealthy behavior inconvenient, expensive, or difficult.

Finally, places may provide access at varying levels to the resources for leading a healthier life, such as physical access to employment, healthcare, shopping, or social connections, for persons of all abilities. It should be noted that not all connections are positive. Some let people indulge in unhealthy behaviors and some social networks are not health promoting, but rather the reverse.

Of course, the place itself is only part of the picture and patterns of use, only partly determined by the detailed specifics of a place, also play a key role. One's social position—occupation, income, education, and the like—as well as wider community networks is crucially important for health. All these are set in a wider context from the economy and the wider media environment to specific policies and programs that shape places and health behaviors and outcomes. Physical places have a role, but there is a lot more happening.

A Trilogy of Investigations and Proposals

This book is one of a set of three books coming from a project at the Harvard University Graduate School of Design, the Health and Places Initiative (HAPI), investigating connections between health and urban environments. Each looks at part of this picture. This book provides a framework for connecting health and place, proposing actions for those planning and designing at the neighborhood and urban scale in middle- and high-income countries. It is the most practice-oriented of the three.

Urban Communities in China: Concepts, Contexts, and Well-Being, by Peter Rowe, Har Ye Kan, and Ann Forsyth, uses a broad health lens to investigate a range of typical residential areas in four cities in China, built or redeveloped in recent decades. China is of interest because it has recently been an area of substantial urban growth and in the near future faces a challenging transition to an aging population. *Urban Communities in China* focuses on ordinary life as it currently exists.

The third book, *Life-Styled: Health and Place,* edited by Leire Asensio-Villoria and David Mah, is a more speculative work using the language of architecture and landscape architecture. It investigates how considering health can trigger design ideas, yielding novelty in design, and explores how computational design—which creates many iterations of a design—can be used as research, not just as a way of developing stylistically intriguing options.

All three books draw on previous HAPI work synthesizing research on the connections between health and place—tools called research briefs—and developing tools for health assessment including checklists and participatory formats. These resources, available for free online, provide the common ground for the three investigations.[4]

Several fundamental ideas inform all three works:

- Research can inform design and planning. A key issue is to look at a balance of evidence from multiple studies.
- Health is a useful lens for investigating urban design and planning issues and can be a trigger for imagining better places.
- While environments are important, there are many other contributors to health from biology and behavior to culture and economics. So humility is needed about how much of a difference a physical place can make.
- There are many aspects of health that are somewhat universal, particularly more physical reactions to exposures such as air pollution. Others are deeply intertwined with an individual's personal trajectory, behaviors, social networks, education, economic situation, and culture.
- Because the issue of an aging population is so large and unprecedented, a key focus is healthy design for longevity.

The three books are not the same, however. They differ in how much they value novelty over reliability, expertise over participation, and quantifiable over more qualitative aspects of health. They also vary in terms of interest in current versus proposed environments, and building versus urban scale. In doing this, they represent a range of approaches across the environmental design disciplines of architecture, landscape architecture, urban planning, and urban design.

As global population growth continues and then slows later in this century, some cities will still grow but others will shrink and the population will generally age.

This guidebook examines how to make healthier urban neighborhoods and districts and proposes a new way of thinking, a new lens, to shape ideas about what makes a healthy place and how to achieve it.

Planning and Design for a Changing World—Transitions

For at least two centuries people have been moving in large numbers to villages, towns, and cities—urban places—where they find work, education, and cultural opportunities. Increasingly an urban life is the only one people have ever experienced. Urban areas have sometimes been places where people were healthier than in rural ones, and sometimes sicker. Over time, however, the balance has tipped toward urban areas being places where lives are longer and less plagued by illness. This is not at all uniform, however. The landscape of disease is also changing, generally from contagious to chronic diseases, though with some complicated new threats.

The urban world in 2050 will also be different to that of today. Even more people, up to about 66 percent of the world's population, will live in urban areas of various sizes.[5] Of course some of those urban areas are quite small, a few thousand people, with currently half the world's urban population in urban areas under 500,000.[6] These smaller cities are important. As global population growth continues and then slows later in this century, some cities will still grow but others will shrink, and the population will generally age. In 1950 5.2 percent of the population was over 65, in 2000 this jumped to 6.9 percent, and by 2050 and 2100 it is projected to increase to 15.9 and 24.4 percent, respectively.[7]

And this is just the start. Environmental changes of various sorts will continue. Poverty will be a continuing problem for many, and inequality will raise other issues. New urban technologies will emerge—particularly in the areas of communication and mobility. Some people will benefit from these technologies but not all.[8] In short, there will be much urban growth in coming decades—giving opportunities for building healthier places. However, even in areas with little growth, rebuilding will occur to evolve with shifts in demographic composition, incomes, natural systems, and technologies.

So the landscapes of both urban places and health are in transition, with implications for how health, wellness, and environments interact. This is an opportune time to explore these interactions. After a decade or so of renewed interest in how health and place are connected, there has been a great deal of progress made: research completed, summaries made, tools developed, case studies prepared, evaluations completed. This work is increasingly international.

How to Read this Book

This book takes health, urbanization, demographic, and environmental challenges and changes as a starting point, providing an overall framework for organizing the various tools, topics, and proposals. It communicates to planners, policy makers, and civic leaders how a health lens can help them understand and improve places, plans, and projects. It does this in a number of overlapping ways structured around a series of principles, propositions, and actions. They deal both with the process of creating a healthier

place and the substance of what that involves. They were developed by reviewing a very broad literature on healthy places and healthy planning processes. Principles include the following:

Principle 1. Importance: Examine how much health may matter in this neighborhood or district. The first principle is preparing to do the work by doing enough investigation to figure out if health is an issue of concern in a neighborhood or district, identifying what kinds of health concerns are raised, and considering if anything is likely to be done from an assessment.

Principle 2. Balance: Make healthier places by balancing physical changes with other interventions to appeal to different kinds of people. This is about understanding how change occurs, particularly that big changes need to have many strategies happening all at once, make informed trade-offs, and demonstrate an understanding of scale and the pathways from environments to health.

Principle 3. Vulnerability: Plan and design for those with the most health vulnerabilities and fewest resources for making healthy choices. The aim is to help undo disparities in how long people live and how healthy they are with a particular focus on the young, the old, those with disabilities, and those who are disenfranchised, such as refugees, marginalized ethnic groups, and those with low incomes.

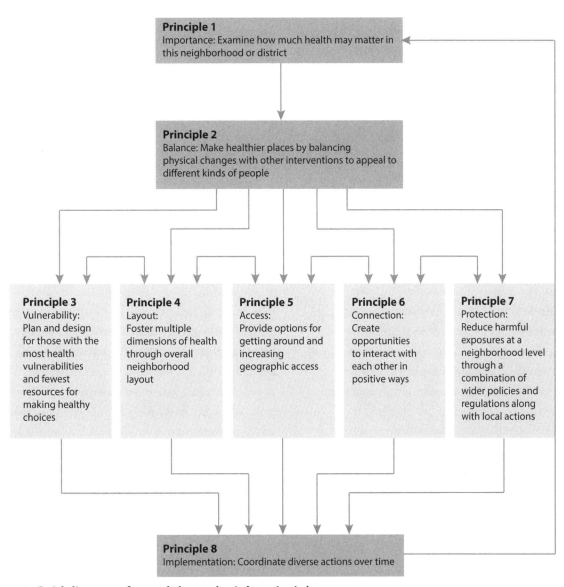

Figure 2. Guidelines are framed through eight principles

The framework includes the process of creating healthier places (dark gray) and the components of such places (light gray).

Source: Developed by authors

Principle 4. Layout: Foster multiple dimensions of health through overall neighborhood layout. This area focuses on the big moves in setting out a neighborhood or district in terms of the locations of activities, distribution of people, the street and path configurations, and green space arrangements.

Principle 5. Access: Provide options for getting around and increasing geographic access. Meeting the mobility and geographic accessibility needs of an entire district or neighborhood is a challenge, so the key is to provide options.

Principle 6. Connection: Create opportunities to interact with each other in positive ways. Neighborhood planning and design can support and supplement the common interests, households and family ties, and events that bring people together; can increase people's sense of belonging in their communities; and enhance informal control of anti-social activities.

Principle 7. Protection: Reduce harmful exposures at a neighborhood level through a combination of wider policies and regulations along with local actions. Reducing harmful exposures is a basic principle of healthy planning—reducing contaminants or hazards at the source, buffering people from exposure, and skillfully designing to mitigate problems.

Principle 8. Implementation: Coordinate diverse actions over time. Implementation is key. Large changes in how environments can support health require multiple strategies. These are not just changes to physical places but to how people use those places.

Principles 1, 2, and 8 address issues that any planning and design process needs to go through, though modified with an eye to how health can make a difference. Principles 3 through 7 draw on the evolving base of research on the connections between health and place related to issues such as urban form, housing, transportation, open space, and infrastructure.

These are operationalized through **20 more specific propositions and 83 action**s that reflect key findings from our review of research. The principles engage larger questions and provide an overall framework for thinking about an issue and connections to other ideas and propositions; the propositions identify more specific areas of intervention related to the preceding principle; and the actions specify what to do. They can be used in two types of situations—creating a new neighborhood or district or retrofitting an older one.

Principles 1, 2, and 8 do not provide a whole planning process but point to how to make health relevant in such a process. They, and the associated propositions, refer to evidence—from experience and academic studies—of implementing complex proposals.

Principles 3 through 6 are based on a different body of evidence, research on the associations between health and place. As was noted earlier, there will never be compete research on all possible variations of places and their inhabitants and where research is missing, we provide conceptual frameworks that build logically from the research base to propose a wider set of solutions. Of course they are interconnected.

Propositions take one of two standard formats. The propositions following Principles 1, 2, and 8 provide the proposition, a clarifying statement, a discussion about how this concept works, specific actions, and connections to other propositions and ideas. Propositions within Principles 3 through 7 include evidence from health and place research, but they also draw on research about the process of planning and design. The connections found at the end of each proposition, and at the end of the introduction to each principle, help readers navigate to other relevant parts of the manual. They list topics that provide background or could allow readers to explore further. Not all possible connections are listed, but those that are listed provide a starting point for exploring linkages between topics.

The two appendices are key. Appendix A includes a complete checklist of all principles, propositions, and actions. Appendix B provides a matrix of specific health topics (e.g., air quality, water quality, social capital) and where they are referenced in the text. A glossary at the end of this introduction defines key terms.

Figure 3. How those in public health can use this book

This book is aimed at planners, urban designers, developers, residents, and civic leaders interested in specific neighborhoods and districts—they are living in them, planning them, and doing projects in them. They start with specific places, and they ask how health may matter.

Public health professionals typically work with populations such as children or those with asthma. Places are settings that expose people to potential health risks and benefits. They may need to go through a long process to decide on which places are key to their work. They start with health issues and ask how and which places may matter.

Given these differences in starting points, public health professionals can use this book to understand how others engage with health issues in neighborhoods. They could also use it to understand specific places, creating a short list of potential neighborhoods using a community health needs assessment (see health assessment in the Glossary) and then focusing in where they are likely to make a difference.

This book helps navigate the research landscape, sorting through evidence and providing clear frameworks linking health and place.

Action Evidence

In each case, actions are classified in terms of their level of certainty:

◆ The action recommendation comes directly from research evidence.

❖ The action recommendation is informed by research.

◇ The action is general good practice, often termed an emerging or promising practice in public health. These will not hurt but, in part because of the topic they relate to, there is not as much evidence as those in the other categories.

The action classification helps experienced planners understand which approaches may be strongly grounded in evidence versus basic good planning. For new planners, non-planner professionals, and community members, they provide an accessible checklist of healthy planning and urban design issues.

Using Research: Evidence-Based Practice in Making Better Neighborhoods

Because what it means to be healthy, well, or whole is so personal, intuitions and experiences are important guides providing compelling insights. But they can also be misleading. It may be commonsense that eating a local fish is a healthy thing to do, except when that fish comes from a polluted waterbody. For a designer, sensitized to the importance of space, it may be clear that a physical public space is needed to make social connections—except that for many people such connections are built or maintained in the buildings of faith communities, in the homes of extended family members, or online.

This is where the move to evidence-based practice—practice informed by research—has a role. It can place commonsense in context, identify causes beyond the obvious, and caution against simple solutions. But of course places—particularly at the urban scale of the block, district, town, and metropolis—are extremely complex, multidimensional, and evolving. There is not and never will be research that can deal with all possible situations. So to make places that promote health, planners and designers need to make leaps of imagination.

This is more complex than it appears. Even where the local environment affects human health and well-being, the exact character of that effect may be difficult to figure out. This is a major reason for creating this book: to navigate the gap between research findings and practice. There are a number of ways in which this gap occurs.

Research availability dilemma

A first issue is the uneven availability of research. As we note, this was a key impetus for writing this book. Potential problems related to research availability are diverse:

- Some topics have a great deal of readily available and relevant research about the effects of environments on health, and other topics have far less. This has to do with patterns of funding, the difficulty of the research, and histories of academic fields. So it is far easier to learn about physical activity, where research has been well funded, than homelessness, for example, where it has not.
- Where there is a great deal of research, considerable effort is required to understand the overall balance of findings. Systematic reviews that carefully compare findings are one source for such overviews, but they are not available for all areas. They may also focus narrowly on specific kinds of studies—like randomized controlled trials—that are not typically available in areas related to urban and neighborhood effects on health. Other kinds of reviews and individual studies fill part of the gap but need to be carefully evaluated.
- Where there is not much research, it can be difficult to find relevant work. In those cases one has to extrapolate from what is known.
- All this is shaped by the problem of publication bias, where studies that find associations between health, wellness, and places are more likely to be published than those that do not. This is because they are more interesting to write, and journal editors and reviewers find them more interesting to review.[9]
- Finally, even if research is available, it is often inaccessible to those outside large institutions as it requires costly subscriptions. So the research that practitioners can obtain may be a very partial list.

Books such as this can help navigate this landscape sorting through evidence and providing clear frameworks linking health and place.

The complicated relationship between health and place

A second issue is the very different pathways from environmental features to health outcomes, which are evident in the various propositions in this book.

Consciousness: Some health outcomes involve a largely involuntary reaction, such as to toxic exposure where the effect on health and well-being is relatively straightforward. Others, however, are deeply affected by perceptions, beliefs, and voluntary behaviors. For example, two people living in the same environment might engage in very different levels of outdoor walking and other exercise related to their perceptions of crime in the area or what is appropriate weather for outdoor activity.

Particularity: Some health outcomes are more universal, such as reactions to chemicals, but others are more influenced by cultural or age differences. Even toxic exposures will have different effects related to age, pre-existing conditions, and individual biology.

Significance and magnitude: Some effects of place on health found in the research are statistically significant but very small in magnitude. This can happen in very large studies where the large sample size means small effects can be detected. Given all the other causes of health, the importance of specific causes can be extremely modest—although if many people are affected, effects on the whole population may be important.

Likelihood: Some aspects of place may have a large effect on health in terms of magnitude, but the effect may be less certain or only apply in particular situations. Examples include flooding or earthquakes.

Other aspects may have a small effect on many people that is more certain—for example, community noise leading to disturbed work patterns. Both need to be considered but in different ways.

Time: Some exposures and events affect people's health very quickly and obviously, and others may only appear over a very long period. It can be very difficult to figure out a cause of something that emerges over decades, and many effects of environment and health are most important in childhood. Ellen et al. talk about the process of "'weathering,' whereby the accumulated stress, lower environmental quality, and limited resources of poorer communities, experienced over many years, erodes the health of residents in ways that make them more vulnerable to mortality from any given disease."[10] This makes it imperative to include the dimension of time in any framework.

Space: Finally, in contemporary society people inhabit more than one place over a day, week, year, and lifespan. As is shown in Figure 4, this makes it complicated or researchers to figure out the effects of any one particular space on health, particularly with conditions that only emerge over time.

The interplay between research, expert knowledge, and local knowledge

A final issue is the interplay between research and other forms of knowledge commonly used in creating local environments.

Local knowledge, such as the wisdom of residents, is crucial. It can tap into key values about health and well-being, identify important ways places are used, and provide a base of ideas for improving places in relevant ways. It can also be wrong—for example, underestimating contaminants in a river or overestimating the problems from a new business. This knowledge can be a problem for the locals if it means they are engaging in less than healthy activities.

In turn, professional judgment relies on prior training, experiences with similar projects, and knowledge of other places. Health research has little to say about the process or planning and design idea generation or implementation, and such expertise is key in filling that gap. However, such knowledge has not always been informed by a rigorous understanding of health, let alone the most recent research. It can be easy to dip into research studies that confirm one's intuition but may not actually represent the balance of evidence.[11] A path forward is to carefully consider all three types of knowledge—local, expert, and research.

It should be clear by now that undertaking evidence-based neighborhood planning and design is not simple, but neither is it impossible. Drawing on research, and logical frameworks to fill in the gaps, much can be done to make places healthier:

- A first set of strategies is to consider how to minimize exposures to hazards such as waterborne diseases, contaminated air, or excessive noise.

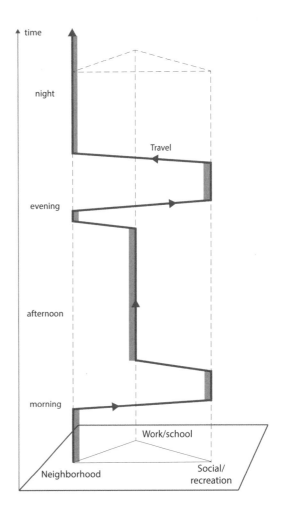

Figure 4. TIme-geography of daily life

Within a single day, people travel to many places and engage in multiple activities, complicating the understanding of how places affect health outcomes.

Source: Developed by authors

Carefully consider three types of knowledge—local, expert, and research.

- Drawing on evidence about the connection between health and place, where it is known, places can be planned to support healthy behaviors and connect people to resources.
- Finally, they are planned in the context of the wider geography and longer term beyond the immediate here and now of neighborhood and district life.

Examples of Healthy Places

How might health be incorporated in specific places? This involves a place performing well in the current period but also over time, for health-related concerns but also in relation to wider concepts of quality of life.

One example is where places have one purpose when built but can age gracefully beyond their initial program. A classic example is classical pleasure ground parks, large green spaces with lawns, trees, and meandering paths.[12] Some nineteenth- and early twentieth-century versions may have been initially designed with the idea of fostering more middle-class behavior among workers.[13] However, over a century or more, such types of parks have

become the setting for many different kinds of behaviors beyond those initially intended, many of them health promoting. These include providing spaces for active sports, social gatherings, and individuals experiencing the restorative aspects of nature. Where there have been problems—such as violent crime in parts with poor visibility—the better places have provoked community networks to solve the problems for the parks and beyond. Such non-physical components—organizations, programs, and policies—are key to successful places.[14]

A related strategy is to have places that nudge healthy behavior in multiple ways, or provide opportunities for people to do healthy things. Many universities make access to campus easy by cycling or walking, with dedicated bicycle and pedestrian paths. They combine pricing and physical design to make driving and parking expensive in both time and money.

But some places may only support healthier behaviors for certain people in certain kinds of places and periods. Planning and design have a history of models that created livable places in one context but tragic environments elsewhere. A high-rise tower can be a positive home environment when well-located units are big enough and residents have resources to get out and about. They may not work so well for large households in cramped quarters in buildings that lack maintenance. A "climb-the-stairs" campaign that promotes beautiful stairs as a focal point for socializing and physical activity may make those in wheelchairs seem like second class citizens, again.

Designs that separate cars from pedestrians and connect destinations along leafy paths (for example, Radburn-style superblocks) may promote traffic safety and community connections in a natural setting. However, ill-maintained spaces can provoke fear.[15]

Cumbernauld in Scotland provides a specific example of Radburn-style planning, dating from the 1950s and 1960s. Its very high-density, award-winning layout almost completely separated people from cars, dramatically decreasing accident rates to under one quarter of the national average in early years. In the core areas, the pedestrian paths are completely continuous with high-quality landscaping and modern architecture.

Over time, however, some of the pedestrian paths faced safety problems (related to crime) that offset the solutions the paths aimed to address (related to traffic). Although surveys in the 1990s found most people were fairly satisfied with life in the new town, vandalism and crime were concerns.[16] While the story is complex—including some problems in privatizing the largely public housing—it does demonstrate how well-intentioned innovations do not always work.

Ponds and lush vegetation offer a restorative setting for people to experience nature, even in a dense, urban area.

Walking paths enable friends to socialize and engage in physical activity.

Youth sports teams take advantage of field space in a neighborhood park.

Figure 5. A pleasure ground style of park featuring lawns and scattered trees
While such parks were created for one set of purposes, over time they have often been reused for different activities.

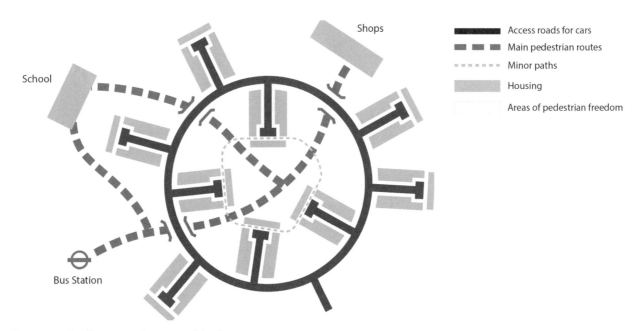

Figure 6. Radburn-style super blocks

This classic Radburn-style neighborhood emphasizes separation between pedestrians and motor vehicles. Homes face a continuous green space so people can walk to major destinations without crossing a road. Such designs have been successful in some locations, but less so in others.

Source: Adapted from United Kingdom Ministry of Transport (1963)

Interventions beyond Place— Combining Types of Initiatives

Intervening in the built environment alone cannot be the sole solution to address health concerns. Approaches should combine a sensitivity to both social and physical aspects of place, and this involves not only changing place but changing relevant policies, programs, and organizations (see Table 1).

One of the book's key arguments is that to make big changes, or to halt large trends, one needs to use many strategies at once—changing physical places, implementing policies that affect how they are used, developing programs, and altering pricing to tip the balance toward creating environments that support positive behaviors, minimize harmful exposures, and enhance healthy connections.

The Health in All Policies (HiAP) approach, described in the following glossary, uses collaboration among agencies, community groups, businesses, and nongovernmental groups to incorporate

Figure 7. Radburn-style planning in Cumbernauld, Scotland

Motor vehicles and cars travel on separate routes in Cumbernauld. In the early years of the development, this layout achieved substantial gains in pedestrian safety. In the 1990s, vandalism and crime became concerns, especially along pedestrian pathways.

Radburn, New Jersey, was founded in 1929 to follow the principles of the Garden City movement in England, with pedestrian paths almost entirely separated from roads.

health-related aims and actions in a variety of areas from transportation to immigration. There are several different tools for doing this work of making places healthier, listed in Table 1.

Overall the aim of the book is to provide a balance between a broad sense of why creating healthy places

matters, evidence–based advice about how to create healthier places at the neighborhood or district scale, and guidance about the process of making changes in neighborhood environments.

Use many strategies at once to tip the balance toward creating healthy environments.

Table 1. Approaches to intervening in places

Approach	Example
Coordinating, educating, and raising awareness	• WHO Healthy Cities and Age-friendly Communities • Health in All Policies • Place-based age-service cooperatives
Assessing health impacts	• Comprehensive approaches (health impact assessment) • One dimension at a time (e.g. food assessment)
Making regulations and policies	• Complete streets ordinances • Pedestrian zoning overlays • Water protection regulations
Proposing places	• Healthy neighborhood plans • Healthy transportation plans
Building physical places	• Single issue such as bike paths • Comprehensive such as new neighborhoods or towns
Using places differently	• Temporary uses (e.g. cyclovia) • Changed uses (e.g. candy store to bike repair)

Sources: Developed by the authors

Glossary

A number of words have specific meanings in health, planning, or design but are used more informally in common speech or by other professions. We explain how we use these words in this book and how to tell the specific meaning from the context. Where we refer to another word in the glossary in an entry, we mark this with an *.

Accessibility: "At its simplest, the ease with which one place can be reached by another."[17] This is related to distance, time, cost, and social barriers and may be measured to a specific destinations or destinations more generally (e.g. access to healthcare facilities). With the rise of new forms of communication accessibility is increasingly distinguished from (geographical) mobility* or ease of movement. One can have access to important resources without being mobile.

Active travel or transportation: Forms of transport that require physical activity, most commonly walking and cycling.[18] The term active travel is most commonly used to refer to all forms (walking, cycling, skiing, etc.); it may also be called physical activity for transport. More specific forms of active transport may be called walking for transport, cycling for transport, and the like. Active travel is a form of non-motorized transport but this is a larger category, and included forms that are not active e.g. riding in a horse-drawn cart.

Activity: This has several uses including physical activity and social activity. In work on mixed use we use it to describe the activities happening in places that are destinations for trips. It is related to activity-based models in transport that "work on the premise that travel demand is derived from the activities that people undertake."[19]

Affordable housing: While there are specific definitions for various cities and countries, broadly this refers lower income people being able to spend a manageable proportion of their income on housing (rent, mortgages, maintenance, and utilities). This often requires government action—providing housing directly, helping support nongovernmental developers, providing rent subsidies, helping lower income first home buyers, providing incentives for private developers to build for a lower-income market, or creating regulations to support innovations.

Cause: "An event, such as a change in one variable, that produces another event, such as a change in another variable."[20] While it sounds straightforward it can be very difficult to precisely identify causes in research on the relationship between health and place because there can be many plausible causes of a health related outcome only some of which can be measured at a particular time. Further, many effects have multiple causes. Much of the research in this area can only find associations which may be causes, but may not.

Density: Is the number of things (people, houses, trees, etc.) in an area. Densities can be measured at different scales from the site to the region; gross densities include the entire land area in calculations and net densities exclude certain components (e.g. parks or industrial areas). This makes it hard to compare density figures. Density is often confused with related terms such as crowding, sometimes called interior density, which is a perception of there being too many people in a space; and building bulk and site coverage which are related to the size of a building on the site.[21]

Destination: A place someone is going to. In the context of mixed-use development this is often an activity generator like a shopping area, workplace, or key recreational site.

District: This is an area akin to a neighborhood but not necessarily residential in character as in an industrial or commercial district. While focused on residential and mixed-use neighborhoods most of the guidelines in this book also apply to districts.

Environment: When people say the environment deeply affects health they do not necessarily mean the environment of neighborhoods, parks, blocks, and streets but planners and designers may mistakenly think they do. The environment is at its base a wider context—it can range from the physical spaces around us to less tangible environments such as media, culture, or family. Planning and design distinguish between the built environment (shaped by people and including landscapes altered by people) and the natural* environment (the environment of vegetation and wildlife, that may also include environments shaped by people). To avoid confusion we talk about the built environment (including landscapes) and wild nature. In health the environment is seen far more broadly than in planning and design and may include the peer environment, family environment, media environment, policy and program environment, economic environment and the like. The food environment, for example, ranges in scale from what is available at a family meal to fast food advertising and international food systems. The actual physical built environment is a small aspect of that.

Exposure: For health exposure is the "contact between an organism and a chemical or physical agent, by swallowing, breathing, or direct contact (such as through the skin or eyes)."[22] Second-hand exposure e.g. to tobacco smoke in a room still involves direct contact. In disaster work it has a different meaning related to the "total value of elements at-risk. It is expressed as the number of human lives, and value of the properties, that can potentially be affected by hazards."[23]

Goals and objectives: Goals are typically broad aims that cannot be easily measured, such as "improving health". Objectives are more specific and measurable aims, such as increasing the number of people who walk or cycle to work. Actions and strategies are the specific approaches you will use to achieve the goals and objectives.

Hazard: A source of potential harm. More technically in the area of weather it is a "potentially damaging physical event that may cause the loss of life or injury, property damage, social and economic disruption or environmental degradation."[24]

Health: Health has a number of standard definitions from the absence of disease to the constitution of the World Health Organization—" a state of complete physical, mental and social well-being and not merely the absence of disease or infirmity."[25] This book typically takes the broader view.

Health assessment: A neighborhood health assessment or audit can take a number of forms. In this book it includes health impact assessment (assessing the effects of policies, plans, projects, and proposals), and healthy community assessment (collaborative approaches to understanding health in a place, taking account of both history and the population).[26] Both can be focused on places at the scale of the neighborhood or district. A neighborhood health assessment is different to typical community health needs assessments or community health assessments used in public health that are often more technical analyses focused on the health status of people in wider communities, risk factors, and preventive measures.[27]

Healthy housing: This is the idea that improving housing can improve health, an issue international concern. One example is the U.S. National Standard for Healthy Housing, developed by the National Center for Healthy Housing and the American Public Health Association[28]. It involves topics such as space, plumbing, lighting, thermal comfort, moisture, waste, chemicals, and personal safety and security.

Health in All Policies (HiAP): This is a collaborative approach to integrating health considerations into policy and planning across a range of sectors from housing and transportation to environment and multicultural affairs.[29]

Healthy neighborhood: In this book it refers to a neighborhood where health is a part of the process of planning as well as a key outcome. It is related to the idea of the complete neighborhood that according to the City of Portland, Oregon, "refers to a neighborhood where one has safe and convenient access to the goods and services needed in daily life. This includes a range of housing options, grocery stores and other neighborhood-serving commercial services; quality public schools; public open spaces and recreational facilities; and access to frequent transit. In a complete neighborhood, the network of streets and sidewalks is interconnected, which makes walking and bicycling to these places safe and relatively easy for people of all ages and abilities."[30] It is one of many kinds of neighborhoods* and districts*.

Irritant: "A substance that produces an irritating effect when it comes into contact with the skin, eyes, nose, or respiratory system."[31]

Knowledge is typically about understanding. For this book the key issue is that knowledge has many sources including scientific information, personal experience, or professional activities. These forms of knowledge have different strengths.

Life course: "An expression denoting an individual's passage through life, analyzed as a sequence of significant life-events, including birth, marriage, parenthood, divorce, and retirement."[32] It is a more contemporary version of the life cycle that does not imply regression to childhood at the end and accomodates varied household types.

Mobility: In transportation it is about movement including circulation (short-term movements outside the home, daily travel, touristic travel, etc.), migration (permanent moves), and social mobility.[33] We typically use it to mean circulation and compare it with accessibility*. It may also be used more loosely to mean getting around even within the home in the context of universal design.

Modifiable (causes of health): Much an individual's health is predetermined by our genetic inheritance, age, and gender. Modifiable causes are such factors as diet and physical activity.

Nature: The issue of importance here is a confusion in the literature between nature as untouched wilderness vs. nature as vegetation and animals which may well be altered by humans. Ecologists often mean the first; environmental psychologists, the latter. We typically do not use the term nature but rather specify the type of environment more clearly.

Neighborhood: this is a controversial term with many different definitions though it typically includes residential activities. Research on perceived neighborhoods has found great variety in terms of size and important components.[34] A functional neighborhood is related to a healthy neighborhood* in that they provide a balance of resource. In this book we see the basic neighborhood as a small area from a few blocks (an area of 4–5 hectares or 10–12 acres) up to a district of a few hundred hectares. At a very brisk 4 miles or 6 kilometers an hour, someone can walk from the center to the edge of round district of 314 hectares or 778 acres in 10 minutes. This is a wide range.

Neighborhood Health Assessment or Audit: See health assessment.

Place: This often refers to space* inhabited by people as a setting for social interaction or in terms of the perceived sense of place.[35] In this book we use it loosely, interchangeable with built environment*.

Plan: Generally one can plan for the future with specific actions in a given timeframe. In this book we use it typically in the sense of a spatial plan related to future actions in a place. This may be a public or private activity but as the scale of a plan gets larger, beyond the parcel or block, the public sector is more likely to be involved. A secondary meaning of plan is of the plan view, or the view from directly overhead.

Policy: general principles about how to act. It may not be related to a specific place but rather provides broader framework. As the United Nations Food and Agriculture Organization (FAO) states: "A policy is a set of coherent decisions with a common long-term purpose(s)…The terms "policy", "plan", "program" and "project" are progressively more specific in time and place. Policies are usually national policies (not district or provincial) and are not normally limited in time: one does not usually speak in terms of "2-year policies" as one does of "2-year programs" or "5-year plans.""[36]

Pollutant: Something that causes pollution or contamination by polluting with "harmful or poisonous substances."[37]

Program: A program is generally an ongoing set of events. Examples relevant to this book include a programs to prevent crime or promote exercise.

Project: A specific collaborative enterprise to achieve an aim.[38] It may be more specifically a development project such as a redevelopment project or a neighborhood upgrading project.

Reliable: In health this means a result can be replicated (and such replication comes in several forms). For tools completed by an expert inter-rater reliability is used to see if two different people get the same result. For tools completed by an individual being studied, the core form is test-retest reliability—will they provide the same answers for stable phenomena over time. There are other forms but this captures key concerns. It is related to the word validity* or truthfulness.[39] In common language however, reliability simply means it can be relied upon.

Resilience: "The rate at which a system regains structure and function following a stress or perturbation."[40] This is related to vulnerability.*

Resources: Refers to "sources of human satisfaction, wealth, or strength."[41] In the context of this book they often refer to the resources to lead a healthy life.

Risk: In disasters the "probable impacts, expressed in terms of expected loss of lives, people injured, property, livelihoods, economic activity disrupted or environmental damage."[42]

Significance: Broadly this is about how meaningful or important a result is. It can be used narrowly to refer to statistical significance, where something is "larger or smaller than would be expected by chance."[43] The key issue here is that something may be statistically significant (that is the relationship is likely to be true within some confidence interval (e.g. one is 95 percent sure) but it can be such a small value or magnitude as to be relatively unimportant. It may also be an unimportant or obvious association. There are many such results.

Social capital/social connections: This is broadly the connections among individuals or groups that facilitate collective action. It can be seen to have a number of components: membership of groups and networks, interpersonal trust and solidarity, collective action and cooperation, social cohesion and inclusion, and improved information and communication.[44] As we describe later, on one side these relate to perceptions of reciprocity and trust (cognitive social capital), and on the other interpersonal networks and engagement (structural social capital). They may be strong bonds of close-knit communities and families or the more distant bridging links between people with not as much in common.[45]

Social Determinants of Health: as the World Health Organization outlines "The social determinants of health (SDH) are the conditions in which people are born, grow, work, live, and age, and the wider set of forces and systems shaping the conditions of daily life. These forces and systems include economic policies and systems, development agendas, social norms, social policies and political systems."[46] Neighborhoods provide some of these conditions.

Space: This is typically a physical area in contrast with place* that has social and perceptual dimensions.

Systematic reviews: These are forms of literature reviews with very clear criteria for inclusion in the review and a systematic approach to analyzing findings. They are often contrasted with narrative reviews.[47] They are common in the area of health and less common in planning and design.

Toxic and toxin: Something that is toxic is poisonous and a poisonous substance is a toxicant. Strictly speaking a toxin is "a poisonous substance that is a specific product of the metabolic activities of a living organism" however it is often used interchangeably with toxicant.[48]

Transit, public transportation, collective transportation, and shared transportation: Public transport or transit involves shared rides along scheduled routes on vehicles available to the public. Common modes are trains, trams, and buses. There is not a good alternative word for demand responsive systems that provide individuals with point to point service, more private forms of group transportation, and including traditional paratransit (vans for disabled people); shared cars and vans; work-based van shares, bike-share systems; and taxis. We divide these roughly into collective transportation (e.g. shared vans, paratransit, and work-based shuttles) and shared vehicles where the riders are often individuals (like bike or car share systems). There is obviously a lot of overlap and this is just to indicate the great range of such systems.

Validity: This refers to a research approach that ensures what is meant to be measured is in fact being measured. In other words, truthfulness of the measure. This is particularly important when one is not measuring a variable directly e.g. using the area of parks to measure park accessibility. There are several forms of validity including face validity (does it appear to be valid), content validity (does it include the broad range of the phenomenon), and criterion validity (does it agree with an external gold standard).[49]

Vulnerability: This has different meanings depending on context. Socially it can refer to the possibility that disadvantaged or vulnerable groups may be affected. Such groups typically involve the young, the old, those with existing disabilities, those with low incomes, and people who are otherwise marginalized in a way that could affect health. Environmentally it is also called fragility and related to the "sensitivity, resilience*, and capacity of a system to adapt to stress or perturbation."[50]

Well-being, wellness: Where people "perceive that their lives are going well."[51] This has a number of aspects including physical, economic, social, emotional, and psychological well-being as well as satisfaction with life and engagement with activities.[52]

Urban heat island: "A dome of raised air temperatures that lies over an urban area and is caused by the heat absorbed by buildings and structures."[53]

Importance

**Assess how health matters
in this place.**

Information is needed to start
investigating a project or place and
figure out if health is a useful lens
for understanding and improving it.
For an existing place—how to make
it better? If making or reviewing
a proposal—how can it be made
healthier?

How It Works

A planning process is starting. A community group wants to improve its neighborhood. A city government aims to redevelop a mixed use district. In each of these cases planners, policy makers, civic leaders, business people, and residents may be interested in incorporating health issues into their activities. This raises questions. What specific health-related issues are in play? Who might be affected? If you identify changes to improve positive health outcomes or reduce negative ones, is there any way to make a difference? Because it takes resources to investigate health issues, are there allies and funding sources?

To start answering these questions, dealt with in subsequent propositions, information is required—about the place or proposal, health concerns, the role of environment in those concerns, and the people and organizations who can make decisions about the place. We refer to the process of collecting this information and reviewing projects, plans, and proposals as a neighborhood health assessment. In the planning and public health disciplines, a health assessment can take many forms and can be customized to meet the needs of the community.

The kind of health assessments most likely to be used includes health impact assessment and healthy community assessment. In a formal health impact assessment the processes of answering some of these questions are called screening (to see if it is worth doing an assessment) and scoping (to determine what

to assess).[1] It is often done prospectively, examining a draft project, policy, or plan to identify how to make it better. This book can be used in this way, but it can also be used to assess existing places, plans, programs, and policies to establish goals for making changes. Health impact assessment can be done in a range of ways from the highly participatory to the more technical and quantified to hybrids that combine approaches; they can be short desktop exercises to months-long processes.

Healthy community assessment is a term used to describe a community-based assessment of an existing community that helps residents prioritize health and well-being concerns, develop organizational skills, increase understanding, and act collectively.[2] While many communities are larger than a neighborhood, or not spatially defined at all, this kind of process can occur at the neighborhood level and involve a variety of stakeholders.

These both differ from more traditional community health needs assessments that evaluate the level of health of a population, identify risk factors, and outline preventive measures.[3] Commonly conducted in public health, these can be extremely useful background studies, though they are generally focused on a wider geographical areas than a neighborhood and a public health toolkit of interventions such as vaccinations or education campaigns.

Figure 8 is a decision tree showing how a neighborhood health assessment might be done as

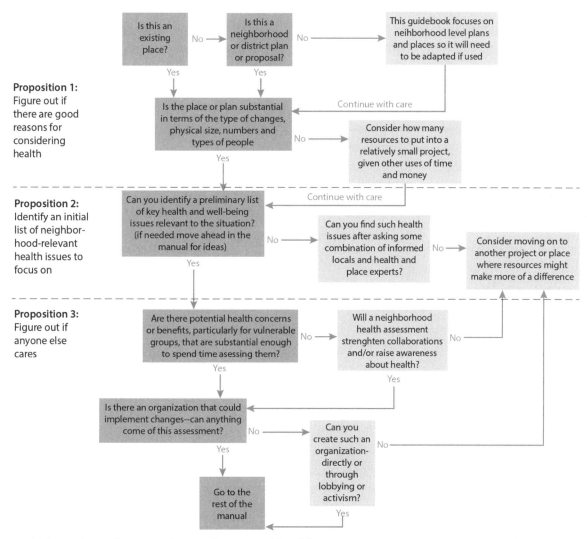

Proposition 1:
Figure out if there are good reasons for considering health

Proposition 2:
Identify an initial list of neighborhood-relevant health issues to focus on

Proposition 3:
Figure out if anyone else cares

Figure 8. Questions about projects, places, and health

The questions in the dark gray boxes, clustered by propositions in this principle, can help decide if and how to incorporate health into planning efforts and projects. They are relevant to planners, policy makers, civic leaders, and activists weighing how to make the biggest impact with potentially available resources.

Source: Developed by authors

part of a planning, design, or redevelopment process. Subsequent propositions provide more detail.[4]

The decision tree does not need to be followed exactly, but it provides a broad sense of the kinds of questions to ask and also the scope of this book—focused on neighborhood and district-level projects, plans, and places. It starts with questions about the kind of place or project, moves to potential health topics, and then focuses on whether an assessment will make a difference. If it will not make a difference, it may not be worth doing unless desired as a learning experience. While it may seem that health is always important, it makes sense to expend effort where you can make a difference. For this reason, at several points the decision tree suggests moving on to another project, plan, or place.

This raises some issues of terminology. The key distinction in this book is between assessing physical places and assessing the rest—spatial plans about specific future actions in a place, projects focused on more specific outcomes, policies or more generalized principles about how to act, and programs of ongoing events (see the Glossary for more detail). When we want to indicate that text applies to something that is not yet a physical place, we often use the terms plans, projects, policies, and programs interchangeably. In these cases, we would say something like programs, projects, and the like, not listing all the options. Indeed the activities often overlap so a component of a neighborhood plan may be implemented by an affordable housing project. Programs or events in a neighborhood park may fulfill a wider policy of being more culturally inclusive. However, at times we use the terms more specifically.

Last is the issue of sources of information about health and about the place. This book draws on a range of forms of knowledge. Key is research-based knowledge about the relationship between health and places. However, the opinions of professionals, residents, and other locals, such as workers, may also be important. Some health problems will be easily observable but others will be harder to detect or may play out over time and space.

Connections

As noted earlier, at the end of the introduction to each principle as well as at the end of each proposition, we list key connections to other parts of the book. Principle 1 connects to:

- **Proposition 1:** Figure out if there are good reasons for considering health
- **Proposition 2:** Identify an initial list of neighborhood-relevant health issues
- **Principle 2. Balance:** Make healthier places by balancing physical changes with other interventions to appeal to different kinds of people
- **Principle 3. Vulnerability:** Plan and design for those with the most health vulnerabilities and fewest resources for making healthy choices

To begin to make a healthier place, information is required—about the place, health concerns, the role of environment, and about the people who can make decisions about the place. In planning, this is often done through a health assessment.

Proposition 1: Examine how much health may matter in this place

Considering the health of neighborhoods or districts takes resources so it is important to know if the health issues are substantial enough, and the likelihood of change big enough, to warrant the work.

How It Works

It may seem totally obvious that health is always important. However, a proposal may be small in scale or a place may be doing well compared with others. In a world of limited resources, it can be best to focus attention on larger or more critical places and proposals. To figure this out, there are two basic steps of a health assessment:

- Understanding if the place or proposal is of a scale to make it worthwhile.
- Figuring out if there are enough reasons to move forward considering health. This is about existing concerns and capacity to make beneficial changes.

Information is vital in order to do any sort of initial review. It is iterative, however. For example, you need to collect information early but you cannot know what to collect until you have done some of the other steps. So you collect some information, assess it, and collect more if needed.

Table 2 provides examples of the key kinds of questions to ask at this preliminary stage. They are in three broad areas:

- Many screening questions aim to identify substantial changes, existing concerns, and places that are big enough so that planning and design affects a large number of people. These are related to the general type and scale of the project or place. Some questions are descriptive—like the type of proposed change. Others, however, look more specifically at health issues like the presence of existing concerns about health.

Here problems of mobility and poverty are apparent. However, even if some places have great need, there may be little local capacity to make neighborhood-scale changes.

Table 2. Preliminary questions for examining a proposal, plan, program, or place

Type of information needed	Type of situation or change	Yes	No	Maybe/don't know
Scale of potential health effects				
Existing health problems	• **Cumulative impact:** Is it a place where specific local health problems have been identified (e.g. traffic safety, air quality, lack of healthy foods, contaminated brownfields)?	☐	☐	☐
Change proposed? (skip if examining an existing place)	• **Type:** Is it building a new neighborhood or district, retrofitting or redeveloping an older one, or something else?	☐	☐	☐
	• **Reversibility:** Are any potential or proposed changes difficult or expensive to reverse once put in place? This is likely to be the case with physical planning and urban design actions such as building housing or laying out a pattern of streets and paths.	☐	☐	☐
	• **Land use:** Does the plan or proposal it substantially change the predominant land use (e.g. from residential to commercial)?	☐	☐	☐
	• **Natural environment:** Will it significantly alter the natural environment even if it does not change land-use patterns (e.g. does it increase or reduce water runoff, air quality or noise)?	☐	☐	☐
Physical area of place?	• **Geographical extent:** Does it apply to a geographic area of neighborhood-scale (a few hectares to a few hundred hectares or acres)?	☐	☐	☐
Population and differential health effects				
Number of people directly affected	• **Population size:** Does it affect a significant number of people (as residents or workers)? Does any proposal substantially increase or displace people?	☐	☐	☐
Demographics of people	• **Population distribution:** Does it involve a vulnerable population group such as children, seniors, people with low incomes, or people with disabilities? Are the health effects on any specific part of the population disproportionate?	☐	☐	☐
Implementation				
Allies and champions	• **Champion:** Is there an identifiable champion of a neighborhood health assessment or of making changes to a place?	☐	☐	☐
	• **Allies:** Is there an organization—such as a government, nonprofit, or business group—interested in health that could maintain momentum?	☐	☐	☐
Specific organizations that could implement changes	• **Making a difference:** Can anything come of suggesting how to make it healthier? (This is dealt with more in proposition 3)	☐	☐	☐

Sources: Adapted from HAPI 2015a. There are numerous other examples of these kinds of tools available (Kemm 2013; Harris et al. 2007) however this one was specifically developed for neighborhood-scale projects and place.

- Other screening questions identify the population affected now or in the future. Certain populations are more vulnerable to health problems, including the old, the young, those without the money to make healthy choices, those with pre-existing health conditions, and those who may be otherwise marginalized in society.[5]
- The questions also focus on implementation and the possibility of making a difference and of finding allies. Specific people with energy and enthusiasm for making healthier places can create links and raise awareness. However, organizations are typically better placed to follow a project in the long haul. Both are important for implementation.

The next proposition is focused on identifying specific health issues and topics. It could well be that only a few questions have yes as an answer, but that would be enough to go forward for further review. Overall, if this basic information is unavailable, it will be difficult to review or assess the project or place further.

As can be seen from these questions, certain kinds of information are needed for just about every place or proposal right at the very start. Potential sources of data include local government planning agencies, census and statistical bureaus, project proponents, and observing of the area.[6] While the specific organization that might supply the information

Table 3. Key sources to consult and types of existing information to gather for a neighborhood health assessment

Sources	Type of information
Local knowledge	Oral history, organizational minutes, letters of complaint, local history archives
Local media	Media reporting, local perceptions/responses
Administrative records	Government documents and databases such as census, property, records, maps
Proponents	Specifics of proposals
Other organizations	Local business and nonprofit activities, political context
Research-based	Most useful at later stages—studies applicable to this type of place

Collecting new data is dealt with in Table 4.
Sources: Adapted from HAPI 2015d; Design for Health 2007g

varies from place to place, the kinds of information providers are fairly consistent.

While some information may be fairly straightforward, such as the physical area of a place, other topics may be contested, and in these cases multiple sources are useful. (Even the physical area may be contested as a small project, for example, may have wider ramifications.) Table 3 deals with data collection using existing documents. Table 4 explains

Table 4: Potential sources of new data for a neighborhood health assessment, including participatory approaches

Category of data collection	Possible method	Example or explanation
Observing people and places	• Locating physical traces	• Paths worn along roads
	• Windshield survey	• Drive-around observations using a checklist
	• Site reconnaissance	• Like a windshield survey but on foot
	• Site audit	• Observation using a highly structured tool like a walkability checklist
	• Photographic site survey	• Photography of an area using a specific protocol of what will be photographed
	• Atmosphere photography	• Photography to communicated qualitative aspects of a place
	• Tomography	• Multiple photographs on a theme to show range and variation
	• Time lapse photography	• Speeding up action shows how spaces are used
	• Participant and semi-structured observations	• Observations in organizations, places, and events
Asking opinions and perceptions	• Unstructured interviews	• Free-form questions, for example in a scoping meeting or correspondence
	• Semi-structured interviews	• Using an interview guide
	• Focus groups, group interviews	• Like semi-structured interviews but with interaction in a group
	• Questionnaires and structured interviews	• In person, over the phone, on papper, and online for more strucutred set of answers
	• Interactive tours	• Visiting and discussing a place
	• Creating image	• Day-with-a-camera (photovoice) where locals take photographs and note their significance, draw mental maps
	• Reacting to images	• Visual preference surveys selecting the best one from a matched pair, voting with dots on preferred images
	• Social media responses	• Reactions to a blog post
	• Interacting with temporary installations	• Responding to temporary street furnishings or signage
Collaborative problem identification and solutions	• Participatory online activities	• Participatory geographic information systems online prioritizing exercises
	• Making maps and models	• Annotating a neighborhood map with key assets and problem areas
	• Prioritizing workshops	• Identifying strengths, weaknesses, opportunities, and threats (SWOT); conducting a future search, prioritizing health impacts in a workshop
	• Developing and prioritizing indicators	• For example, community health indicators

Sources: CommunityPlanning.net 2016; Gaber and Gaber 2007; Handcock and Minkler 2005; Krieger 2011; Participation Compass 2016; U.S. CDC 2015b; University of Kansas 2015a

key types of new data collection. Some are simple and will occur naturally as a result of participatory and collaborative processes, and others require more effort. How much data collection is needed will depend on the situation, though many of these methods will be in use already in a neighborhood planning or redevelopment process and could be modified to incorporate health. The first categories—observing, asking—can be done by professionals, activists, civic leaders, or local residents/workers, with groups working alone or in combination. The final category—engaging—needs to involve multiple groups.

It may also seem that it is always good to collect new information from local residents and engage them in planning and analysis. However, they too have limited time, and it is vital to respect that and not exacerbate participation fatigue. Observations have the benefit of obtaining data often with less of a burden on local participants, who may suffer from participation fatigue from too many engagement processes. It is also important to note that at this stage the information is largely about the place and any proposals or plans—later parts of this book deal with information from research evidence, which requires particular care.[7]

Actions

Do not just jump into considering health, but rather step back to consider if a project is important enough.

◇ **Compile information from multiple sources, particularly where there might be controversy or different perspectives.**
Health concerns can be identified by taking account of multiple sources of information and knowledge in early phases—from local perceptions to administrative records. Compiling this information can minimize the risks that major problems will be missed.[8]

◇ **Move forward in the book if there are any open questions relevant to health including large or irreversible changes, large physical areas or populations, existing concerns about health problems, and differential effects on vulnerable groups.**
There are many factors that may indicate if it is useful to conduct a health assessment. At this stage it is important to take a broad perspective.[9]

◇ **Be cautious in moving forward if there seems to be no possibility of making changes.**
Health assessments and reviews take time. In a world of limited resources, it may not be a good use of time and money to do such a review if the project or place will not change. However, a health assessment should not be rejected out of hand.[10] Even in this situation it may raise awareness among those who go through the

exercise. For example, public health professionals may start to see planners and urban designers as allies, or civic leaders may see how health is a local concern.[11]

Connections

Assessing whether to spend resources to incorporate health in a rigorous way into a project is a key step. To understand this proposition better, go to:

- **Principle 1. Importance:** Examine how much health may matter in this place

To further investigate, look at:

- **Proposition 2:** Identify an initial list of neighborhood-relevant health issues
- **Proposition 3:** Figure out if anyone else cares
- **Principle 2. Balance:** Make healthier places by balancing physical changes with other interventions to appeal to different kinds of people
- **Principle 3. Vulnerability:** Plan and design for those with the most health vulnerabilities and fewest resources for making healthy choices

Environments may have open questions about healthy making them worth further investigation. This pedestrian and cycling path provides opportunities for physical activity and is well lit. However, it is cut off from other activity and fairly narrow, potentially leading to conflicts between users going at different speeds.

Proposition 2: Identify an initial list of neighborhood-relevant health issues

It could be that there are many health issues that are obvious early on in a neighborhood health assessment; it may also be that you start with one or two key insights or questions. However, not all connections between health and place are equally understood, equally well researched, or equally influential.

How It Works

Finding obvious and less obvious health and well-being topics

Identifying the different kinds of intersections between health and environments is a key step often referred to as scoping in the neighborhood health assessment process.[12] This can help narrow or focus attention on important issues but also help broaden the agenda beyond what initially seems obvious. For example, it might seem obvious that a roadway redesign or transportation plan has implications for physical activity but more important may be such issues as traffic safety, air quality, accessibility to services, social connections, and mental health.

As a preliminary step, it can be useful to have a checklist of issues. Because many health assessment tools are designed to have very broad applications— from national policies to interior designs—the range of such issues is large. Table 5 provides indicators relevant to neighborhoods and districts. This is not an exhaustive list but selects key health indicators at the neighborhood scale that are fairly well supported by

evidence. Places with these features may be healthy enough, but this list indicates some red flags. The issues raised are dealt with in more detail later in the book.

If any of the indicators in Table 5 are highlighted, it is worth doing more investigation. If none are highlighted, there may still be concerns—for example, there could be issues related to droughts or

This space has a playground and urban greening, but is not clear how well this is used, and there are signs of vandalism.

Table 5. Example indicators of potential health concerns

Exposures	
Air quality	• Nearby major roads with 6 or more lanes; smokestack industry; wood, dung, or similar fuel sources.
Disasters and climate change	• Low elevation zones; flood plains; hazardous industries (nuclear power plants etc.); areas with substantial paved areas and little vegetation; areas where people are close to locations with disease vectors like mosquitoes.
Noise	• Major roads with 6 or more lanes; high speed roads; airports; entertainment districts.
Toxics	• Problematic past, current, or proposed uses such as nuclear facilities, heavy manufacturing, and busy traffic corridors; areas with older housing with likely contaminants (chemicals mold).
Water quality	• Un-sewered areas; areas without clean drinking water.
Connections	
Accessibility to services/ employment	• Areas without relatively frequent transit service within 500 meters; Areas where clinics are more than 20 minutes by available transportation.
Physical accessibility/ universal design	• Mobility-impaired residents and workers cannot get around except by private car.
Sociability/ social networks	• Public community centers and/or gathering spaces are more than 1km or 15 minutes by available transportation.
Health-related Behaviors and Supports	
Healthy eating options	• Areas where there are no sources of fruits and vegetables within 2km or 20 minutes by normal transportation.
Mental health supports	• Areas of 5 hectares (12 acres) or greater with no vegetation (2 hectares or 5 acres if densities are relatively high for the location); crowded units (many people per room).
Physical activity options	• Areas with more than 500m to a park or trail; major roads that do not have sidewalks and safe crossings, particularly in locations with children and older people
Safety (accidents, crime)	• Transportation routes are not lit at night.

The left-hand column of this table lists the intersections between health and the built environment featured in this book, with a number of examples of how these intersections operate at the neighborhood-scale.

Sources: Adapted HAPI (2015a) based on HAPI (2014o)

specific traffic safety problems or local perceptions not captured in the more numerical indicators. The specific numerical thresholds, while drawing on research evidence, may not be quite appropriate for a specific situation. However, the list at least provides a systematic starting point.

Underlying the indicators is a concern with the different effects on groups such as children and those with few financial resources. This is an important additional lens.[13]

It is also possible to create a checklist specifically about one dimension of the environment such as access to healthy food. Such frameworks can be helpful, but a strength of more comprehensive lists such as in the figure is that they help make the multiple connections between health and place clearer.[14]

When identifying health issues, it is important to consider groups vulnerable to negative health impacts from the environment. For instance, children are more susceptible to toxins and other harmful exposures because they have little control over their surroundings and are still physically, mentally, and emotionally developing.

Actions

◇ **Identify an initial list of health issues, balancing a need to focus on important topics with a need to understand links that are less obvious.**

Planners and designers also already do many assessments. But one conducted through a health lens can identify opportunities and problems in that specific domain.

◇ **Consider the potential for differential effects on population subgroups such as children, older people, and those with low incomes and pre-existing conditions and who are otherwise marginalized.**

Most health effects vary with the population group exposed to or interacting with the environment.[15]

◇ **Use numerical indicators to aid this process of scoping as well as more qualitative assessments such as resident and professional perceptions.**

Many times local perceptions and practices tap into sources of knowledge unavailable to outsiders or those relying on research and administrative evidence.

Connections

Coming up with a set of key topics can frame the rest of the project, plan, or assessment. To understand this proposition, better go to:

- **Principle 1. Importance:** Examine how much health may matter in this place

To further investigate, look at:

- **Proposition 3:** Figure out if anyone else cares
- **Proposition 4:** Understand that trade-offs are inherent in planning for health at all scales and this is true of neighborhoods as well
- **Proposition 5:** Appreciate that there is no ideal size for a healthy community, but different dimensions of health relate to different scales
- **Principle 3. Vulnerability:** Plan and design for those with the most health vulnerabilities and fewest resources for making healthy choices

Proposition 3: Figure out if anyone else cares

If you are the only one who cares about the health of a place or proposal, you can perhaps do something. With allies you can do a great deal more.

How It Works

One of the most important aspects of the health lens can be the way it brings people together. Health can be a common interest that links people who have very different views on other matters—just about everyone is interested in health.[16]

This is not necessarily the case, however, when considering the links between environments and health. Some people may have a very specific view of how healthy places are created—for example, focusing on providing health care. Others may feel uncertain about how their interests relate to place. There can also be rivalries between professionals within disciplines who feel that they have specific expertise—public health and medicine, engineering and planning, environmental management and education. Some people may be interested in a different scale from the room to the region—the neighborhood or district may just not be as relevant. Residents may have different priorities.

This proposition involves two basic activities. First is looking at community and institutional concerns as outlined in Table 6. This involves considering whether there are at least some parties concerned about health in relation to themselves or others, understanding if examining health will create new ties or visibility, and

assessing if there is capacity to do a review within a time frame to make changes. There also needs to be an opportunity to actually make those changes. It is not necessary to say yes to each statement at this stage but it is important to be able to confirm a substantial number of the statements, as they indicate whether there will be allies in the work and if it will make a difference.

Health concerns can be a way to bring people together from public and private organizations and the community.

◆   Directly from research evidence   ❖   Informed by research   ◇   General good practice

Table 6. Checklist of community and institutional concerns, benefits, and capabilities

Concerns, benefits, and vulnerable groups	Yes	No	Maybe/ don't know
1 Concerns: There are professional or community questions about negative health effects inside and outside the project/place.	☐	☐	☐
2 Benefits: There are professional or community interests in the potential health benefits of the proposal or place. Assessing these could help reinforce these benefits.	☐	☐	☐
3 Affected groups: There is some evidence that the project or place has health effects on vulnerable groups such as children, older people, those with low incomes, or those with disabilities.	☐	☐	☐
Wider benefits			
4 Beneficial linkages: Doing a health review or assessment would strengthen ties between planners, public health professionals, project stakeholders, local residents and workers, and developers.	☐	☐	☐
5 Awareness-raising: By conducting a health assessment, health will be more visible as an issue in public and professional discussions.	☐	☐	☐
Capacity and readiness			
6 Institutional capacity to make changes: There is interest and/or capacity of local government, nonprofit, and private organizations to address any potential problems—that is, something will get done following the assessment. For example, there is a potential champion of the process AND there is an opportunity to change the plan or the place.	☐	☐	☐
7 Institutional capacity to do a review: There is internal expertise or a capacity to bring in outside experts to complete a health assessment.	☐	☐	☐
8 Timeliness: The health assessment or review can be completed within a time frame that is useful for influencing decision making.	☐	☐	☐

Source: Adapted from HAPI 2015a

Table 7. Interest groups and stakeholder analysis matrix

Interest groups and stakeholders	Interest in the place, plan, or proposal	Knowledge base and expertise	Ability to change the proposal
Decision makers			
Elected officials	Varies	Political	Moderate/high
Agency staff	Varies	Professional	Moderate/high
Project development team	Proponent	Professional	High
Experts			
Local practitioners (health, planning, design, social work, real estate)	Provides professional and local perspective	Professional	Varies
Academics and researchers	Provides expert knowledge so health interventions actually make a difference	Research	Varies
Community groups	Making a place where they can live more healthy lives	Local experience	Via political/ negotiation process
Service providers		Professional/ local experience	Via political/ negotiation process
Populations affected			
Residents	Making a place where they can live more healthy lives	Local experience	Via political/ negotiation process
Business owners and employees	Making a place where they can live more healthy lives/ health of customers	Local experience	Via political/ negotiation process
Visitors	Varies	Time-specific experience	Low
Community groups	Making a place where they live more healthy lives	Local experience	Via political/ negotiation process
Service providers	Health of customers	Professional/ local experience	Via political/ negotiation process

Source: Developed by authors

Involving a broad base of individuals and organizations interested in health can bring time, money, and knowledge to the process.

Second, beyond some very small-scale activities, cooperation is required to get things done. For this reason it is important to identify potential alliances and opportunities for engagement.

A starting point can be to brainstorm which individuals and groups may care about the issues already identified in terms of the place, the topics, and the people affected. This includes professionals but also residents, workers, politicians, and others with an interest in using places as well as designing and managing them. They can come from different sectors—public, private, and community based. Often, within governments, key actors will come from different levels—planning at the city level and health at the county or state level, for example.

It can help to list individual and organizational interests in health-relevant issues and the larger plan or place, specific expertise, and level of control. There can be a great deal of mismatch between who knows a lot about a subject, who cares, and who has power to change a proposal or place.

Consider whether the inventory of stakeholders is comprehensive enough—perhaps there are others who might be interested in the process? Creating a matrix such as the one in Table 7 and filling in the cells with more locally specific answers can help structure this kind of review.

The reason for identifying alliances and opportunities for engagement is to have a broader base of individuals and organizations interested in health, which can bring more time, money, and knowledge to the process.

Actions

◇ **Identify allies by figuring out who they are, understanding their roles and resources, and potentially making contact.**

The list of potential allies includes governments, residents, businesses, nonprofits or nongovernmental organizations, and people from a range of specialties.

◇ **Involve others in the project in a way that respects their time, capitalizes on their knowledge, and encourages joint ownership of a solution where that is needed.**

While there is an idea that more involvement is always better, people have limited time and healthy neighborhoods are only one topic of interest. Figuring out how to involve the various stakeholders is likely to be an iterative task that depends on many factors including your own position in the project. Ideally health is integrated into larger processes of planning so it does not need to involve extra work.

◇ **Identify strategies that aim to have multiple health benefits (e.g., physical activity options and mental health benefits from a park) in order to gain support and also make it more likely that a proposal will help at least one group.**

A narrow proposal may be the only workable compromise, but more likely a broader view of health can engage more people and draw on more resources. This is related to the next principle—on appealing to different kinds of people—but focuses on the work of doing the health assessment rather than its outcomes.

Connections

Having allies is key to many parts of the planning and design process, including implementation. To understand this proposition better, go to:

- **Proposition 1:** Figure out if there are good reasons for considering health

To further investigate, look at:

- **Principle 2. Balance:** Make healthier places by balancing physical changes with other interventions to appeal to different kinds of people
- **Proposition 4:** Understand that trade-offs are inherent in planning for health at all scales and this is true of neighborhoods as well
- **Principle 5. Access:** Provide options for getting around and increasing geographic access
- **Principle 8. Implementation:** Coordinate diverse actions over time

Health assessment processes should involve people in a way that respects their time and expertise.

Balance

Make healthier places by balancing physical changes with other interventions to appeal to different kinds of people.

It may seem that there are easy solutions to making healthier places, but this is rarely the case. This principle is about several interconnected issues: Successful places fulfill needs for different people, using multiple kinds of strategies, and they do this at different but interconnected scales. Just one kind of intervention is typically not enough.

People vary in their needs, and environments affect different people differently. Altering the environment alone is not enough to improve health.

How It Works
Different needs

A key message is that environments affect different people differently. Designing a place so that, say, adults will walk more for transportation may not help people in other age groups much; they may need other kinds of environments to target other kinds of activity. Strategies and innovations that are widely adopted to improve health often satisfy many needs and desires.

A research finding on how larger programmatic changes are made is that they tend to involve multiple activities done simultaneously appealing to multiple groups.[1] Such places with broad appeal create allegiances—for political support, funding, and collective maintenance over time. For example, suburbia was a solution to the need for low-cost housing, ideas about family life, economic stimulus, and more; for some groups it was seen as the socialist thing to do (good homes for the working class), and

in others it fostered markets (making a population of property owners).[2] Similarly major highway systems helped personal travel and freight, often served military purposes, and generated new urban development opportunities.[3] Similar arguments could be made for many of the widely adopted urban movements of the 20th century—urban renewal districts, public housing projects and redevelopments, and open space systems.

Of course, as ideas not all of these were good in and of themselves or might be seen as good for health. There was also a great deal of variety among such places—different kinds of suburbs and highways— with excellent examples and poor adaptations. However, they gained their support from multifaceted appeal to the public and decision makers.

Multiple kinds of interventions

Building or altering an environment is not enough to improve health, however. A new environment can improve health in some areas such as exposures to pollutants and irritants. Generally, however, other dimensions such as programs, pricing, education, social pressure, and the like may be equally or more important for improving health. They can more directly change behaviors and work at scales both larger and smaller than the neighborhood. Of course, programs, education, and policy alone may not work either. This is the story of trying to stop smoking; in spite of a multifaceted approach, short of banning it completely it has been very challenging to stop. However, banning it in or around buildings can eliminate it from those spaces.[4]

An example from bicycling highlights these issues too. Pucher et al. summarized case studies from 14 cities that implemented "packages of mutually supportive pro-bicycle policies" showing that in many of the cases bicycling increased dramatically.[5] Exceptions were cases where the economic base of the area changed—for example a move to long-distance commuting in Davis, California, meant that cycling was no longer viable for many. Interventions ranged from infrastructure and regulations to education and promotional programs. It seems logical that such packages of programs, projects, and policies are likely to have at least some approaches that work, and are more likely to have specific actions that appeal to particular groups who may be left out of narrower interventions. As Pucher et al. conclude, "The cases reviewed here suggest that a comprehensive approach produces a much greater impact on bicycling than

individual measures that are not coordinated. The impact of any particular measure is enhanced by the synergies with complementary measures in the same package."[6] The situation in the Netherlands is outlined in Figure 9. It seems plausible that this need for multiple interventions would also occur with the more comprehensive goal of making healthy communities.

Public space should serve mulitple health functions for a variety of people. These goals can be achieved through complementary policies and programs.

Case: Cycling infrastructure in the Netherlands

How the Netherlands maintained its trips by bicycle is one of the better examples of creating successful large change. Since the 1970s, the Netherlands combined every available strategy to support pedestrians, cyclists, and public transportation: community design, infrastructure and facility improvements, changing pricing incentives, policies, and educational programs. This creates a much safer and convenient cycling environment, especially important for women, children, and the elderly. As of 2005, 27 percent of all trips were by bicycle in the Netherlands.[7] By comparison, only 1 percent of all trips are made by bicycle in the United Kingdom, Australia, and the United States.[8]

Examples of strategies[9]

Community design:

- Road design and urban form that prioritizes cyclists over cars (a)
- Infill and redevelopment prioritized over new development, mixed-use zoning
- Transportation and land-use planning integrated across levels of government with regional coordination
- Cycling and walking facilities required in new suburban developments

Infrastructure and facility improvements:

- Extensive systems of separate cycling facilities, including along highways (b)

- Intersection modifications and priority traffic signals (c)
- Traffic calming and low speed limits (d)
- Bike parking (e)
- Coordination with other transportation modes and facilities, such as bike parking at public transit stations, bike rentals at transit stations and "park and bike" parking lots (e)

Changing pricing incentives:

- Tax breaks to purchase a bike
- Higher taxes for automobile ownership and use (sale, excise, parking, license)
- Access to inexpensive or free bikes via rentals and company bikes

Policies:

- Cyclists have legal right of way over motorists (children and elderly especially protected)
- Strict enforcement of cyclist rights by police and courts
- Public participation in bike planning (such as surveys, bike councils)

Educational programs:

- Traffic education and training for both cyclists and motorists
- Trip planning websites and comprehensive bike maps (f)
- Public awareness campaigns, events, and competitions

(a) Cyclists have right-of-way

(b) Separated cycling facilities

(c) Intersection modifications

(d) Crosswalk striping to signal pedestrian crossing

(e) Bike parking and rentals adjacent to transit

(f) Comprehensive bike maps

Figure 9. Cycling infrastructure in the Netherlands

Train station
①

Pedestrian and
cyclist paths
②

Dedicated
busway
③

Bicycle
parking
④

Views of
green
⑤

Figure 10. Different kinds of transportation modes connect different scales or distances
Healthy places connect physical places and programs; they also perform multiple functions from transportation to mental restoration.

To make big changes use many strategies at once.

Overall, different people may need different kinds of incentives and may also be more influenced or affected by some parts of the environment than others. Thus, to make big changes, or to halt large trends, one needs to use many strategies at once—changing physical places, implementing policies that affect how they are used, developing programs, and altering pricing to tip the balance toward creating environments that support positive behaviors, minimize harmful exposures, and enhance healthy connections. Environments may be only a small part of the whole picture. But of course you have to start somewhere.[10] In addition, environmental change can be complex enough to achieve, even without the whole range of public health interventions. Even small areas may need multiple interventions as is shown in Figure 10.

Connections

The interdependence of place, policies, and programs is a key feature of how neighborhoods support health. To further investigate, look at:

- **Proposition 4:** Understand that trade-offs are inherent in planning for health at all scales and this is true of neighborhoods as well
- **Proposition 5:** Appreciate that there is no ideal size for a healthy community, but different dimensions of health relate to different scales
- **Principle 5. Access:** Provide options for getting around and increasing geographic access
- **Principle 6. Connection:** Help people interact with each other in positive ways
- **Principle 8. Implementation:** Coordinate diverse actions over time

Proposition 4: Understand that trade-offs are inherent in planning for health at all scales, and this is true of neighborhoods as well

There are many competing approaches to make an environment healthier, and it is not possible to do everything at once.

How It Works

Creating healthy places relies on more than just understanding how to limit exposures to contaminants, irritants, or hazards; foster connections; and support healthy behavior choices for different populations. Rather these typically need to be combined into comprehensive strategies that represent priorities and trade-offs: among health-related issues, between the needs and priorities of different groups, between health and wellness outcomes, and between perfection and cost.

Different health issues, groups, and outcomes

The idea of a healthy neighborhood or district implies a comprehensive approach that integrates multiple health issues. However, as will become obvious from the rest of the book, there are many sorts of environments that can be healthy, and one kind of environment is unlikely to be equally strong in supporting all kinds of health.

The differences between a more compact and a more decentralized approach to development highlight these kinds of issues.[12] Table 8 outlines some of these trade-offs. It could cover other approaches, including access to green space, social connections, and safety. The core story is that each has strengths—in some areas one form of development is clearly stronger and the other weaker, but overall both have benefits. Compact development provides more accessibility to services and potential for active transportation; decentralized approaches provide better air quality and less noise. Creating a healthy neighborhood is a process of balancing needs over time. Such trade-offs can be found in other domains—for example, between:

- Accessibility for people with disabilities and recreational routes that may involve rough terrain, steps, or other mobility challenges
- Transportation systems that favor bicycles, which may move quickly along separated routes or on roads, and those that favor pedestrians, who move more slowly and less predictably

Table 8. Comparison of health trade-offs in compact versus decentralized approaches to neighborhood and district planning

Theme	Compact	Decentralized/ecological protection
Core approach	High residential and employment densities bring people and activities close together; along with connected pedestrian patterns, non-motorized travel is fostered. Saves land on the urban edge and provides an environment that is both efficient and vibrant.	Lower residential and employment densities allow ecological functions to be incorporated into the planning and design of the neighborhood that uses landscape to frame development. Brings nature and people close together with on-site water treatment, food production, and other natural processes.
Example Tensions		
Access to services (a)	A strength—services likely closer and more accessible by multiple modes or forms of transport.	Services may be further away unless the neighborhood is well located in a smaller town or city.
Air quality (b, c)	A problem—even if on average people drive less, and industries are more regulated they are closer together. Air pollution hotspots cause health problems.	May use more motorized transport but densities are low and pollution dispersed.
Noise (d, e, f, g)	Traffic, neighbors, events.	A strength—fewer problems.
Physical activity (h, i)	Walking and cycling for transport is easier but people are more exposed to air pollution.	Transportation walking is more difficult but recreational walking may be pleasant; cycling may be preferred; space for other exercise and active pursuits e.g. gardening.
Water quality (j, k, l, m, n, o)	More intensive development leads to more runoff; need more engineering solutions but have development intensity to pay for them.	Less intensive development allows easier on water treatment.

Source: Adapted from Crewe and Forsyth 2011; Jacobson and Forsyth 2008; Neuman 2005; Berke and Smith 200; (a) Levine et al. 2012; (b) Mansfield et al. 2015; (c) Schweitzer and Zhou 2010; (d) Babisch et al. 2014; (e) Berglund et al. 1999; (f) Fritschi et al. 2011; (g) Murphy and King 2015; (h) Forsyth and Krizek 2010; (i) Reviews in Big Ideas 4 and 5; (j) Barbosa et al. 2012; (k) Brabec et al. 2002; (l) Burton and Pitt 2002; (m) Goonetilleke et al. 2005; (n) Jacobson 2011; (o) Wang 2015

- "Walkable" environments that favor exercise and minimize stops versus those favoring a sociability and liveliness where there may be more standing than walking[13]

Perfection and cost

The final trade-off is between perfection and cost. It may seem that some of the trade-offs identified above can be resolved through design and planning—for example, vegetated roofs could absorb water in higher density environments or noise walls could reduce annoyance and irritation. However, all of these interventions have costs—vegetated roofs often require more maintenance and stronger building structures, or they can be more expensive to install.

An example from the field of sustainable urban development can help illustrate these trade-offs.

Almere in the Netherlands and Hammaby Sjöstad in Sweden are two much lauded planned developments, created by government agencies to provide housing and jobs. Almere, a larger development, provides a very high percentage of social housing and a wide variety of employment in a transit-oriented development that also supports walking and cycling with an extensive system of paths. But it is built on filled wetlands (a polder), which in the long run has environmental if not health implications.

Hammarby Sjöstad, built on a brownfield site, features many environmental innovations—from recycling to noise reduction—in a high-density, midrise format that also includes well-planned and diverse open spaces providing views of water or green from every unit. However, brownfield clean up was extraordinarily expensive, meaning that

The Village Homes in Davis, California, are not extremely dense, but offer benefits of views of green and quiet.

Table 9. Key data for Almere, Netherlands and Hammarby Sjöstad, Sweden

	Almere	Hammarby Sjöstad
Scale (incl. gross density)*	Large: almost 25,000—36% forests/ag.; density of core node "Almere Stad" (100,000 +residents) is over 40 persons/hectare (16/ acre) or 15–20 homes per hectare (6–8/acre)— still under development	Small: 200 hectares; 45 homes per hectare (18/ acre)
Developer	Rijksdienst voor de IJsselmeerpolders of Netherlands Government	Projekt Hammarby Sjöstad is within the Stockholm Real Estate and Traffic Admin., partnership with Stockholm City Planning
Designer/ Planner	Rijksdienst voor de IJsselmeerpolders and various consultants	Master plan developed by Stockholm City Planning Bureau, with Jan Inghe-Hagström as lead architect
Metro area/ state	Amsterdam outer suburbs	Stockholm, inner suburbs
Population in early plans	250,000, now increased to 400,000	22,000 increased to 25,000 residents + 10,000 employees
Starting date	Planned in 1970s; first residents 1976	early 1990s planning; First phase (north) completed in 2000

The key features of Almere, Netherlands and Hammarby Sjöstad, Sweden—two planned developments—are quite different from another, demonstrating how varied approaches can be to create healthy neighborhoods. Illustrations are on the next page.

Source: Adapted from Crewe and Forsyth 2011; * All else being equal, gross densities are always lower for larger developments that include more nonresidential uses.

Exposures	Connections	Supports for Behavior

Almere

Separated cycling and pedestrian paths reduce users' exposure to air pollution from motor vehicles.	Pedestrian and bicycle paths connect to bus rapid transit and trains to provide multiple option for those without cars.	Open spaces include parks, planted forests, a network of pedestrian and bicycle paths, and shared streets.

Hammarby Sjöstad

Noise walls protect residents from traffic while maintaining visual contact.	Services are provided on-site—accessible by walking, cycling, and ferry—and the area is linked to light rail and bus routes, connecting to the surrounding region.	Open spaces include lush, reed-filled wetlands along the waterfront, unbuilt hillsides, and formal open spaces used as parks and paths.

Figure 11. Almere and Hammarby Sjöstad comparison

Source: Adapted from Crewe and Forsyth 2011

although publicly developed, housing costs are mainly affordable for upper-income groups.[14] Of course, it is possible, for instance, to subsidize some of the housing in Hammarby Sjöstad but at a cost to the wider society. It is also much smaller than Almere. Overall, these examples demonstrate the complexity of creating a solution that works well on every dimension, indicating the need to prioritize health outcomes. In addition, some aspects of health may be better served by interventions beyond neighborhood planning and design such as regulating industrial emissions or noise, or making healthier food less expensive.

Actions

◇ **Understand that designing and planning a healthy neighborhood involves engaging multiple needs and goals.**
It can be tempting to think that there is a best solution but both human health and places are complex. Instead, use this tension as a productive start for discussion among the planning and analysis team and the wider community.

◇ **Recognize and prioritize health trade-offs systematically.**
Given that neighborhood planning and design is an ongoing process, it is important to continue identifying tensions between different aims and strategies.

◇ **Identify actions beyond planning and design that can help foster a healthier place, mitigating some of the less-than-optimal characteristics in any design and planning approach.**
Planning and design are not the only tools for improving health in neighborhoods. Programs and policies that shape how places are used—from the cost of parking to programs for active commuting—can make a big difference.

Connections

It is very difficult to address all dimensions of health at once; knowing how to prioritize is crucial. To understand this proposition better go to:

• **Principle 2. Balance:** Make healthier places by balancing physical changes with other interventions to appeal to different kinds of people

To further investigate, look at:

• **Proposition 5:** Appreciate that there is no ideal size for a healthy community, but different dimensions of health relate to different scales

• **Proposition 11:** Create a connected, "healthier" travel circulation pattern for pedestrians, bicyclists, and transit users—the vehicular pattern can be different

• **Proposition 14:** Adopt policies and planning practices to create safe neighborhood transportation options for all types of road users

Proposition 5: Appreciate that there is no ideal size for a healthy community, but different dimensions of health relate to different scales

A small village, a large metropolis, and many urban types in between can form healthy communities.

How It Works

This proposition is about two issues—whether there is an ideal size for a healthy environment and how different health issues relate to different scales of intervention.

Ideal size of a city or town

Many have investigated the ideal size of a city or town. They have done so through utopian literature, urban theories, and empirical analyses.[15]

- Economists have sought to find the most economically efficient city. However, a city that is efficient locally may not be the most efficient when looked at from a national perspective or from the perspective of different kinds of industries.[16] Economists may also consider how larger cities with more diversified economies foster creativity.[17]

- Environmentalists have looked for the most sustainable metropolitan area size but this varies when considering different dimensions (e.g., optimum for transportation energy efficiency versus water use). It has been difficult to assess

this through research studies because there are so many variables at play.

- Planners, designers, and residents considering quality of life may trade off issues like being small enough to be convenient but large enough to support substantial cultural activities.[18]

- Typically these discussions are at scales beyond the neighborhood, and the sizes of cities studied were often very large, in the millions.

Ideal size of a neighborhood or district

A second level of consideration is the ideal size of districts and neighborhoods. This has often focused on perceptions or proposals rather than outcomes.

- Some studies have examined the size of perceived neighborhoods, finding that they vary substantially from some blocks to vary large areas. They do so related to the kinds of people in localities—with richer, more privileged, car-driving people having physically larger perceived neighborhoods.[19]

- Clarence Perry's neighborhood unit, proposed in the 1920s, suggested a district the size of a catchment for a primary or elementary school.[20] Even in that period, Perry proposed a range of neighborhood sizes depending on household structure, ranging from 5,000 to 10,000 people. However, at different times and in other places, such schools have varied a great deal in size, meaning a neighborhood catchment could be smaller. There would be still more variation in size if the catchment of a shopping center was used.[21]

- Yet others have proposed that neighborhoods need a certain scale to foster political engagement. Alexander et al. suggest a political community of no more than 10,000.[22]

All these topics—employment, sustainability, quality of life, neighborhood services, and engagement—have some relation to health and well-being. One key issue is the common assumption that people conduct a large part of their activities within the neighborhood. However, people use services outside the neighborhood related to issues such as transportation connections, options offered, and personal preferences.[23]

No one ideal

Eventually, researchers came to the conclusion that there is no one ideal size for a city or a part of a city, such as a neighborhood or district, but rather:

- Each size of overall metropolitan area has advantages and disadvantages. Most obviously, larger populations can support more varied

A small village, a large metropolis, and many urban types in between can be healthy places.

services but tend to be larger in area and/or more congested than smaller communities.

- Even among services, different kinds of programs, facilities, and economic activities require different population thresholds to be viable. Many of these thresholds have changed over time or vary across places. For example, the population to support an elementary or primary school, the base of the classic neighborhood unit, depends on the number of children per household and the size of the school that is preferred in that society. This has changed with smaller households and changes in the approach to school size.

- Overall community size is irrelevant for some topics—what matters is the planning and design of the house, block, and district or larger systems of regulation and policy. For example, exposure to toxic chemicals in paint is related to the scale of the building as well as the wider policy context that determines what chemicals can be put into paint.

That said, there is a range of areas in which normal daily life is conducted, particularly if using walking and cycling, as is explained in later propositions. As we explain in the Glossary, at a very brisk 4 miles or 6 kilometers an hour, someone can walk from the center to the edge of a round district of 778 acres, or 314 hectares, in 10 minutes. This generic human activity leads to something that can be roughly called a neighborhood-scale (Figure 12).

Actions

◇ **Consider how planning and design proposals are framed by scales beyond the neighborhood.**

The neighborhood is nested between other health-relevant scales of intervention. At the larger scale are such systems as transportation, media, and health care finance. Metropolitan areas, cities, and towns provide the settings for neighborhoods and districts. At the much smaller scale is the environment of the household, home, or school. Making changes at the neighborhood level generally requires understanding of these other contexts.

◇ **Focus on good planning and design relevant to the size of a neighborhood or district.**

Different sizes of districts have different strengths and weaknesses. How they fit in a region also affects neighborhood performance—for example, how the district is exposed to air pollution or has access to services. These kinds of considerations are more important for making a healthy neighborhood or district than finding an ideal size.

Connections

There is no one ideal neighborhood size. To understand this proposition better, go to:

• **Principle 2. Balance:** Make healthier places by balancing physical changes with other interventions to appeal to different kinds of people

To further investigate, look at:

• **Proposition 10.** Provide enough density of population to support services for a healthy lifestyle

• **Proposition 13:** Coordinate land-use planning and urban design with transit to increase efficiency, access, and mobility

• **Principle 6. Connection:** Create opportunities for people to interact with each other in positive ways

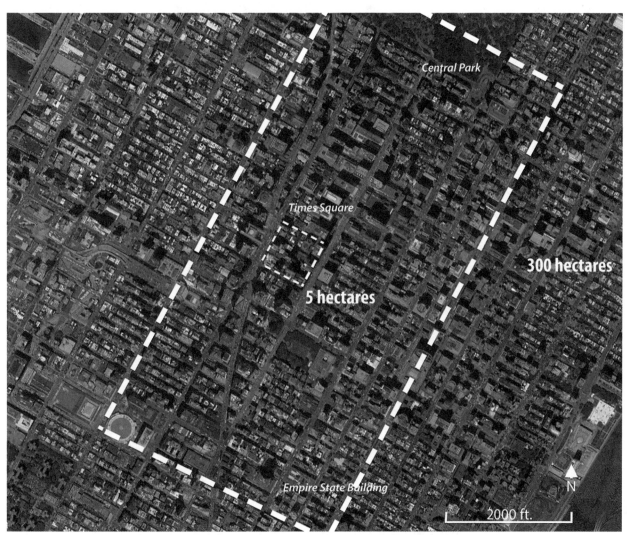

Figure 12. Size range of neighborhoods or districts dealt with in this book, illustrated in New York

Neighborhoods in this book range from a few hectares to some hundreds of hectares—the immediate vicinity of a home to a wider

area that is walkable and can provide services. For instance, a person could walk from the inner five-hectare (12-

acre) square near Times Square to the edge of the 300-hectare (700+-acre) rectangle near Central Park in about 10 minutes.

Source: Developed by authors using Google Maps

Vulnerability

Plan and design for those with the most health vulnerabilities and fewest resources for making healthy choices.

Many groups most vulnerable to health problems—the young, the old, those with existing illnesses, and those with low incomes—may spend much of their time in or around their residential neighborhood making the local environment particularly important for their health.

Certain demographic groups are also disproportionately burdened with problems stemming from the built environment, do not have the resources to deal effectively with those problems, or both.

Low-income people, infants and children, older adults, and other vulnerable groups often have the most health risks.

How It Works
Demographic issues

The groups that come up again and again in public health literature, in individual studies, and in major reviews such as the 2014 World Health Organization–sponsored *Review of Social Determinants and the Health Divide in the WHO European Region* include:[1]

- **Low-income people:** They are the most disadvantaged group across all health and place connections. They have much less ability to make healthy choices or to create healthy places.

- **Infants and children:** They are vulnerable to environmental health risks because they are still physically, mentally, and emotionally developing.

- **Older adults:** The physical and psychological changes that happen with aging mean that older adults are more likely to have mobility disabilities and chronic illnesses—making them more vulnerable to environmental hazards. They may also have less control over their environments, especially if they are low income or no longer able to care for themselves independently.

- **Ethnic and cultural minorities** In many countries, ethnic and cultural minorities face issues related to prejudice, neighborhood neglect, and historic spatial segregation, which can lead to disparate health outcomes. They may also have language barriers to accessing information and health care.

Focusing on these groups makes sense for multiple reasons. First is an ethical purpose, helping the most vulnerable to participate as fully as possible in society and to live with dignity and good health. Another reason is efficiency as preventing health problems in these vulnerable populations saves time and money for individuals, families, and the wider society.

Place Issues

Urban and rural places each have their own distinct challenges for public health and vulnerable groups:

- Vulnerable populations living in cities can be more prone to problems of the built environment because they may live in areas that are more exposed to air pollution, urban heat island effects, certain natural disasters, toxics, noise, traffic safety issues, and crime.
- Those in rural areas may face pollution from agricultural or mining industries, and issues related to accessibility and mobility. Rural areas generally have lower-density development patterns which can make it more difficult to get around, and have less variety of community resources like healthcare, food, and transit. In low-income countries, access to clean water and sanitation is also a major health issue.

Many of these problems are not focused at the neighborhood scale. However, some neighborhood-scale actions are possible. Like everyone else, vulnerable groups live and work in neighborhoods and districts. In existing neighborhoods, understanding where the most vulnerable groups are located will help identify the health and environmental problems they face (See Table 10). New neighborhood can be designed to improve access to resources and minimize problematic exposures. Areas of particular concern include environmental hazards, housing opportunities, universal design, comprehensive approaches to street design to enable mobility, and access to community services such as food outlets.

Connections

If there is a fundamental idea in this handbook, it is that vulnerable groups should be a key focus of healthy planning and design. To understand this proposition better, go to:

- **Proposition 1:** Figure out if there are good reasons for considering health

To further investigate, look at:

- **Principle 2. Balance:** Make healthier places by balancing physical changes with other interventions to appeal to different kinds of people
- **Principle 5. Access:** Provide options for getting around and increasing geographic access
- **Principle 6. Connection:** Create opportunities for people to interact with each other in positive ways
- **Principle 7. Protection:** Reduce harmful exposures at a neighborhood level through a combination of wider policies and regulations along with local actions

Table 10. Vulnerable populations and their health risks from negative place-related health outcomes

	Air quality	Climate/ Heat-illnesses	Disasters	Housing	Noise	Toxics
Low-income	●	●	●	●	●	●(a)
Children	●	●	●	●	●	●
Older adults	●	●	●	●	●	
Chronically ill	●	●	●	●(g)	●	
Women	●(j)	●(k)	●		●(l)	●(l)
Ethnic minorities		●(d)	●	●		●(a)
City dwellers	●	●	●	●(n)	●	●(a)
Rural populations						●(o)
Heavy labor employees	●	●			●	●(q)
Those socially isolated		●	●			

Source: Based on HAPI 2014 a–n; (a) residential proximity; (b) low-income countries; (c) mixed findings; (d) especially U.S.; (e) especially those under 5 years old; (f) traffic, fear of crime; (g) certain disabilities; (h) mobility difficulties; (i) traffic, mobility difficulties; (j) indoor; (k) some locations; (l) pregnant; (m) rape, domestic violence; (n) slum resident; (o) agriculture; (p) contaminated water source, sanitation; (q) occupational exposure

Water quality	Access to community resources	Social capital	Mobility/ Universal design	Access to healthy food	Physical activity	Safety
●(b)	●(c)			●(d)	●(c)	●(b)
●(e)		●	●	●		●(f)
		●	●			●(f)
	●(h)		●(h)			●(i)
						●(m)
				●(d)	●(c)	
						●
●(p)	●		●	●(d)		
		●				

Dots indicate which population groups (listed in left column) are most vulnerable to certain health risks that are covered in detail throughout this book (listed in top row).

Proposition 6: Create a variety of housing options to promote housing choices within the neighborhood

With mixed housing types, sizes, and tenures (various forms of ownership and rental), neighborhoods can provide housing options for households of varying ages, sizes, incomes, and preferences. This can support household stability and health over the lifespan.

How It Works

This proposition deals with how housing is related to general well-being. Specific evidence for housing having strong health effects is less clear, though Figure 13 summarizes results of multiple studies showing some effects. There is a need for more qualitative research to better understand the mechanisms that contribute to health.[2] This involves three interlinked issues:

- **Having housing that is of sufficient physical quality.** It seems obvious that housing should provide enough space, clean water, good waste water treatment, sufficient lighting, thermal comfort, waste disposal options, nontoxic surfaces, good ventilation, and personal safety and security.[3] However, in many places (including many new developments) it does not. Access to outdoor areas, even a balcony, is often limited. While it can be tempting to create a minimal house of the smallest possible size—and necessary in some locations—having enough space to change household structure (e.g., add children,

host aging parents), incorporate a home business, and the like adds flexibility. On the other hand, many communities defend excessive lot sizes and setbacks by citing quality, when good design can make much denser housing forms work well.

- **Having options for healthy housing across a person's lifespan within the neighborhood.** People may not live their entire lives in a single neighborhood, but wherever they live they should have access to appropriate housing. One way to do that is to mix housing types (single units, small apartments, larger and taller buildings, housing with services like meals and home care), housing sizes, and housing tenures. The mix need not be one unit or parcel at a time—often called salt and pepper. It also does not mean that every neighborhood has to have every possible kind of unit for every type of person. It can be appropriate for an apartment building to house mainly smaller households or even disabled people needing collective services,

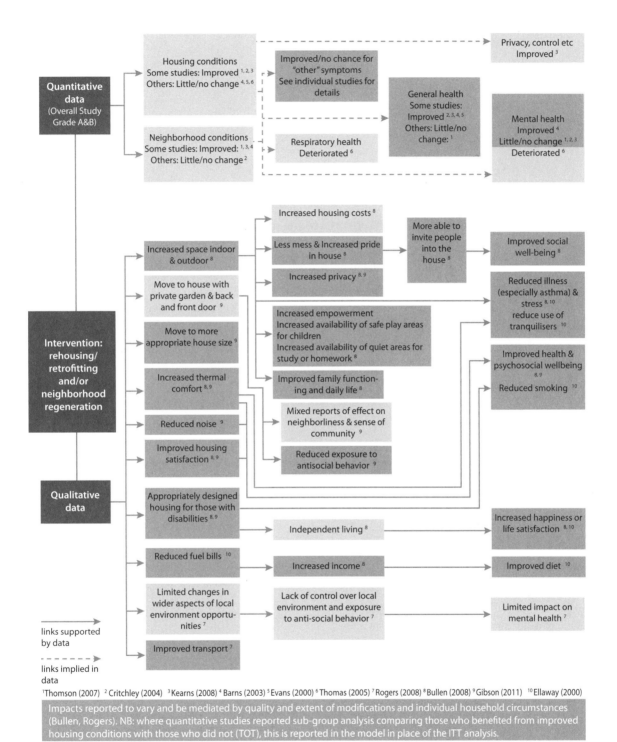

Figure 13. How housing retrofitting and neighborhood regeneration relates to health

This conceptual diagram illustrates the connections between housing and health, based on Thompson and Thomas's 2015 systematic review. Light gray boxes are negative and dark gray boxes are positive.

Source: Thompson and Thomas 2015

Table 11. Housing affordability problems and strategies

Housing component	Problem	Affordability strategy
Land (a)	High-cost land in "hot" housing markets and in locations with good amenities (schools, employment centers, transit, services) increases cost of housing	• Increased density so more units on the same land • Public and non-profit housing for rent and sale • Community land trusts to separate cost of land from housing unit
Construction Materials and Labor	Construction materials and can drive up the cost of development	• Permit modular homes to reduce construction costs
Regulatory costs (a, b)	Complying with complex building codes, environmental and land-use regulations, impact fees, and administrative barriers can add time and resources to the planning and development pipeline	• One-stop shops to access building permits and information • Expedite permitting and development/review processes for affordable housing • Have project facilitators to navigate the regulatory process • Adopt rehab codes to streamline improvements to existing homes
Energy use. maintenance, and taxation (long-term)	Costs of owning and operating a home can be high in initially inexpensive homes	• Standards and incentive programs for higher quality and energy efficient uses • Home modification and weatherization programs • Making homes help provide income (e.g. space for home businesses, accessory rental units)
Mortgages and lending (c)	Interest rates and down payments can be a barrier.	• First-time homebuyer programs • Low-interest or deferred-payment loans • Shared-equity programs to preserve affordable housing subsidies (b)

Most of these strategies to increase affordability involve government programs, policies, and regulations.

Sources: (a) Forsyth et al. 2015; (b) Schill 2005; (c) Lubell 2014, 203–230

for households with children to seek homes close to schools, or for older people to want to be very close to shops and even clustered in the same building. However, on balance in the neighborhood, there need to be options.

- **Providing housing that is not too expensive, draining other resources.** Households that spend more than they can afford on housing-related costs (rent or mortgage, plus utilities) may be susceptible to health risks. Table 11 describes some of the affordability challenges along with strategies for mitigating them. In addition, households with fewer resources often live in less advantageous areas (termed locational disadvantage)—further from jobs and other resources. They may also be forced to move more often due to cost, severing positive social ties.

One problem is that healthy housing areas are attractive and may increase in value, a phenomenon termed gentrification in some situations, potentially excluding those who need such locations the most. Providing a range of housing sizes, densities, and construction technologies is a start in creating a healthy housing mix. Smaller homes and styles with more units on the same amount of land can provide inexpensive options. Another strategy is to use less expensive construction techniques, such as manufactured housing or owner-built methods. However, even these may not solve all the affordability problems.

This means that additional strategies are needed to ensure affordability, which are dealt with in the actions. Most are at the dwelling or wider policy scales, however, and only indirectly affected by neighborhood planning and design. They include providing housing outside the market through public ownership, subsidies, or collective land ownership and increasing housing supply through additional construction or the dividing up of large units. Generally, they require either direct actions by city, state, and national governments, or policies that support private and nonprofit initiatives. This issue of the cost of a healthy environment is a crucial one.

Evidence about Health
Housing quality

Housing quality—the condition of the physical dwelling—can be linked to health. Older homes, poorly maintained homes, and those with structural deficiencies can increase the risk of negative physical and mental health outcomes (Table 12). A systematic review of housing improvements and health outcomes found some housing improvements can yield modest health improvements, but inconsistently and not always directly (see Figure 13).[4] Of 14 New Zealand and UK studies reviewed on warmth and energy efficiency improvements and health, the authors find conclusive evidence to support health improvements in units of inadequate warmth, with the strongest benefits for residents with existing respiratory disease.[5] Other housing improvements that lead to increased

Table 12. Health issues associated with poor housing conditions, and neighborhood-level responses

Health Issue	Cause	Neighborhood-level Response
Relevant to neighborhood-scale		
Gastrointestinal illness (a)	Poor water, sanitation, and hygiene conditions (sewer, plumbing)	District or higher level clean water and sewage system
Mental health (e.g. aggression, withdrawal, psychological distress, depression)(a, b, c)	Overcrowding (many people per room), inadequate lighting, multifamily housing (e.g. 3 or more units), high-rise housing (particularly for low-income families with children), noise, fear of crime	Low-rise housing options or larger units for low-income families with children
Respiratory and allergic effects (a, d, e)	Secondhand smoke, dampness, mold, poor ventilation, VOC exposure, pests, pets, particulate matter, inadequate warmth	Building siting for good natural ventilation, shading, and passive solar
Relevant to other scales		
Asthma (a)	Allergens, dampness, mold, pesticide exposure	*
Cancer (a)	Secondhand smoke, radon, asbestos	*
Cardiovascular effects (c)	Secondhand smoke, excessive heat/cold, VOC exposure	*
Injuries (e.g. falls, fires/ burns, choking/ suffocation, drowning/submersion) (a)	Structural deficiencies, lack of accessible features, lack of safety devices	*
Mortality (c)	Secondhand smoke, carbon-monoxide poisoning, injury, nonworking smoke alarms, excessive hot or cold conditions	*
Neurological damage (a)	Carbon monoxide poisoning, polychlorinated biphenyls (PCBs) in water, lead poisoning	*

Sources: (a) U.S. HHS 2009, 5–14; (b) Evans 2003, 536; (c) Jacobs 2011, S118; (d) Gibson et al. 2011; (e) Thompson and Thomas 2015, 208

Older adults often desire to stay in their home or within their communities as they age, increasing the need for options.

living and usable space, better housing design, housing satisfaction, and control over the living environment may support improved health and well-being, though evidence is mixed. Long-term health effects of housing improvements were not evaluated in the studies reviewed.[6]

A review of housing by type, floor level, and neighborhood quality and its effects on mental health found that high-rise housing as a type is linked to self-reported psychological distress, which is most pronounced among low-income mothers with young children, and possibly the children themselves due to restricted recreation and play activities.[7] Less is understood about the specific mental health effects of high-rise housing based on floor level.[8] In addition, high-income high-rise dwellers have rarely been studied but presumably avoid health problems due to larger units and an ability to go out and about more easily. A systematic review of reviews on housing and health indicate research on housing tenure and health has not been studied in enough depth to make conclusions about the health effects of owning or renting a unit.[9]

Housing and the lifespan

The housing life cycle, generally based on the nuclear family, and the more contemporary concept of the life course, based on significant life events, are ways to understand how housing needs change over time. Housing to meet the needs for older adults is especially important as the global population of persons over age 65 reaches unprecedented numbers. Between 2050 and 2100 the 65+ population is projected to increase from 16 and over 24 percent.[10] Overwhelmingly personal preference surveys and focus groups indicate that older adults desire to age in place—that is, staying in their home or within the same community as they age.[11] Good quality housing is linked to psychological well-being in older adults, and older adults living in higher-quality homes tend to feel more attached to where they live.[12] But the condition and cost of housing is a critical factor that determines whether this is desired or even possible.[13]

Though there is a lack of research evidence to support specific planning and design interventions that enable aging in place, ensuring access to affordable and stable housing options is key (including multigenerational options, seniors-only assisted living, and supportive services). Strategies that eliminate mobility barriers within the home, offer access to nearby services, and provide opportunities for social interaction are generally recognized as features that support households in different stages of life.

Costs and health

Research summaries and reviews on housing affordability and health suggest that to cover housing costs, households may be forced to make trade-offs on food and medical expenses, live in overcrowded units that can increase exposure to stress and infectious diseases, or occupy units of substandard condition. As mentioned in the section on housing quality, residents living in units of compromised quality face increased risk of injuries and exposure to lead, radon, or other toxics associated with cardiovascular problems, cancer, respiratory and allergic effects, asthma, neurological effects, and mental health issues.[14] Tsai's systematic review of 42 publications on foreclosure, health, and mental health found that, at an individual level, foreclosure—a delinquent or unpaid mortgage—has adverse mental health effects due to stress, which is linked to poorer health.[15]

Struggles to keep up with housing expenses may lead to housing instability, defined as frequent or unplanned moves, which is linked to stress, depression, and other psychological disorders. A policy piece on housing and health suggests that housing instability may also undermine "the ability of individuals with chronic health problems to maintain a consistent treatment regime."[16] Research reviews on housing insecurity, housing instability, mobility of children, the built environment, and mental health present consistent evidence that among children frequent moves are linked to a higher incidence of ear infections, asthma, developmental risk, lower body weight, and socioemotional problems.[17]

A literature review of 92 articles on the physical, social, and economic environments of local communities and residents' health found that "poor conditions in homes and neighborhoods tend to cluster together, compounding the risks for adverse health consequences."[18] Other studies have attempted to understand how improving neighborhood conditions may contribute to health. Gibson et al. reviewed two studies of US-based government interventions to move disadvantaged populations to lower-poverty areas. Of participants who moved, there were reductions in the proportion of participants reporting depression and an increase in the proportion of participants reporting good or excellent health.[19] However, it is unclear if the improvements were a result of the new neighborhood conditions or the new housing conditions.[20]

Actions

◇ **Take a life course approach to creating a housing mix.**
Promote different building types—accessory dwelling units, single-family and multifamily

homes to accommodate residents of different ages—and ensure that options employ universal design features to minimize mobility barriers within the home.

◆ **Provide housing of high physical quality.**
Much of housing quality is related to building-level decisions such as internal air circulation, structural integrity, and maintenance. However, there are site and neighborhood-level dimensions, including housing that has access to usable open spaces, is protected from external noise, has proper lighting and shading to enhance thermal comfort, and is located in safe areas.

◆ **Use strategies beyond size and density to protect affordability, particularly in high-cost areas.**
Housing policies and programs can expand and preserve the supply of affordable housing —rental and ownership—to households that need it most. Several models provide innovative tenures, such as community land trusts that own the land while the resident owns the home, nonprofit ownership, and government ownership. Other techniques can reduce cost, such as helping owners build all or part of the home themselves, subsidizing interest, and promoting rent-to-own models and shared equity programs.

Connections

Housing variety is a key strategy for improving many dimensions of health—physical, social, mental. To understand this proposition better, go to:

- **Principle 2. Balance:** Make healthier places by balancing physical changes with other interventions to appeal to different kinds of people

To further investigate, look at:

- **Principle 4. Layout:** Foster multiple dimensions of health through overall neighborhood layout
- **Proposition 10.** Provide enough density of population to support services for a healthy lifestyle
- **Proposition 12:** Increase access to a variety of locally relevant recreational facilities and green spaces
- **Principle 7. Protection:** Reduce harmful exposures at a neighborhood level through a combination of wider policies and regulations along with local actions

Proposition 7: Integrate universal design principles into neighborhood planning and design

Places should incorporate mobility consideration to facilitate ease of use for persons of all ages and abilities. This requires both removing mobility barriers on streets, sidewalks, and other public and private spaces and creating a more enabling environment.

How It Works

The mobility of many people, especially those with physical disabilities, is affected by the condition of pedestrian infrastructure in public spaces and the design of building structures.[21] Most people will experience mobility difficulties at some point in their lives due to illness, injury, caregiving for an older parent or young child, or aging. But too often the built environment is unpleasant, difficult to navigate, or inaccessible for walking, cycling, or exercising for those with impairments.

Universal design is an approach to designing products and features in the built environment aimed at eliminating barriers, at little or no extra cost, that are more likely to be burdensome for older adults and populations with physical, cognitive, or sensory disabilities.[22] Examples of universal design features include ramps with handrails instead of stairs and countertops at a height accessible for persons in wheelchairs. Internationally, similar design concepts are known as barrier free planning, normalization, inclusive

design, and design for all.[23] Universal design is guided by a set of seven principles demonstrated in Table 13, that when applied benefit persons of all ages and abilities, including adults with small children in strollers, injured persons, and those without any impairments.[24]

Although it is implied that universal design concepts will foster increased mobility and opportunities for physical activity, research indicates that universal design features in the environment alone may not be enough. Other factors to improve mobility, highlighted in systematic reviews and guidebooks, include high-quality transportation, destinations close enough for walking or wheeling, and amenities like public toilets, seating, and lighting.[25]

Evidence about Health

How much one is able to engage in physical activity is partially associated with ability or disability, though most research on this topic comes from United States. The US Centers for Disease Control's Behavioral Risk Factor Surveillance System data from 2009 indicate that the rate of physical inactivity among Americans with a disability is 22 percent, as opposed to only 10 percent for Americans with no disability. Disabled people also have increased risk of secondary conditions, some of which can be prevented or maintained by regular physical activity, including overweight and obesity, diabetes, asthma, and arthritis.[26]

Most research on universal design, health, and place makes a general link between the built environment and physical access and general convenience. However, not enough is known about how specific features facilitate or act as barriers to one's involvement in daily activity, especially among older adults.[27] Whether universal design increases healthy behaviors or improves health outcomes is not well understood, and there are no studies that measure the physical, psychological, and social benefits of accessible neighborhoods.[28] An in-depth review of 95 instruments to measure levels of walking, cycling and recreation "with respect to disability and universal design" found only approximately a third of the tools consider people with disabilities and only a few universal design principles are consistently demonstrated across the tools, suggesting a lack of consideration at the neighborhood-scale for the needs of all users.[29]

Actions

Tables 13 and 14 provide examples of universal design interventions to make the built environment more accessible for people of all ages and abilities.

Universal design features are helpful for people of all ages and abilities.

Table 13. Universal design principles and neighborhood examples

Principle	Neighborhood examples
Equitable Use: The design is useful and marketable to people with diverse abilities	• Paths that separate people and vehicular traffic • Sidewalks, separated bike lanes, rights-of-way, crosswalks
Flexibility in Use: The design accomodates a wide range of individual preferences and abilities	• A downtown that is able to accommodate increasing numbers of residents as increasingly people want to live near where they work • A greenspace which accommodates different activities, e.g. children's playground, sports fields, scenic walking paths, formal garden with benches
Simple and Intuitive Use: Use of the design is easy to understand, regardless of the user's experience, knowledge, language skills, or current concentration level	• Clear and accurate wayfinding and directional signs
Perceptible Information: The design communicates necessary information effectively to the user, regardless of ambient conditions or the user's sensor abilities	• Signs, wayfinding, and crosswalks engage more than one sensory mode (e.g. visual, auditory, tactile) • Using images, sounds, and changes in horizontal surface textures to communicate
Tolerance for Error: The design minimizes hazards and the adverse consequences of accidental or unintended consequences	• Disaster evacuation plans • Connectivity of street pattern to ensure access for emergency vehicles
Low Physical Effort: The design can be used efficiently and comfortably and with a minimum of fatigue.	• Affordable and accessible mass transportation (e.g. bus rapid transit, taxis, subway) • Wide and well-maintained sidewalks with curb cuts
Size and Space for Approach and Use: Appropriate size and space is provided for approach, reach, manipulation, and use regardless of user's body size, posture, or mobility	• Complete communities with a balance of housing, transportation, and services to meet daily needs • Pedestrian amenities provided (e.g. benches, public toilets)

The commonly recognized definition of universal design includes seven core principles, aimed to design products and features in the built environment to eliminate barriers, that are more likely to be burdensome for older adults and populations with physical, cognitive, or sensory disabilities (left-hand column). The examples in the right-hand column, and photos in the adjacent array, illustrate how these principles can be implemented at the neighborhood or district scale.

Sources: Modified from HAPI 2014c, 4; The Center for Universal Design 1997; Nasar and Evans-Crowley 2007, 17–24

Paths that separate people and vehicular traffic

Disaster evacuation plans for vulnerable areas

A downtown with live-near-work opportunities

Clear and accurate wayfinding and directional signs

Accessible mass transit

Crosswalks that engage more than one sensory mode

Pedestrian amenities (e.g. seating)

◇ **Use the core universal design principles as a checklist for neighborhood planning, design, and redevelopment.**
The universal design principles in Table 13 and interventions in Table 14 can be used to assess how accessible and user-friendly a place is. Incorporating universal design principles starting from the initial design and planning phase of any project is ideal, as retrofitting an existing site can be a time- and resource-intensive process.[30]

Universal design interventions include wide, accessible, and unobstructed routes with well-maintained, non-slip pavement. Ramps and elevators should be available, if neccesary, to provide an alternative to stairs.

Connections

From a life-course perspective, just about everyone needs universal design features at some point in their lives, but these features are not yet ubiquitous. To further investigate, look at:

- **Proposition 11:** Create a connected, "healthier" travel circulation pattern for pedestrians, bicyclists, and transit users—the vehicular pattern can be different
- **Proposition 12:** Increase access to a variety of locally relevant recreational facilities and green spaces
- **Principle 5. Access:** Provide options for getting around and increasing geographic access
- **Proposition 14:** Adopt policies and planning practices to create safe neighborhood transportation options for all types of road users
- **Principle 6. Connection:** Create opportunities for people to interact with each other in positive ways
- **Proposition 16:** Create publicly accessible neighborhood spaces, programs, and events to support healthy interactions and behaviors

Table 14. Universal design interventions for different types of places

Place (a,b,c)	Example
Streets and sidewalks	☐ Curb cuts (d, e, f, g)
	☐ Wide accessible access routes (d, e, f)
	☐ Well maintained and even pavement (d, e)
	☐ Traffic signals that can be seen and heard
	☐ Numerous crosswalks and signs (g)
	☐ Handrails (f), seating, and street furniture (h, i)
	☐ Warning strips (g)
	☐ Gradients/incline no more than 6% (e)
	☐ Public toilets (h)
	☐ Wayfinding signage (g)
Public spaces (indoor and outdoor)	☐ Wayfinding (signage, direct visual access, simple decision/reference points, wheelchair entrances, textures and sounds for the blind) (j, k)
	☐ Street furniture (h, i)
Outdoor spaces (parks, gardens, civic squares)	☐ No stairs or obstructions in paths (b)
	☐ Wide paths and sidewalks (b)
	☐ Well-maintained, non-slip paths (b)
Building entrances	☐ Wide doorways (f)
	☐ Adequate disabled parking spots (3–5% of spaces) (f)
	☐ Motorized door opening (f)
	☐ Setting down points where passengers can be dropped on and off
	☐ Ramps (f)
Transit planning and public transport	☐ Locating transit stops within a 10–15 minute walk from residential neighborhoods (l)
	☐ Universal design features on public transit and stations (m)
	☐ Door-to-door transit schemes (m)
	☐ Wayfinding signage (g)

Sources: Adapted from HAPI 2014c, 9 and (a) Centre for Accessible Environments 2012, 22–42, 48; (b) Preiser and Smith eds. 2011, 17.9; (c) Skiba and Zuger 2009, 17–20, 21, 26, 30, 34, 67–68, 72; (d) Clarke et al. 2008; (e) Li et al. 2012, 602; (f) Rimmer et al. 2004, 421, 424; (g) University of Kansas 2013; (h) WHO 2007 (i) de Nazelle et al. 2011, 775; (j) Passini 1996; (k) Marquardt 2011, 80; (l) Doerksen et al. 2007, 52; (m) Green 2013, S125

Proposition 8: Increase choice, access, and exposure to high-quality, diverse, and healthy food options, especially in low-income areas

Eating habits are based on a number of factors, including personal and cultural preferences, income, marketing, education, availability (seasons, accessibility), and cost of food. But ensuring consumers have a range of options to purchase affordable and nutritious food is necessary to facilitate healthy choices.

How It Works

Maintaining a healthy and nutritious diet is an important part of basic health that can reduce the risk of obesity, hypertension, diabetes, and other related health conditions.[31] As Figure 14 shows, food consumption habits are based on a number of factors that include the neighborhood food environment (places outside the home, school, work, or other settings where food is consumed). But the figure also shows most of what can be done to improve healthy eating lies outside the area of neighborhood design—from marketing, labeling, and education to pricing, workplace culture, and school offerings. The neighborhood built environment is a very small part of the food environment picture. Even the much-publicized US food deserts in low-income areas, not replicated in other countries, are not necessarily lacking in healthy food options but rather the cost of healthy foods may be a greater barrier.[32]

Evidence about Health

The modest importance of neighborhood

A commonplace assumption is that neighborhood proximity to healthy food options is the primary driver behind one's food consumption habits. In the United States, systematic reviews of research studies consistently find that neighborhoods with predominantly low-income populations (both rural and urban) and ethnic or racial minority groups have an overabundance of fast food options, or lack access to food outlets that source affordable, nutritious food.[33] These areas are also known as "food deserts." However, it is far less clear whether this affects actual food consumption as so many other factors are at play.

Whether "food deserts" are a problem in other high-income countries is also less clear. Black et al. conducted an international systematic review on neighborhood food environments. A total of 123 articles were reviewed (United States, United Kingdom, Canada, Australia and New Zealand represented). The authors were able to conclude, "There is evidence for inequalities in food access in the U.S. but trends are less apparent in other developed countries."[34]

More importantly, other scales of the food environment, as well as the larger macro-level factors appear to be more substantial influences on what people eat than the neighborhood scale[35] (see Figure 14). Several sample studies from the United States find this to be the case. For example, a survey of over 500 residents in Philadelphia found that nearly 95 percent of participants shopped at large chain grocery stores outside of their neighborhood, as opposed to the local convenience stores.[36] Similarly, a study on shopping patterns of 1,682 participants in King County, Washington, found that only one in seven respondents shopped at the supermarket nearest to their home. Rather, respondents typically traveled to the nearest full-service supermarket.[37]

On the other hand, the cost of healthy food (economic access) is a global concern because healthier diets cost more. Several US-based studies examine food costs in relation to its nutritional value.

- Aggarwal et al. looked at the relationship between the nutrient intakes, diet cost, and socioeconomic status of individuals in King County, Washington

The cost of healthy food matters just as much, if not more, than proximity to food outlets.

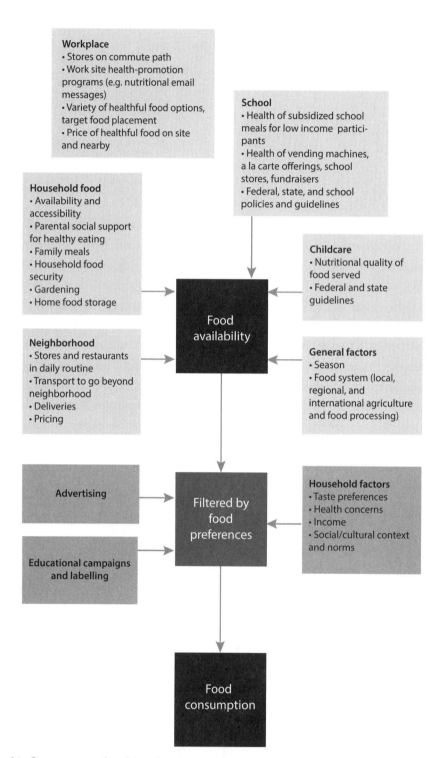

Figure 14. Broad influences on food intake

Food consumption habits are based on numerous factors that operate at multiple scales from individuals and households, to schools and workplaces, the larger media environment, and the food system.

Source: Adapted from Forsyth et al. 2010a; Story et al. 2008

(n=1,266). The study found that "nutrients commonly associated with a lower risk of chronic diseases were associated with higher diet costs" and vice versa. The cost discrepancy "may help somewhat explain why lower income groups fail to comply with dietary guidelines and have the highest rates of diet related chronic disease."[38]

- Drewnowski compared the cost versus nutritional value of foods using the U.S. Department of Agriculture Food and Nutrient Database for Dietary Studies and the Center for Nutrition Policy and Promotion food prices database. "The highest prices per serving were found for meats, poultry, and fish, and the lowest prices per serving were for the fats category. These price differentials may help to explain why low-cost, energy-dense foods that are nutrient poor are associated with lower education and incomes."[39]

Given this situation, a reasonable path forward is to provide options within or near neighborhoods, ensure transportation is available to link homes to stores, and ensure that the trend of home delivery of healthy food is accessible to those with lower incomes.

Actions

- ❖ **Create a flexible neighborhood plan to make it possible to adjust to the geographically varied and evolving food retail landscape.**

   The food landscape is evolving and varies by place. For example, in some locations grocery and meal deliveries are rare, in dense neighborhoods or districts with an economy of scale they are commonplace, and in others they are on the rise.

- ◆ **Focus on providing access to lower-cost sources of healthy food.**

   Price is a key barrier to purchasing healthy foods, and neighborhood and district planning should not make it worse. Depending on the location, this may involve accessing health promotion funding to support individual vendors and markets, grocery stores, or supermarkets in offering healthy food at different price ranges. It may also mean helping people travel out of the neighborhood to obtain cheaper food through strategies such as revised bus routes, shopping shuttles, and shared rides.

- ◇ **Concentrate most food stores in locations where people already walk, cycle, and take transit.**

   Convenience may be important, so food stores and restaurants should be located where people can take transit, walk, and cycle. This also means that the food store can be a destination for active travel.

- ◇ **Carefully locate food retail and dining places, including convenience stores, restaurants, food vendors, or public markets, considering both access and commercial viability.**

   Proximity to food outlets is not the primary factor behind consumer shopping behavior, as

Figure 14 illustrates, but increasing food vending and shopping opportunities in strategic locations can help provide options. However, in research on mixed use new development, Grant and Foord separately describe how some developments in Canada and the United Kingdom have struggled to attract street-level retail and commercial tenants due to lack of customers, contrary to the planners' and designers' assumptions that they would be ideal locations for shopping opportunities.[40] The implication is that food retail locations need to be realistic.

◇ **Use food-related activities to generate health benefits beyond nutrition.**
Food related activities such as community gardens may only produce food for a few months of the year, but they help gardeners make social connections for far longer. Home gardening can provide mental health benefits. Buy-local programs can help the local economy with the indirect effects on health.

Connections

Improving access to healthy food options does not necessarily mean that consumers will change their eating habits, but it does mean that they have options to make healthy choices about their diet. To understand this proposition better, go to:

- **Principle 3. Vulnerability:** Plan and design for those with the most health vulnerabilities and fewest resources for making healthy choices
- **Proposition 9:** Create mixed use neighborhoods with a balance of activities that support good health
- **Proposition 10:** Provide enough density of population to support services for a healthy lifestyle
- **Proposition 12:** Increase access to a variety of locally relevant recreational facilities and green spaces
- **Proposition 13:** Coordinate land-use planning and urban design with transit to increase efficiency, access, and mobility

Community gardens and urban farms can encourage social connections, support the local economy, and provide valuable educational programs on healthy eating.

Layout

Foster multiple dimensions of health through overall neighborhood layout.

A well-planned or healthy neighborhood, designed holistically, can benefit many dimensions of health through appropriate densities of people and activities, connected street patterns, and well-design open spaces. It is easiest to coordinate these features when an area is initially developed, but better design can be retrofitted over time in existing places.

How It Works
Overview of Practice

How the neighborhoods and districts where people live, work, learn, and socialize can support healthy behaviors varies by the kinds of people and environments. For example, some places provide more options for recreation and others may reduce exposure to hazards, and these may be more important for some age groups.

Generally, however, a healthy neighborhood or district is one in which people are able to have convenient access to employment and housing, everyday services and institutions, transportation, and green spaces (Figure 15). In particular, access to resources such as healthcare facilities, recreation spaces, and healthy food outlets can provide options that support healthy behaviors. Many styles of neighborhood and district environments can support health, from small towns to areas of major metropolitan regions—however, several dimensions are key. These are outlined here and dealt with in more detail in later propositions.

Activities: Typically some mixture of activities is needed in neighborhoods and districts. While planners often call these land uses, we use the more general term activities as they may occur over time in a way that a static land-use mix does not account for well.

For largely residential areas, these would start with schools, markets or shops, jobs (or some way of getting to them), places to recreate, and other places for sharing information (from libraries to coffee shops). Some of these residential neighborhoods are self-contained towns and villages and others are connected to larger metropolitan areas.

For employment areas, they would include many of the activities above. However, in some circumstances, they may have few or no residences but rather may be linked to residential areas.

Activities also include more temporary happenings, such as cyclovias (where streets are closed to vehicles so cyclists and pedestrians can take over), farmers markets, and street vendors.

Density: As the glossary demonstrates, density has a range of meanings. In this situation, it is broadly the number of people in an area and may be measured in terms of residents, housing units, workers, visitors, or some combination of these. It is related to the physical size of buildings, though different numbers of people can inhabit buildings of the same size. It is also related to land-use activities. Healthy neighborhoods need to have a minimum density so that there are enough people in an area to support services like shops and so that people can reach those services quickly using available transportation.

However, given this premise, there is a very broad range of potential densities for a healthy neighborhood, some quite leafy and spread out and others very intensely built up.

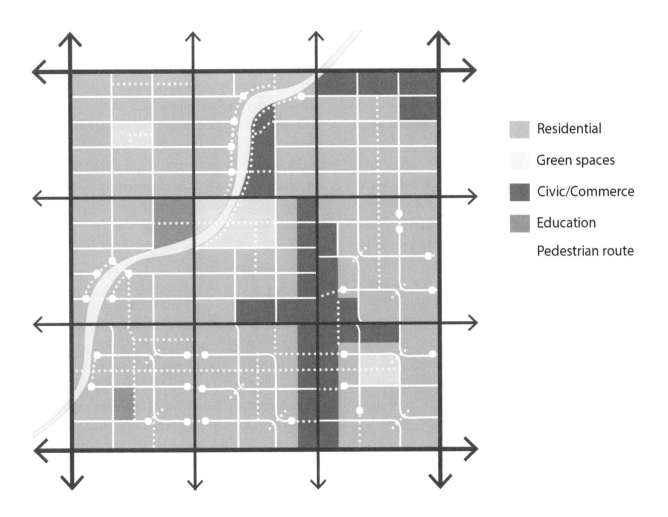

Figure 15. Internal arrangement of neighborhood and district, with services and connections

Healthy neighborhoods provide space for the various activities of daily life. They also help people connect within the neighborhood and outside. This neighborhood uses a fused grid layout to combine traffic safety and pedestrian circulation. The fused grid is explained in Proposition 11.

Source: Developed by authors and Yannis Orfanos

Street and path pattern: How blocks, streets, and paths are laid out is also key to healthy neighborhoods, as these connect people with each other and with services. Large blocks make getting around more circuitous and can discourage pedestrian travel, although paths that cut through blocks can remake those links.

Open spaces, natural, and recreational areas: A final dimension of a healthy neighborhood is the balance between indoor and outdoor spaces, and in

particular how open spaces, natural, and recreational areas are inserted into districts. Too few open spaces limit people's options for interacting with nature and engaging in outdoor recreational activities; too many open spaces may lower densities so much that it is hard to get around. Balancing these dimensions is not simple.

At lower density levels, the problem is having enough people to support services like shops and having ways for people to get around if they cannot drive cars (including the young and the old). At

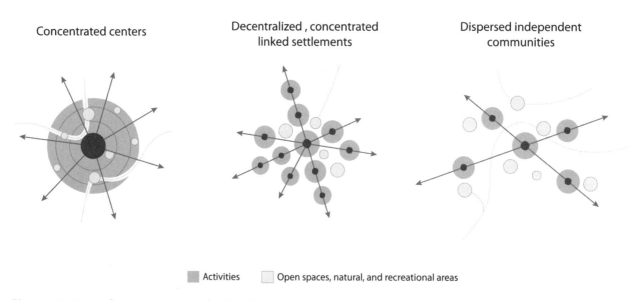

Concentrated centers

Decentralized, concentrated linked settlements

Dispersed independent communities

Activities   Open spaces, natural, and recreational areas

Figure 16. Varied arrangements for healthy neighborhoods

Healthy neighborhoods can be clustered in different ways—packed close together in a compact town or city and linked along transportation routes, such as trains or bus lines.

Source: Developed by authors and Yannis Orfanos

greater densities, the problem is some of the negative side effects of having concentrated numbers of people and economic activities, ranging from air quality problems to not having places where people can find refuge from traffic and noise. This section tackles how to balance these problems and potential benefits in particular places.

Connections

How neighborhoods are laid out physically—streets, buildings, open spaces—is fundamental and expensive to change. To understand this proposition better, go to:

- **Proposition 4:** Understand that trade-offs are inherent in planning for health at all scales and this is true of neighborhoods as well

To further investigate, look at:

- **Proposition 9:** Create mixed use neighborhoods with a balance of activities that support good health
- **Proposition 10.** Provide enough density of population to support services for a healthy lifestyle
- **Proposition 11:** Create a connected, "healthier" travel circulation pattern for pedestrians, bicyclists, and transit users—the vehicular pattern can be different
- **Proposition 12:** Increase access to a variety of locally relevant recreational facilities and green spaces
- **Principle 5. Access:** Provide options for getting around and increasing geographic access

- **Principle 6. Connection:** Create opportunities for people to interact with each other in positive ways
- **Principle 7. Protection:** Reduce harmful exposures at a neighborhood level through a combination of wider policies and regulations along with local actions

A certain density threshold is required to support public transportation and widely accessible community resources.

Proposition 9: Create mixed use neighborhoods with a balance of activities that support good health

In neighborhoods and districts that have a well-balanced land-use mix, people have easy access to the kinds of places and services that enable healthy behaviors along with good transportation to link to destinations elsewhere.

How It Works

What gets mixed and why

Neighborhoods with mixed land uses and other more temporary activities provide some of the health advantages of a healthy neighborhood. A mixed use approach increases proximity (access) to resources, including open space and recreational facilities; supports walking or cycling to destinations through connected street patterns or paths; and can support the density needed for public transportation. However, such neighborhoods vary a great deal. Some provide access to services for residents' daily needs—to places such as food stores, medical offices, and schools—and are connected to other resources in the wider city by means including buses, trains, and bicycles as well as cars. Others have a more substantial mix so that almost all of one's life can be conducted there.

A key issue is what is mixed in such a neighborhood? In other words, what are the uses or activities that are combined?:

- Mixed uses in this context typically include housing and other activities. However, housing types such as apartments and detached homes may also need to be mixed to attract different kinds of households, from families with small children to living for older adults.
- Similar proposals may be made about businesses, green spaces, or institutional uses such as schools and hospitals, which are the four big categories at the base of most land-use schemes. Within each category there typically needs to be a mix.
- In general, a healthy neighborhood provides the basics of daily life nearby, but residential neighborhoods may need to be connected to other areas for employment opportunities and other needs; the reverse is true for employment districts.

Grain of mix: This mix of activities also needs to be planned at a certain spatial scale or grain. It is not much good to mix three uses—or three types of one use, like housing—in very big clumps of hundreds

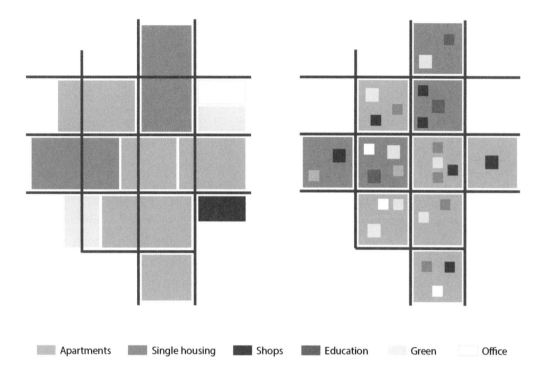

Apartments   Single housing   Shops   Education   Green   Office

Figure 17. Diagram of clumps versus a random fine-grained mix

These two diagrams show the same grid pattern and same mix of activities. They differ in different in how the activities are clustered. The left-hand diagram shows different activities laid out in big clumps, whereas the right-hand diagram displays the same activities in a random fine-grained or "salt and pepper" mix. A middle ground places some important activities like shopping in clusters close to most people.

Source: Developed by authors and Yannis Orfanos

of acres each as this lumpiness defeats the purpose of mix. However a random fine-grained or "salt and pepper" mix of, say, stores and offices, eliminates the benefits of clustering as in a town or neighborhood center. Clusters provide easy and convenient access or proximity to destinations and services. The scale or grain of mix matters.

Bad mix: It is also important to point out that mixing land-use activities is not necessarily good in and of itself—imagine a mix of housing with automobile megastores, gravel pits, and waste transfer stations—even if it is at a good grain and well clustered. Rather it is important to have a balance of healthy uses and

to carefully locate and regulate others that may be harmful to human health.

Healthy mix as a balance

In terms of health, mixing land-use activities requires a balance.

Positive interactions: On the one hand, bringing people closer to each other and to services means that most people can find support and resources nearby. This is particularly important for those who cannot travel with ease because they are old, young, unwilling or unable to drive, or do not have a car. However, even for others without these travel barriers, proximity provides options in terms of being able to do things locally and use walking and cycling to get there if they want.

Negative conflicts: On the other hand, bringing all these activities together can sometimes cause problems—conflicts between groups, exposures to noise and pollution, increases in crime or traffic congestion, and safety concerns.

Evidence about Health
Mixed use supporting healthy behavior
Summary reviews of research studies on neighborhood layout and adult physical activity provide consistent evidence that areas with a mix of uses foster walking for transportation.

McCormack and Shiell's review of 20 cross-sectional and 13 quasi-experimental studies published between 1996 and 2010 on the built environment

Figure 18. Mixed land use is not always positive
Residential proximity to uncontrolled waste can increase risk of disease and birth defects. Pregnant women and children are particularly vulnerable to the health risks of waste exposure.

and physical activity and Ewing and Cervero's meta-analysis of over 60 studies on the built environment and travel patterns identify that a mix of land-use activities supports walking for transportation, thereby providing greater opportunities for one form of physical activity.[1]

Ewing and Cervero explain that walking is "strongly related to land-use diversity, intersection density, and the number of destinations within walking distance."[2] However, evidence for a link between mixed use and walking is somewhat less consistent for other age groups in similar environments. Sixty-three percent of 103 papers reviewed on youth, physical activity, and the built environment supported associations of land-use mix attributes, but the others did not.[3]

There has not been much research on mixed use and access to services, but it seems logical that if services are close by, people at least have the advantage of having options.

Potential problems of mixed use

While there are advantages to mixed use, there are a number of disadvantages that need careful planning and design to overcome.

One commonly cited advantage of mixed use neighborhoods is increased interaction among residents and activity on the street. Foord's review of policy and research literature, and a London-based neighborhood case study on mixed use neighborhoods, finds insufficient evidence that mix contributes to social cohesion and urban vitality. According to Foord's review, mixed use neighborhoods rarely include housing and schools necessary for all residents, especially for families with children, and older adults.[4] In neighborhoods without these supports, job centers, and other services available in the immediate area, access to other neighborhoods and districts is critical.[5] Residents surveyed as part of Foord's case study indicate they trade off exposure to noise, litter, low levels of community cohesion, disturbance, and limited open space in exchange for the locational advantages the neighborhood offers.[6] This single case paints a stark picture but highlights the need to carefully consider designing mixed use for different groups.

Mixed use and exposures to health hazards

Proponents of mixed use layouts argue that co-locating activities in a neighborhood or district has the potential to improve environmental quality. The evidence base paints a complex picture. For example, a neighborhood can be designed to reduce driving and potentially overall air pollution. However, slow traffic speeds and congestion in mixed use areas can increase local air pollution, and multiple studies have found air pollution to be worse in higher density and presumably mixed use areas.[7]

Water quality may also be compromised. Areas with high levels of impermeable surfaces may increase pollutants and contaminants in rainwater and stormwater that run off into sewers, streams, and bodies of water instead of flowing into the ground.[8]

At the same time, mixing incompatible land-use activities can increase risk of exposure to harmful health hazards, especially if the hazard is located in close proximity to areas where people live, work, or recreate. Principle 7 deals with a number of chemical and noise exposures that are exacerbated by mixed use. Research on mixed use layout and safety, described in more detail in Proposition 18, suggests that mixed use settings are more prone to crime compared to homogeneous land-use areas, which can influence personal safety and stress levels associated with mental health outcomes.[9]

Actions

❖ **Mix the right kinds of activities for daily life in a neighborhood or district.**
Healthy neighborhoods offer the advantages of co-locating different uses, but only if an appropriate mix of activities is in place.[10] Planners should ensure that neighborhoods have (or have access to) the basic services and amenities needed in daily life, including schools, daycare, community and senior centers, recreation opportunities, employment, and shopping.

◇ **Consider specific uses carefully, including how they are spatially mixed and whether there are useful clusters of activities within the district.**

An activity mix that is too large in scale or homogeneous (lumpy) or too fine-grained (random, salt and pepper) defeats the purpose of mixing uses. Rather, clusters of complementary activities within the neighborhood or district are best.

◆ **Identify potentially problematic uses for special treatment (e.g., moving or buffering, as is explained in later sections).**
For example, it is important to buffer toxic land-uses or noisy roads from residences. This is described in more detail in Principle 7.

Connections

Mixed use is about more than convenience but can provide livelihoods and life-enhancing resources. To understand this proposition better, go to:

• **Proposition 5:** Appreciate that there is no ideal size for a healthy community, but different dimensions of health relate to different scales

To further investigate:

• **Principle 4. Layout:** Foster multiple dimensions of health through overall neighborhood layout
• **Proposition 11:** Create a connected, "healthier" travel circulation pattern for pedestrians, bicyclists, and transit users—the vehicular pattern can be different
• **Principle 5. Access:** Provide options for getting around and increasing geographic access

- **Proposition 13:** Coordinate land-use planning and urban design with transit to increase efficiency, access, and mobility
- **Proposition 16:** Create publicly accessible neighborhood spaces, programs, and events to support healthy interactions and behaviors

- **Proposition 17:** Design the public realm to reduce street crime and fear of crime
- **Proposition 18:** Reduce pollutants and chemicals at the source, and separate people from toxins

Mixed use spaces may provide close proximity to different shops and services, and support walking or cycling for physical activity.

However, mixed use areas must be planned carefully to include resources for all ages, such as schools, day care facilities, and senior centers.

Proposition 10. Provide enough density of population to support services for a healthy lifestyle

Services like shops and public transportation need a critical mass of daytime and nighttime users. Careful design and planning can help minimize the negative aspects of congestion at higher densities.

How It Works

Density is controversial. At its base, as the glossary has outlined, it is the number of people (or things such as housing units) in a given area. However, there are many ways to measure it—leading to substantial confusion even among professionals. It is also often confused with related terms such as crowding (people per room or per bed) and building bulk or coverage. Partly because of this confusion, there is a great deal of fear about density.

In terms of health, the issue of involves a number of trade-offs between low- and high-density values, although the problems of higher densities (as opposed to high-rise buildings) have not been much studied.

In general:

- **Population densities need to be high enough to support services in a reasonable radius of where someone works or lives.** That radius varies by mode of transport (walk, bike, bus, train), and how often people need to access to a service (refer to Table 19). For

an activity center such as a shop or a school or a transportation stop, the density also needs to reflect the numbers of people needed in a catchment. Such catchments vary in size. For example, schools are typically larger and more specialized in terms of grade level the United States than many other countries and so need a larger catchment; trains need larger catchments than buses to keep full.

- **Higher density areas generally use resources more efficiently.** These areas save land and energy and enable more equitable transportation choices like public transport and walking.

- **Population densities that are very, very high by international standards can have other problems.** These include environments such as the most intensively developed low-rise densely packed informal settlements with many people per room or in some large high-rise developments with small units and little landscaping. Here there may be issues of the spread of contagious diseases, poor air quality, overcrowding, and increased exposure

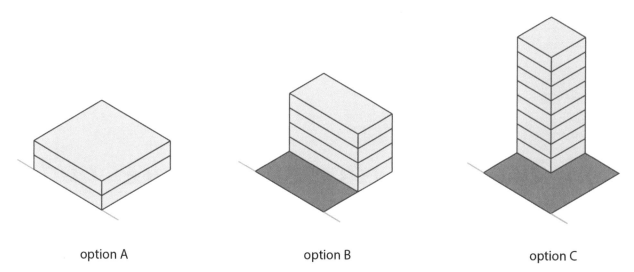

option A option B option C

Figure 19. Density is a complex phenomenon

The same building, population, or unit density can be achieved from different building layout and land coverage configurations.

Source: Developed by authors and Yannis Orfanos.

to pollutants and noise.[11] Depending on the neighborhood design and the heights of buildings, it also may be difficult to access green space.

Low-income populations are also a concern. For example, in dense urban areas they may be concentrated in neighborhoods more prone to flooding or other natural disasters and hazards, and in general these hazards will likely affect many more people in such locations.[12]

Planners and architects are typically strong proponents of higher densities as they have many advantages, particularly at the density ranges prevalent in middle- and higher-income countries. Landscape architects have often focused on the opposite, intrigued by designs that integrate development with natural settings. New technologies like driverless cars could increase the amount of time in a lifespan it is possible to drive or be mobile, and new energy sources could reduce the environmental costs of doing so, making lower densities more viable.

For health, however, there needs to be a balance that allows the option of walking or cycling for those who are interested, buses to run, and the sharing economy to function. For all this to happen, some minimal level of density is important.

Evidence about Health

Research related to density includes work on density per se but also proximity to resources.

Access to resources

Neighborhoods and districts that accommodate high densities may achieve an economy of scale appropriate for services that directly or indirectly support health. For example, the viability of transit services relies on residential and employment densities at certain levels, discussed earlier and in more detail in Proposition 1. A GIS analysis of 52 metropolitan regions in the United States on the opposing influences of speed and proximity found that higher densities can improve accessibility to

Density supports access to services and walking or cycling for transportation, but can have health problems as well.

resources and improve transportation outcomes more than low-density development patterns.[13] It helps to have people close to each other.

Physical activity

Areas that support walking and cycling for transportation need very concentrated activities (high-density housing, employment centers, shopping). Forsyth and Krizek's (2010) international review of 300 empirical studies on promoting bicycle and pedestrian activity found that a strong predictor for higher rates of pedestrian activity for transportation is the urban form—including density and street pattern—along with proximity of nearby destinations.[14]

Potential problems of population density for health

Higher-density areas, however, suffer from some health problems in relation to air pollution, disasters, water pollution, and waste. Many of these problems stem from poor planning and design or problems with regulation. A healthy neighborhood would focus on mitigating these issues.

Actions

◆ **Create a critical mass of people to support daily services within walking, cycling, or transit distance.**
There is no one-size-fits-all standard for density levels. Setting the appropriate neighborhood or district density depends largely on the activity but also on the area and population being served. Figure 19 shows how the same density levels can be laid out differently.

◆ **Focus on the very young, the old, and those who do not have cars, ensuring that neighborhoods and districts have centers that can be a focal point for activities and transportation, while avoiding congestion.**
As with many health issues, the young and old are likely to be particularly vulnerable because they are less able to get out and about or have control over their environment. Areas with very low and very high densities provide particular stresses—of congestion that may create a barrier

◆ Directly from research evidence   ❖ Informed by research   ◇ General good practice

Table 15. Health problems associated with density

Health topic	Detriments to health
Air quality (a, b, c, d)	• Proximity to busy roadways and biomass fuel is linked to increased exposure to particulate matter and vehicle emissions • Dense areas are associated with greater frequency of respiratory disease and bronchial allergies
Disasters (e, f, g, h, i, j, k, l)	• Numbers of people living in large cities mean there are more people and infrastructure affected by disasters
Housing (m)	• High-rise housing is linked to self-reported psychological distress, and is most pronounced among low-income mothers with young children. It should be noted that high rise is not equivalent to high density
Noise (n, o)	• Greater density is associated with higher noise levels
Social capital (p, q)	• Community and social interaction may be less positive in denser areas • Compact forms may worsen neighborhood problems and dissatisfaction
Waste (r, s, t)	• Residential proximity to hazardous waste sites, landfills, and older incinerators has been associated with many diseases and birth defects although this can also be a problem at lower densities • Uncontrolled urban waste is a health concern for pregnant women and children
Water quality (u, v, w, x,y, z)	• Urban runoff and wastewater often carry large amounts of contaminants with it • Large areas of impermeable surface (asphalt, concrete, rooftops) increases risk of flooding and water runoff.

Sources: (a) D'Amato et al. 2010, 95; (b) Hitchins et al. 2000, 58; (c) Mansfield et al. 2015; (d) Schweitzer and Zhou 2010; (e) Adger et al. 2005, 1036; (f) Douglas et al. 2008; (g) Galea et al. 2006; (h) Gaspirini et al. 2014, 2–3, 68–69; (i) Joffe et al. eds. 2013, 2; (j) Kidokoro et al. 2008, 4, 18, 100–101, 107; (k) Pelling 2003; (l) Wamsler 2014, 21–23, 82, 86, (m) Evans 2003, 537; (n) Babisch 2014; (o) Berglund et al. 1999; (p) Bramley and Power 2009, 34, 36; (q) Williamson 2010(r) Brender et al. 2011, S38, 49; (s) Mattiello et al. 2013; (t) Porta et al. 2009; (u) Barbosa et al. 2012; (v) Brabec et al. 2002; (w) Burton and Pitt 2002; (x) Goonetilleke et al. 2005; (y) Jacobson 2011; (z) Wang 2015

for those unsteady or slow on their feet, or alternatively, a lack of nearby services.

◆ **Mitigate against noise and air pollution, and provide green space to support physical activity and mental health in very high density areas.**
To ensure the health of residents in very dense neighborhoods, it is important that there is access to outdoor recreation opportunities for physical activity and green spaces to support mental health. Neighborhood designs should consider building height so that residents can have views of green, include building layouts that minimize street noise while providing access to outdoor space (yards, balconies), and reduce proximity to negative exposures such as vehicle emissions from busy roads.

Connections

Getting density right involves a comprehensive approach. To understand this proposition better go to:

- **Proposition 7:** Integrate universal design principles into neighborhood planning and design

- **Principle 4. Layout:** Foster multiple dimensions of health through overall neighborhood layout

To further investigate look at:
- **Proposition 11:** Create a connected, "healthier" travel circulation pattern for pedestrians, bicyclists, and transit users—the vehicular pattern can be different
- **Proposition 12:** Increase access to a variety of locally relevant recreational facilities and green spaces
- **Principle 5. Access:** Provide options for getting around and increasing geographic access
- **Proposition 16:** Create publicly accessible neighborhood spaces, programs, and events to support healthy interactions and behaviors
- **Proposition 17:** Design the public realm to reduce street crime and fear of crime
- **Proposition 20:** Reduce unwanted local noise exposure at the source and separate people from noise through buffers, technology, or design

◆ Directly from research evidence   ❖ Informed by research   ◇ General good practice

Balconies provide access to the outdoors

Mixed use areas cluster residential and commercial uses

High rise next to a park, formal greens, tree lined streets

High density doesn't have to be high rise

Figure 20. Higher density environments can vary in character

Proposition 11: Create a connected, "healthier" travel circulation pattern for pedestrians, bicyclists, and transit users—the vehicular pattern can be different

Create a connected network for people to get around—on streets or on other paths—so people can get access to important resources and have options for using active transport.

How It Works

Look at aerial photos from around the world and it is obvious that there are a great variety of street patterns—that is, the basic layouts of roads. Three major types stand out, with numerous variations and hybrid forms (Figure 21):

- **The lattice or grid:** Regular and rectilinear patterns like central New York City or organic ones like central London have many connections.
- **Tree structures:** Where cul-de-sacs and loops link to larger roads and still larger ones, as seen in many suburban areas.[15]
- **The superblock:** Where basic blocks are large and most vehicular traffic is on the edge. The center is reached by short and dead end streets, from Beijing's hutongs to New Jersey's Radburn model to modernist blocks. More contemporary examples include the fused grid.

Within these larger layouts, the street itself can be designed differently in terms of width, furnishings, and more specific design. These issues are dealt with in more detail in Principle 5.

The big issues in road network design for healthy neighborhoods are the balancing of traffic safety needs, and pedestrian and cyclist convenience. The important tradeoff is that road structures like grids are convenient for pedestrian and cycling circulation but have more traffic accidents than other types.[16]

The key design strategy for a well-designed, complete neighborhood is to keep a pedestrian and cycling network continuous while slowing, but not stopping, traffic. This often involves treating the two networks separately through traffic calming interventions, creating pedestrian passageways between routes, and implementing other strategies to make car travel slower (safer and more cumbersome)

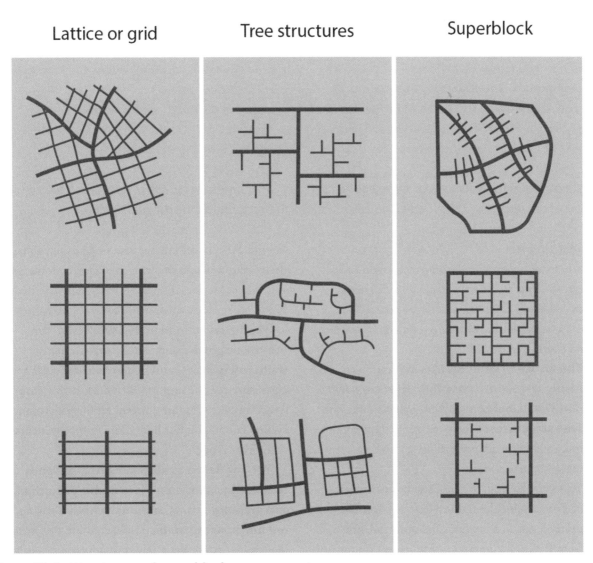

Figure 21. Lattice, tree, and superblock arrangements

Within the three main types of road layouts—lattice or grid, tree structures, and superblocks—there are numerous variations and hybrid forms.

Source: Partially adapted from Marshall 2005

and active transport more direct (quick and attractive). Four main approaches to these "healthier streets" are used (Figure 22).

- **Delinking vehicular road connections in grid and lattice structures** while keeping pedestrian and cycling routes in place. Examples are the fused grid and the diagonal diverter street-calming pattern.
- **Connecting pedestrian and cycle routes** across tree structures and superblocks. This is classical Radburn planning.
- **Warping the grid or lattice** with staggered or offset intersections or with some missing links, which slows traffic without inconveniencing pedestrians too much. This prioritizes traffic safely over pedestrian and cycling convenience, however.
- **Retrofitting signage, crossings, furnishings, and plantings; altering travel lanes; and widening sidewalks** to change the way that people use the spaces without changing the underlying street pattern.

Given the idea is to connect routes for pedestrians and cyclists, cars may well need to travel much further to reach the same destination. Bus and tram routes may also be altered due to this rerouting. Equity may be affected as people using buses on ordinary streets already need to wait for vehicles to come and then to pick up and drop off other passengers, and their already slow travel times could be exacerbated by

rerouting. Pedestrians and cyclists also do not always share spaces well so approaches that mix them can also be a problem. However, putting bicycles with cars raises other problems. With no perfect solution, minimizing distances for pedestrians is key.

Evidence about Health
Physical Activity

High intersection density and street connectivity, as provided by lattice or grid structures, increases the efficiency of the street network, increases route options for residents, and makes it possible to get to destinations more directly.[17] On balance, evidence shows street connectivity matters more for physical activity for able-bodied adults and adolescents than for young children and older adults.

McGrath et al.'s systematic review and meta-analysis (23 studies from 2000 to 2013) found mixed or uncertain evidence of the connection between street connectivity and physical activity of children and adolescents. Likewise, Giles-Corti et al.'s review of 113 articles found that street connectivity mattered more for older than younger children's physical activity. A comprehensive review of 17 empirical studies from 1990 to 2010 on the effect of the built environment on mobility in older adult populations (ages 60+) found that a high density of intersections, shorter walking distances, and proximity to destinations are the most likely factors to affect levels of mobility and pedestrian activity.[18] However, other recent comprehensive and systematic reviews show

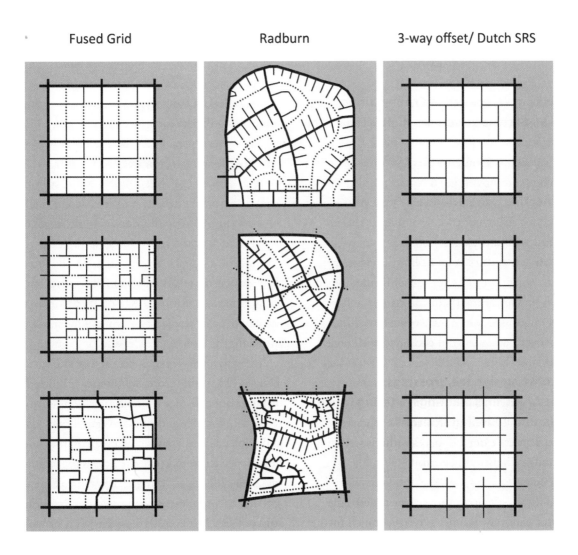

Fused Grid | Radburn | 3-way offset/ Dutch SRS

Figure 22. "Healthier circulation" street patterns

Retrofitting standard street patterns by delinking lattices, connecting trees, and warping grid can improve travel circulation, calm streets, preserve pedestrian and cycling routes, and improve traffic safety, thus making them "healthier" for non-motorized travel. Pedestrian routes are not shown in these diagrams but in each case they link loop and dead-end streets to a network of paths for easy access.

Source: Partially adapted from Sun and Lovegrove 2013

weak or no relationships to street connectivity and physical activity among older adults.[19]

Safety

Grid and lattice patterns with high intersection counts

Traditional grid patterns create a high number of intersections and provide good connectivity, though findings on these characteristics and vehicle accidents are mixed.

Marshall and Garrick analyzed data from over 230,000 vehicle crashes in 24 California cities that took place over 11 years. After controlling for possible confounders, they found that denser street networks with higher intersection counts (which can occur in many street patterns) were associated with fewer crashes of all severity levels. However, increased street connectivity (such as grid patterns) and additional travel lanes were correlated with more crashes.[20]

Lovegrove and Sayed created collision prediction models using data from 577 neighborhoods in and around the Vancouver, British Columbia, metropolitan area and found the grid network to be predicted the least safe by nearly three to one over other street patterns.[21]

Cul-de-sacs and loops—variations on tree structures

Cul-de-sacs and loop road patterns differ from grid and lattice street patterns in that they feature roads that are discontinuous or dead ended and/or have limited access.

Wei and Lovegrove's qualitative literature review citing 34 articles on vulnerable road users (i.e., pedestrians and cyclists), volumes, and safety found that cul-de-sacs have low traffic volumes but can have limited access for emergency vehicles.[22] They also have pedestrian and cyclist safety issues where neighborhood roads intersect with larger arterial roads.[23] However, because of low traffic volumes, cul-de-sacs may promote physical activity for young children by enabling them to play on the street within sight of home.[24]

Variations on superblocks: Offsetting and delinking both vehicular and pedestrian routes

A three-way offset street network converts all four-way intersections into three-way "T" intersections, which attempts to blend accessibility and safety. Dutch Sustainable Road Safety networks are different in that they allow for more four-way intersections (see Figure 22 for comparison). Lovegrove and Sayed's collision prediction models (described previously) found that three-way intersections significantly reduced collisions.[25] Lovegrove and Sayed went on to analyze their collision prediction models to statistically test neighborhood network structures and safety.[26] They found three-way offset networks were predicted to be the safest overall. Grid patterns were found to be the least safe, as previously mentioned. A potential downside to the three-way offset or Dutch Sustainable Road Safety network is that pedestrians and cyclists do not have special, more direct networks

Table 16. Major types of urban street patterns: advantages, problems, and potential improvements

Types	Advantages	Problems	Improvements
Lattice or Grid	• High connectivity and accessibility • Promotes physical activity for transportation (adults) (a,b) • Can build at higher densities (sustainability)	• Speeds can get too high • Can cause traffic-cut through and safety issues for pedestrians and cyclists (c) • More permeability has been associated with higher levels of crime (a) • Can be more expensive than cul-de-sacs (use more land) (a,d)	• Traffic calming (e) • Pedestrian and cyclist infrastructure • Close off certain roads to protect against vehicles but still allow pedestrians and cyclists, creating a fused grid
Tree Structures (includes cul-de-sacs and loops)	• Slow traffic speeds • Can promote physical activity for young children (f, g, h) • Highly liked residential choice in N. America, UK, and Australia (i)	• Criticized for automobile dependence • Doesn't usually support walking or cycling for transport (longer trip lengths, inconvenient) (i) • Limited access for emergency vehicles (i,j) • Safety problems where cul-de-sacs intersect with larger arterial roads	• Where possible, connect cul-de-sacs to each other and destinations with off-road trails for pedestrians and cyclists (j) • Put signalization or roundabouts at major intersections (j)
Superblock	• Safety (j,k) • High accessibility and connectivity for pedestrians and cyclists (over cars)(l) • Still good access for emergency vehicles	• No prioritization of pedestrian/cyclist connectivity over vehicles —in block edge they all share the same network • Retrofitting likely difficult • Implementation and costs may be a barrier (m) • Maintenance of green corridors (m)	• Add in additional off-road pedestrian, cyclist, or transit routes • Green space along pedestrian and cyclist paths

Sources: (a) Cozens and Hillier 2008, 63; (b) Ewing and Cervero 2010, 276; (c) Marshall and Garrick 2011; (d) Sun and Lovegrove 2013, 35; (e) Sun and Lovegrove 2013, 44; (f) Ding et al. 2011; (g) McGrath et al. 2015; (h) Sallis and Glanz 2006; (i) Sun and Lovegrove 2013, 38; (j) Wei and Lovegrove 2012, 147 (k) Lovegrove and Sayed 2006b, 620; (l) Frank and Hawkins 2008, 5; (m) Mang 2013.

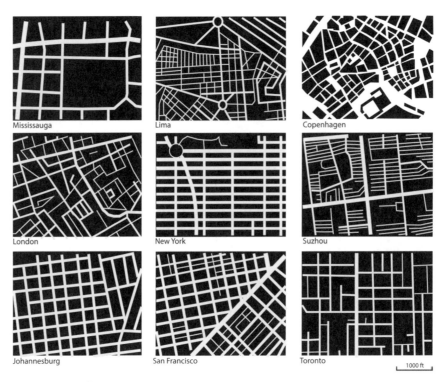

Mississauga

Lima

Copenhagen

London

New York

Suzhou

Johannesburg

San Francisco

Toronto

1000 ft

Figure 23. Variations on grid patterns
Cities around the world have different variations of the main types of street patterns (lattice or grid, tree structures, and superblock).

and still share exactly the same accessibility and connectivity as cars.

Superblocks with fine-grained pedestrian networks separate to vehicles

Fused grids take a grid and remove some vehicular links within a district. The fused grid then overlays a diagonal network of offroad walking, biking, or transit routes.[27] In their literature review, Wei and Lovegrove conclude that "the three-way offset and fused grid community patterns can be reasonably expected to experience 60 percent fewer road collisions than similar neighbourhoods using conventional road patterns."[28] This is similar to Radburn designs. As mentioned in the Introduction, Cumbernauld in Scotland achieved accident rates one quarter of the national rate with a comprehensive Radburn plan.[29] The tricky issue with this model is whether the off-street parts of the path network will be perceived as safe, particularly at night. This has often been a problem.

Actions

◆ **Provide multiple route options to encourage pedestrian and bicycle travel.**

As the slowest users of roads and paths, cyclists and pedestrians find directness is a key issue (particularly for pedestrians). To increase the likelihood of walking or cycling, it helps to have multiple route options, no matter what the street pattern. This means prioritizing connectivity for pedestrians and cyclists over cars.

◆ **Connect cul-de-sacs to each other and to destinations (where possible) with pedestrian and bike paths.**

Cut-through pedestrian and cyclist paths that link cul-de-sacs to other streets and green spaces can increase connectivity, which may significantly increase the mode share of walking and cycling.

❖ **Minimize distances between destinations to avoid penalizing non-vehicular traffic.**

Re-routing traffic to slow vehicular speed may inadvertently affect transit riders, pedestrians, and bicycle passengers as well. To avoid penalizing non-vehicular traffic and collective transportation modes, it is best to minimize distances between destinations. It may also be worth considering bus- or transit-only lanes.

❖ **Deal with each kind of underlying pattern differently, moving toward healthier patterns where possible.**

Each kind of basic underlying street pattern can be healthy but needs different treatment. Examples include adding traffic calming to grids, connecting pedestrians and cyclists to tree structures, and making sure pedestrian networks in superblocks perceived as safe. For more actions related to these issues see Proposition 14.

Connections

A well designed street pattern can do a great deal to safely connect people to the resources they need to live healthier lives. To understand this proposition better, go to:

- **Principle 3. Vulnerability:** Plan and design for those with the most health vulnerabilities and fewest resources for making healthy choices
- **Principle 4. Layout:** Foster multiple dimensions of health through overall neighborhood layout

To further investigate, look at:

- **Principle 5. Access:** Provide options for getting around and increasing geographic access
- **Proposition 13:** Coordinate land-use planning and urban design with transit to increase efficiency, access, and mobility
- **Proposition 17:** Design the public realm to reduce street crime and fear of crime

◆ Directly from research evidence   ❖ Informed by research   ◇ General good practice

Proposition 12: Increase access to a variety of locally relevant recreational facilities and green spaces

Green spaces and recreational facilities have a multitude of health benefits including urban cooling, opportunities for physical fitness and ecological education, the promotion of water and air quality, a refuge from traffic and noise, and improved mental health.

How It Works

Green spaces and recreational facilities come in a range of forms from gyms and children's playgrounds to trails and nature parks. Well-designed or healthy neighborhoods include these spaces in a coordinated way to provide options for different kinds of users and also multiple benefits from single interventions. These benefits can include physical activity, safety from traffic, mobility and universal design, healthy diets, natural cooling, water-quality protection, and psychological well-being. For example, a community garden may be a space that facilitates education about food systems and provides mental health benefits for gardeners and access to healthy and seasonally available produce. To achieve this kind of outcome, several issues need to be considered:

Landscape structure is the overall pattern of green and open spaces, from yards and pocket parks, to tree-lined streets and off-road trails, to larger district

and regional parks and natural areas. Through the lens of human health, three factors are key:

- Access (visual and physical) from residences and work places to green and recreational areas. Physical closeness is particularly important for groups who have trouble getting around (the old, young, less affluent, mobility-impaired).[30]
- Connections between spaces so that people can move between them easily and make them part of walking or cycling circuits, for example. This requires at least some public spaces in addition to private spaces such as yards.
- Variety in terms of facilities and character so that people can engage in different types of activity when they need to and so that spaces appeal to people across the lifespan.

Space planning and design can support multiple users and multiple uses within each space and across spaces, and also allow different functions in the same location (e.g., recreation and stormwater management).

Parks are a great resource, especially in urban neighborhoods (as pictured above). They provide opportunities for urban residents to get physical activity outdoors and offer mental health benefits associated with greenspace.

Management and programming should provide an impetus for people to gather, interact, and socialize—for example concerts, festivals, or farmers markets.

Evidence about Health

Mental Health

Over the past several decades, research has clearly shown that contact with nature aids mental health, cognitive function, and stress.

While some green space preferences may be innate and influenced by human evolution, these preferences and ways of using the environment are greatly modified by socioeconomic, environmental, and cultural influences.[31]

An analysis of 10 British studies on exposure to green exercise found that as little as five minutes of activity outside was enough for mental health improvements.[32,33] A meta-analysis of 25 studies on health in natural environments (e.g., parks, wildlife preserves, university campuses) and synthetic areas (e.g., gyms, shopping centers) found that self-reported positive emotions ranked higher for walking and running in a natural environment when compared to synthetic environments.[34] Additionally, a review of 11 studies on indoor versus outdoor exercise found that outdoor exercise was linked to better self-reported measures of stress, mood, and energy levels.[35] Natural environments have even been shown to improve symptoms of people with attention deficit disorder, Alzheimer's disease, and dementia.[36]

Exercise

Increased recreational activity or exercise is less consistently tied to the built environment; rather, other factors ranging from cost to personal preferences seem to be more important.[37] However, access to recreational facilities can play a role in providing opportunities for recreation, especially for children or older adults.[38] Christian et al.'s literature review of studies over the past 30 years found for young children (less than 7 years old) "strong empirical evidence that neighborhoods which are safe from traffic and which have green spaces (i.e., nature, public open space, parks, playgrounds) are associated with behaviors (i.e.,

Table 17. Types of green space and associated positive health behaviors and outcomes

Green space type	In other words	Health behaviors and outcomes
Urban parks	Parks of all sizes, including pocket parks for a variety of different people and uses	• Physical activity options • Protection from heat (a) • Stormwater infiltration (water quality protection)(a) • Socializing (a, b, c) • Psychological well-being (a, b)
Recreational facilities (other than parks)	Playgrounds, beaches, pools, community centers, picnic areas, sports fields, exercise equipment, etc.	• Physical activity (d, e, f, g) • Socializing (b) • Relaxation and psychological well-being (b)
Off-road trails, paths, and greenways	Linear parks that connect people and places	• Physical activity (h) • Access to community resources (h) • Safety from traffic (h)
Tree canopy	Street trees, trees on public and private property	• Protection from heat (urban cooling) (i, j) • Climate change mitigation (carbon dioxide removal) • Psychological well-being (i) • Buffers from traffic and noise (k)
Landscaping and gardens near buildings	Especially for schools, retirement homes, and hospitals, etc.	• Stormwater infiltration (water quality protection) (l, m) • Protection from heat (urban cooling) • Buffers from traffic and noise (k) • Psychological well-being (i)

Research studies associate different types of neighborhood green spaces with positive health outcomes.

Sources: (a) Forsyth and Musacchio 2005, 3–5, 144; (b) Barton and Pretty 2010; (c) Harnick 2006, 57; (d) Ding et al. 2011; (e) Rosso et al. 2011; (f) Van Cauwenberg et al. 2011; (g) Wendel-Vos et al. 2007; (h) Dallat et al. 2014; (i) Maller et al. 2009, 59, 62, 66; (j) Stone et al. 2010, 1427; (k) Daigle 1999, 139, 153; (l) Austin 2014 154–172; (m) Burke 2009

outdoor play and physical activity) that facilitate early child health and development."[39]

Actions

◆ **Plan for a network of spaces with varied functions and users to achieve different, and hopefully multiple, health outcomes.**
Small parks within a neighborhood or district can be planned as a system, providing the ecological, social, physical, and psychology benefits of larger parks. This can enable individual park space to differ by function and character, while remaining accessible and also linked to a larger system of open spaces.[40] This is especially important for children living in higher-density residential areas.[41]

◆ **Make the spaces physically and/ or visually accessible to likely users, and in particular those with health vulnerabilities and a likelihood of using such spaces (e.g., the young and old).**
Parks and neighborhood recreational green spaces should be accessible to every neighborhood and useable by those from any mobility or income level.[42] Ideally, they will be located within easy walking distances (optimally 0.25–0.5 miles, or 400–800 m) from all residences. Where possible, they should be located adjacent to transit to increase accessibility.

◆ **Link spaces so that people can travel between them as parts of tours or loops for exercise and recreation.**
Wayfinding, pedestrian and cyclist paths, and marketing efforts can link spaces together as a network and encourage visitors to travel between them. The success of trails that link places together often depends primarily on accessibility, proper maintenance, safety, and ongoing funding.[43]

◆ **Plan spaces to allow for multiple uses and reduce problematic conflicts.**
Programing and management in public spaces can prioritize different activities throughout the day for different users, helping to reduce conflict over use of the space.[44] For example, teen sports can be scheduled for after-school or weekend hours, whereas community events for older people can be prioritized during school hours.

◆ **Plan green spaces near buildings for increased mental well-being, improved cognition, reduced stress, and better healing.**
Locating green space near buildings and ensuring visual access to vegetation aids mental health. Green spaces need not be uniform or of a specific size. In urban areas with limited space, they may include small parks, tree lined streets, pathways, and even views of vegetation and greenery from buildings.

◆ Directly from research evidence ❖ Informed by research ◇ General good practice **123**

Connections

Recreational opportunities and green spaces increase opportunities for physical activity, potentially with greater mental health benefits as well. To further investigate, look at:

- **Proposition 8:** Increase choice, access, and exposure to high-quality, diverse, and healthy food options, especially in low-income areas

- **Proposition 15:** Ensure adequate pedestrian and cyclist infrastructure and amenities

- **Proposition 16:** Create publicly accessible neighborhood spaces, programs, and events to support healthy interactions and behaviors

- **Proposition 17:** Design the public realm to reduce street crime and fear of crime

Green spaces need to be physically accessible and usable for persons of all age and mobility levels. This urban open space is near buildings, with wide and level paths.

◆ Directly from research evidence   ❖ Informed by research   ◇ General good practice

Time spent outdoors in green spaces has well-documented benefits for mood, attention, and energy, and has been shown to improve attention-deficit disorder, Alzheimer's disease, and dementia.

Access

Provide options for getting around and increasing geographic access.

There is no one-size-fits-all transportation solution to meet the mobility and geographic accessibility needs of an entire neighborhood, so the key is to provide options.

How It Works

Gaining access to resources to live a healthy life is in part about moving people to resources but also about bringing resources to the neighborhood (e.g. freight goods and services, health care facilities, grocery stores). Not all connections require mobility of people or things; a phone conversation or Internet use can provide access to many resources.

Transportation networks and infrastructure aim to improve mobility, or the ability to move between places. Mobility can provide indirect health benefits enabling people to travel quickly, safely, and conveniently. Neighborhoods that enable walking and cycling to nearby destinations and transit can also provide opportunities for physical activity. However, multiple options are needed to serve the diverse transportation needs of the community. What is a viable mode of transportation also varies with the size and density of the neighborhood and surrounding areas.

Access and Mobility

Most urban neighborhoods are in close proximity to some range of community resources. The question is: How quickly and easily can residents reach those destinations? Can they be reached without using a car? Groups who may be unable to drive include the young, the old, those with low incomes, and those with certain disabilities. These groups can face geographic accessibility and mobility disadvantages, but this is not always the case and it depends on the specific place. For these people, other mode options—transit (or paratransit and shared transport like shared vans, taxis, and ride-sharing), cycling, and walking—are important alternatives.

Several key considerations frame the connection between transportation and health at a neighborhood level: who or what is being transported and transportation availability and service, along with individual-level and system-level factors.

What and who is transported

- People: Personal transportation or moving people around.
- Freight goods to businesses and homes: For example, moving items to a new house or apartment, stocking stores, or moving things that have been produced locally.
- Emergency services: Services such as ambulances and fire engines.

Range of transport options and services

- Mode or means of travel: Relevant at the neighborhood level are modes including walking, cycling, driving, and transit.
- Service and convenience: Schedules, safety, cost, customer service, infrastructure maintenance, travel time, and navigability.

Range of user- and system-level factors

- User-level factors: Some groups are not able to use the full range of transportation modes for various reasons, such as personal preferences against

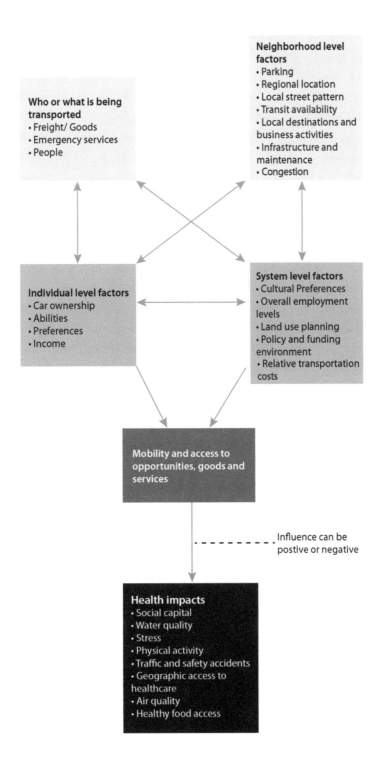

Figure 24. Factors affecting transportation options

Many factors affect transportation options for people and goods and their health effects can be positive or negative. Intervening at

the neighborhood level is important but requires care.

Source: Expanded from Rodrigue et al. 2006; Taylor and Fink 2013

particular modes, physical mobility challenges, not owning or being able to drive a car, or public transportation service and area deprivations.

- System-level factors: Many affect individuals and transportation availability, such as the overarching policy and funding environment, land-use planning (or lack thereof), overall employment levels, and cultural norms.

There is a complex relationship between these factors and their effects on mobility and geographic accessibility, and consequently both positive and negative health outcomes (see Figure 24). The underlying research behind this diagram is described in this section and related propositions.

Cars may be needed in lower-density areas.

Providing options

In the United States, many transportation and planning agencies use the term "complete streets" to describe policies and plans aimed at achieving "equity objectives by giving non-drivers a fair share of road space."[1] Zavestoski and Ageyman's 2009 inventory of 80 state and local complete streets policies found shortcomings in terms of inclusiveness. All policies reviewed included pedestrians and cyclists but only one-third addressed transit users, less than one-third addressed the needs of older road users, and only one-tenth and one-sixth included motorists and freight vehicles, respectively.[2] Some critics also claim that there is neighborhood bias in the areas that receive multimodal road projects and that policies and plans serve as a catalyst for neighborhood investment that leads to gentrification.[3] While these are US-based critiques, many international examples of healthy transportation planning featured prominently in their book likewise focus on places catering to young and healthy pedestrians and cyclists. Healthy neighborhoods need to go further and to carefully consider the full range of options.

Cars: Automobiles and vans are a highly flexible and fast (but low capacity) option that works best in lower-density areas because they have a greater spatial reach and may be the only way of getting around.[4] Currently there are several health problems with this approach for neighborhood planning and design: not everyone can drive, including the young and the very old; emissions cause localized problems like air pollution (fossil fuel use is a larger concern); car accidents cause injuries and death; and cars take up valuable space on the road and when parked.

New technologies are changing some of this landscape in relation to health in neighborhoods and districts. Driverless cars may extend the age range of mobility, at least at the older ages. Electric cars are reducing local air pollution. Some new technologies may reduce accidents. Shared vehicles will likely require somewhat less parking in individual homes and parking lots. However, there will still be people who cannot drive due to age, infirmity, or income, and the problem of congestion on roads will remain. Even a shift to shared or driverless cars will not necessarily solve all problems because while there may be fewer cars, they may well be on the street more (saving parking spaces but not road space). In order for there to be real transportation options, alternatives need to be available and competitive: flexible, fast, convenient, and affordable. Measures to put some restrictions on the flexibility of the car—such as carpool only lanes, parking restrictions, and speed limits—may incentivize other travel options.[5]

Transit: Transit, such as trains or buses, can match the speed of a car and has higher capacity but is not as flexible.[6] Collective and shared transport options, such as taxis and shared-ride vans, fill some of this gap in many places. To be financially viable (filled with a reasonable number of paying riders) and

successful, transit requires a certain level of residential or employment density surrounding station areas and bus routes, as described in the following proposition (Proposition 13).[7] It needs to link important destinations—for example, fairly concentrated residential areas and employment hubs.

Walking and cycling (or non-motorized modes): Walking and cycling operate at slower speeds and have less spatial reach than cars or transit, but they are highly flexible. Walking in particular has high capacity; nearly everyone can walk to some extent and pedestrians take up little space.[8] Cycling has the advantage of people being able to go farther

Walking has many health benefits, but can be a slow transportation mode unless activities are in denser areas.

than walking in the same time, making lower-density environments more accessible.

Communications technologies: Postal mail, telephones, and the Internet allow people to have increased access to goods and services without personal mobility. In many urban areas, there is an increasing ability to have almost anything delivered from online stores. Car services—such as Uber, Lyft, taxis, and shuttles—can bring drivers to one's doorstep. Increased home deliveries may put increased pressure on road networks in residential areas but simultaneously offer an opportunity to support health

Transit (such as trains or buses) can match the speed of a car and has higher capacity, but is not as flexible.

and sustainability strategies by providing greater access to goods and services and doing this in an efficient way through fleet optimization.[9]

Freight and emergency services: Urban planners and policy makers often overlook freight and emergency services issues when considering the transportation network or complete streets policies.[10] Freight is essential to moving goods and services to where they need to be so people can access them. A common difficulty for freight being delivered to urban neighborhoods or central business districts is a lack of road or loading space.[11] While new transit and rail services, as well as methods to reduce cars on the road, may positively affect the mobility of urban road freight transport (generating less congestion), other measures, like increasing pedestrian areas and cycle infrastructure, may have a negative effect on freight mobility (affecting distance speed).[12] If carsharing reduces the need for automobile parking spaces, these may not be in locations where freight needs them. The main takeaway is there are trade-offs, and freight transport should be considered in transportation planning.

Providing enough emergency services (fire, police, and ambulance) in the right places is an important issue, as well as ensuring they can get to where they need to go quickly. In the United States and Canada, a conventional measure of adequate geographic access to emergency health care is 30 minutes for many places, but there is not often clear evidence for this standard.[13] Cul-de-sac road designs have been criticized as having limited access for emergency vehicles.[14]

Evidence about Health
Physical activity

Systematic reviews suggest that walking or cycling to destinations (as opposed to driving) likely increases overall levels of physical activity; however, the evidence is inconclusive and the effects are not particularly large.[15] Providing opportunities for walking to destinations is worth doing, however, because it has multiple benefits—social and mental as well as physical.

Safety

Pedestrians and cyclists are among the most vulnerable to road injuries and deaths, according to the World Health Organization[16] and therefore need infrastructure and policies to protect them. Coordination between transportation and land-use planning activities, policy efforts to increase safety for all road users, and pedestrian and cyclist infrastructure are key. These design strategies are described in the following propositions in this section.

Disadvantages

Transportation can also pose health risks, such as exposure to air pollution, water quality issues, from paving and pollution, noise, traffic accidents, and stress. Presumably increased forms of remote communications also pose health risks—they might encourage sedentary behavior or increase stress,

for example. Many of these negative effects of transportation are dealt with in other sections and can be reduced through new technologies and regulations.

Connections

Having multiple ways of accessing resources is a key to health equity. To understand this proposition better, go to:

- **Principle 3. Vulnerability:** Plan and design for those with the most health vulnerabilities and fewest resources for making healthy choices
- **Proposition 10:** Provide enough density of population to support services for a healthy lifestyle
- **Proposition 11:** Create a connected, "healthier" travel circulation pattern for pedestrians, bicyclists, and transit users—the vehicular pattern can be different

To further investigate, look at:

- **Proposition 13:** Coordinate land-use planning and urban design with transit to increase efficiency, access, and mobility
- **Proposition 14:** Adopt policies and planning practices to create safe neighborhood transportation options for all types of road users
- **Proposition 15:** Ensure adequate pedestrian and cyclist infrastructure and amenities
- **Proposition 16:** Create publicly accessible neighborhood spaces, programs, and events to support healthy interactions and behaviors

Public transportation

Collective transportation

City buses

Paratransit

Subway

Privately owned shuttles

Light rail

Privately owned ferries

Figure 25. Public, collective, shared, and individual transportation options

Shared transportation

Individual transportation

Taxis

Bicycles

Bike share

Walking

Car share (e.g. Zipcar)

Cars

Proposition 13: Coordinate land-use planning and urban design with transit to increase efficiency, access, and mobility

Transportation options depend on the built environment to be functional. Transit needs a critical mass of riders.

How It Works

Connecting transport with overall neighborhood land use and urban design is a crucial aspect of healthy place making. Public transportation or transit is a vital part of that picture. Several neighborhood-level strategies are important:

- **Aligning activities or land uses with transportation options.** For example, walking and transit station areas need very concentrated activities (high-density housing, employment centers, shopping); buses and bicycles can reach farther; and cars, trucks, and vans are well suited for very dispersed patterns.
- **Developing appropriate infrastructure:** Each kind of transportation mode needs the right infrastructure, from parking areas to station areas, while keeping health front and center.
- **Prioritizing modes that support those with transportation disadvantages.** For young, old, mobility-impaired, low-income people, transit options (bus, train, subway, light rail) combined with adequate road, bicycle, and pedestrian

infrastructure can expand choices to get around by creating transportation networks that connect neighborhoods and destinations. They can also provide supplementary health benefits.

Transit: A key part of the transportation toolbox

A great deal of work on making healthy places has focused on how to encourage walking and cycling. The larger transportation planning system engages the key issues of cars and trucks. In between are forms of public and shared transportation—vehicles on fixed or scheduled routes (like buses and trains) or more flexible collective and shared services (Table 18). There is a great deal of current excitement about more flexible services, but scheduled transit is vitally important for a number of reasons:

- It can serve a great many people at once.
- It encourages efficient land uses because its more fixed nature allows long-term investment decisions. This means that it is part of the infrastructure allowing denser development.

- It gives reliable options to those who cannot drive for various reasons.

There is no one set of policies and interventions that guarantee ridership and cost effectiveness of a transit system.[17] Transit options that work well in one neighborhood might not work well in another. That said, the following aspects of the built environment can support transit viability:

- **Employment and residential density:** Residential and employment densities are "critical determinants" of transit use by providing points of origin and destination within reach of the system.[18] Table 19 provides recommended minimum residential and employment densities

to support different transit modes and service frequencies.

- **Distance to transit:** There is no consensus on the distance that passengers are willing to travel to transit since it varies by mode and neighborhood conditions. Reviews find people are willing to walk 0.4–0.5 miles (600–800 meters) or even more from a residential area to reach transit.[19] However, for children distance is a barrier walking to school[20] and is likely to be one for transit as well. Cyclists will go farther, 1.2–6.2 miles (2–10 kilometers) depending on the study.[21]

- **Parking availability:** This is one of the strongest influences on transit ridership. Studies

Table 18. Vehicle and line capacities, and maximum frequencies of different transit modes

Unit/ Mode		Vehicle capacity	Max frequency (a)	Line capacities (b)
		Spaces per vehicle (sps/veh)	Transit unit per hour (TU/h)	Spaces per hour (sps/h)
Private	Auto on Street	4–6, total	600–800	720–1050 (c)
	Auto on Freeway	1.2–2.0, usable	1500–2000	1800–2600 (c)
Street transit	Regular bus	40–120	60–180	2400–8000
	Streetcar	100–250	60–120	4000–15,000
Semirapid transit	Bus rapid transit	40–150	60–300 (c)	4000–8000–20,000 (c)
	Light rail transit	110–250	40–60	6000–20,000
Rapid transit	Rail rapid transit	140–280	80–100	10,000–70,000
	Regional rail	140–210	80–130	8000–60,000

Source: modified from: Vuchic 2007, 76

Notes: a) For auto, lane capacity; for transit, line (station) capacity in transit unit per hour (TU/h); (b) Values for line capacity are not necessarily products for the extreme values of their components because these seldom coincide; (c) With multiple parallel lanes and overtaking at stations

Table 19. Recommended residential densities, employment center sizes, service levels, and station spacing, based on transit modes

Modes	Typical stop/ station spacing	Service Levels (minimum service levels)	Minimum Residential Density	Central Business District Size (commercial/office space)
Local Street Transit Local bus, streetcar	1/8–¼ mile 0.2–0.4 km	20/day	4–15 units/ acre 10–37 units/ ha	2.5–10 million sqf 230,000–930,000 sqm
Rapid Street Transit Rapid or express bus, streetcar	1/5–1/3 mile 0.3–0.5 km	120/day	3–15 units/acre 7–37 units/ha	7–35 million sqf 650,000–3.25 million sqm
Semi-rapid Transit BRT, LRT	1/3–2/3 mile 0.5–1.1 km	5-minute peak-hour headways	9 *units/acre 22 units/ha	21– 50 million sqf 1.95–4.65 million sqm
Regional Transit Commuter rail	¾ –3 mile 1.2–4.8 km	20/day	1–2 units/acre 2.5–5 units/ha	50–70 million sqf 4.65–6.5 million sqm
Rapid Transit Heavy rail	1/3–1 1/3 mile 0.5–2.1 km	5-minute peak-hour headways	12** units/acre 29 units/ha	50 million sqf; Only largest downtowns 4.65+ million sqm

For a corridor of 25–100 square miles or 64 to 260 square kilometers (km).

** For a corridor of 50–100 square miles or 130 to 260 square kilometers.

Source: adapted from: Chatman et al. 2014, 7–8; Design for Health 2007a, 5; Regional Plan Association 1976; Pushkarev and Zupan (1977; 1982); TCRP (1995)

find that a greater number parking spaces, such as in the central business district, is associated with a decrease in transit trips.[22] Strategies to increase parking costs in high demand areas are more effective at increasing transit mode share than strategies to increase the frequency or accessibility of transit service.[23] In contrast, having more affordable and available parking at commuter rail stations may increase ridership, but the evidence is less certain.[24]

At a larger scale, coordinating and integrating land use and transit is a long-term, time-consuming endeavor, requiring a lot of cross-sector coordination.[25] In order for public transportation to be successful, it needs to be effectively located within a neighborhood with the density necessary to generate sufficient transit demand (see Table 19).[26]

Evidence about Health

Physical Activity

Transit access and proximity has also been shown to be related to physical activity for those 65 and younger. There is not necessarily a connection between transit proximity and access and physical activity for older adults.[27]

Appropriate infrastructure and support for those with physical disadvantages

Everyone has physical difficulties at some point in their life: parents with strollers; little children; older people; and those with injuries or sensory, cognitive, or mobility disabilities. Infrastructure and support for these groups should include universal design features for public transit vehicles, stations (e.g, no step entry, ramps, elevators), door-to-door systems (paratransit), adequate disabled parking, and wayfinding signage.[28]

Actions

◆ **Locate transit close to activity generators and the reverse.**

Land-use density, mix of land-use types, and development patterns complement transportation plans and policies that aim to improve safety and accessibility for all users.

◆ **Prioritize and cluster transit, health, and social services near where vulnerable populations live.**

Since transit can increase land prices and displace low-income and other vulnerable residents, policy makers and planners should integrate mixed-income housing and preserve affordable housing opportunities close to health centers, social service agencies, and transit.[29]

◆ **Co-locate transit stops with pedestrian and cyclist-friendly infrastructure and amenities.**

A pedestrian and cyclist-friendly network of streets within station/stop areas can enable pedestrians and cyclists to actively travel to transit.[30] This also enhances transfers between modes.

❖ **Ensure continuity across neighborhood and jurisdictional boundaries.**

Neighborhood transportation infrastructure like sidewalks, cycle lanes, and public transportation should be created with a regional perspective. They should be coordinated across municipal lines and/or government agencies to provide safe, continuous routes for all users to travel to and from destinations.

Connections

Transit systems do not operate in isolation of the surrounding built environment. To understand this proposition better, go to:

- **Proposition 9:** Create mixed use neighborhoods with a balance of activities that support good health
- **Proposition 10:** Provide enough density of population to support services for a healthy lifestyle
- **Proposition 11:** Create a connected, "healthier" travel circulation pattern for pedestrians, bicyclists, and transit users—the vehicular pattern can be different

- **Principle 5. Access:** Provide options for getting around and increasing geographic access

To further investigate, look at:

- **Proposition 14:** Adopt policies and planning practices to create safe neighborhood transportation options for all types of road users
- **Principle 6. Connection:** Create opportunities for people to interact with each other in positive ways
- **Proposition 19:** Separate people and infrastructure from areas vulnerable to natural disasters and build in resilience through technology or design

Pedestrian and cyclist infrastructure located at transit stops, such as bike parking, can support cycling to transit and transferring between modes, extending the reach of public transportation.

Proposition 14: Adopt policies and planning practices to create safe neighborhood transportation options for all types of road users

Roads should be designed to serve all users—including pedestrians, bicyclists, motorists, and transit riders—making different modes of transportation viable and safe.

How It Works

This guideline is about designing roadways and paths for comfort and safety with a particular focus on vulnerable road users: pedestrians, cyclists, and motorcyclists. According to the World Health Organization, 50 percent of road deaths worldwide in 2010 happened to vulnerable road users.[31]

Several neighborhood-level issues are important:

- Policies and practices that treat the street as shared public space and attempt to accommodate the multimodal travel needs of all can enhance safety and accessibility for pedestrians, bicyclists, motorists, and transit riders alike.
- The speeds at which road vehicles travel and traffic volumes can influence the risks of accident and injury to drivers and their passengers, motorcyclists, bicyclists, and pedestrians.
- Traffic flow can be managed by street design. The introduction of traffic calming measures such as diagonal street parking, bulb-outs or curb extensions, sidewalk widening, conversion

of one-way streets to two-way, the addition of street trees to give the perception of narrower streets, or the addition of chicanes (street curves or barriers) can slow traffic through physical and visual cues that provide information to drivers on safe and appropriate operating speeds.[32] See the actions section that follows for a summary of strategies and examples.

Evidence about Health

Safety and traffic speed and volume

Vehicles operating at greater travel speeds significantly increase the risk of a traffic accident resulting in fatality for both drivers and pedestrians.[33] Slower travel increases drivers' visibility to potential hazards, such as pedestrians crossing the streets, and increases reaction time to respond to such hazards. Figure 26 shows that the risk of pedestrian fatality is reduced considerably with lower vehicle speeds.

The relationship between speed and safety is well documented but there are "complicated interactions" that make it "difficult for researchers to isolate the

141

effect of speed… on safety", such as whether drivers or pedestrians are they obeying road laws, traffic volumes, and other people using the street.[34]

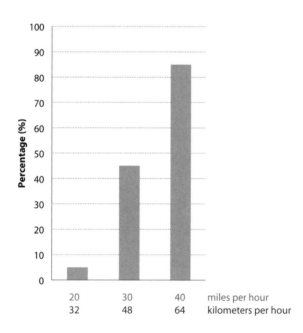

Figure 26. Probability of pedestrian death resulting from accidents at various vehicle impact speeds

It is well documented that reducing speed limits and implementing traffic calming measures can play an important role in traffic and pedestrian safety.

Source: Adapted from Donnell et al. 2009, 8

Litman and Fitzroy's review of 200 international sources consistently found that increased distance traveled per capita is also related to increased traffic fatalities.[35] Also, if traffic speeds are too slow, this can cause congestion, increasing local air pollution and travel times for vehicles.

Safety and traffic calming

Studies consistently show a connection between traffic-calming strategies and greater traffic safety. A review of seven detailed traffic-calming studies from Scandinavian countries, Israel, Greece, Australia, and Great Britain highlights "positive and well-documented safety effects, which appear to be independent of the extensiveness of the implementation of the measures."[36] An international review of 28 systematic reviews on the effectiveness of transportation interventions on improving public health found that area-wide traffic calming measures that reduce traffic speeds and discourage non-local traffic from using residential streets decrease accidents by 15 percent, on average, across all countries studied.[37] Most studies on traffic calming have been conducted in high-income countries, and more research is needed for low- and middle-income countries; however, logically the effects should be similar.[38]

Physical activity

Reviews show low traffic speeds and volumes are strongly related to physical activity for younger

Appropriate speed limits

On-street parking with bike buffer

Barriers

Street trees close to roadways

Sidewalk widening

Bulb-outs at intersections

Speed bumps

Chicanes

Traffic circles or roundabouts

Figure 27. Various traffic calming measures

children, in part because parents allow them out and about more in areas they perceive to be safer. However, evidence is mixed for able-bodied adults—some reviews found a connection while others found no relationship, and some found mixed results. Interestingly, reviews mostly found no connection between traffic speeds and volumes and physical activity of older adults.[39]

Actions

◆ **Create speed limits appropriate for the type of street.**

Slower speeds reduce traffic collision rates and severity, as well as reduce injury risk for pedestrians and cyclists. Speed limits should be lower (18–31 mph or 30–50km/hr) on local streets located in densely built areas, residential neighborhoods, and near schools, and where there is a mix of vulnerable road users and car traffic.[40] Just lowering speed limits can be frustrating for drivers; rather, combining them with the traffic-calming measures discussed in later actions will make these lower speeds feel more natural.

❖ **Provide a variety of street parking, but buffer it from cycling infrastructure.**

Street parking gives visual cues for drivers to slow down. Back-in parking maximizes pedestrian safety. On-street parallel parking can be problematic for cyclists getting "doored" without a buffer or wide bike lane.

◆ **Retrofit problematically fast roads with a variety of traffic calming measures.**

Ewing and Dumbaugh (2009) reviewed over 100 articles on the built environment and traffic safety. The authors conclude that in dense, urban areas "less 'forgiving' design treatments . . . appear to enhance a roadway's safety performance when compared to more conventional roadway designs."[41] These measures include widening sidewalks, bulb-outs or curb extensions at intersections, speed bumps, street trees, or chicanes.

Connections

Transportation safety is affected by accidents on roads and security on paths. To understand this proposition better, go to:

• **Principle 3. Vulnerability:** Plan and design for those with the most health vulnerabilities and fewest resources for making healthy choices

• **Proposition 13:** Coordinate land-use planning and urban design with transit to increase efficiency, access, and mobility

To further investigate, look at:

• **Proposition 17:** Design the public realm to reduce street crime and fear of crime

• **Proposition 19:** Separate people and infrastructure from areas vulnerable to natural disasters and build in resilience through technology or design

◆ Directly from research evidence   ❖ Informed by research   ◇ General good practice

Proposition 15: Ensure adequate pedestrian and cycling infrastructure and amenities

The presence or absence and quality of sidewalks, footpaths, bicycle lanes, and pedestrian rights-of-way influence the perception of safety and people's willingness to travel by foot or bicycle. Design is also an important factor in ensuring pedestrian and cycling infrastructure is safe, accessible, and appealing.

How It Works

Bicycle and pedestrian travel offer health benefits by increasing mobility options and opportunities for physical activity in the community, whether for recreational or travel purposes. Walking and cycling infrastructures are a relatively low-cost, commonsense way to support people getting out and about locally by increasing the safety of vulnerable road users. Such infrastructure can be integrated with almost any type of existing street.

Ensuring adequate infrastructure requires creating a network of walking and cycling routes, ensuring safe road crossings, and incorporating features that can be used by people of different ages and abilities and at different times of day, including adequate lane and path width and lighting. Well-designed pedestrian amenities also make the public realm more comfortable, accessible, aesthetically beautiful, and enjoyable. These pedestrian amenities can include seating, public toilets, drinking fountains, signage, lighting, garbage receptacles, public art, and trees and plantings.

Evidence about Health
Physical activity
Pedestrian amenities and aesthetics

Although pedestrian amenities and aesthetics create an enjoyable and pleasing environment, the weight of evidence suggests they are not strongly related to physical activity. While some systematic reviews and large qualitative studies have shown a moderate positive relationship between high-quality amenities or aesthetics and physical activity, most studies have found mixed or no significant connection. There is somewhat more evidence for aesthetics and recreational walking versus walking for transportation.[42]

However, high-quality pedestrian amenities and aesthetics are more important for other health reasons, such as improved mental well-being from viewing nature and benefits for older adults and children, who are more likely to need places to rest and rejuvenate.[43]

Sidewalks

Reviews find mixed evidence for sidewalks supporting walking for able-bodied adults, with some studies finding a relationship.[44] The bulk of the evidence agrees that sidewalks are important for children walking to school[45] and may benefit pedestrian accessibility and safety, especially for those with physical impairments. Special consideration should be given to pedestrian and cycling infrastructure connectivity to avoid instances where sidewalks are suddenly discontinued or wide streets that allow bicyclists to share the road abruptly narrow.

Pedestrian safety infrastructure

Other pedestrian safety infrastructure, such as crosswalks and controlled intersections, was also found to be important for children walking to destinations.[46] There is mixed evidence for older adults.[47]

Cyclist infrastructure

For cyclists, there are two issues—infrastructure availability and quality. A key aspect of availability is having a complete network and "the literature consistently suggests that the dearth of cycling infrastructure is a major detriment in terms of spurring cycling."[48]

Safety

Pedestrian crossings are the source of most collisions,[49] and they can be dangerous and challenging on streets with multiple lanes, heavy traffic volumes, or high traffic speeds. In the United States, road crossings at midblock locations account for more than 70 percent of pedestrian fatalities.[50] Unlike pedestrian accidents,

most bicycle accidents occur at street intersections, not midblock.[51] The evidence connecting bicycle infrastructure with increased ridership and perception of safety is strong.[52] What is less clear in the research is whether physically separated bicycle facilities, such as cycle tracks, where cyclists have a barrier between them and traffic but periodically need to cross streets and intersections where they may be conflicts with cars, are safer or more conducive to cycling than on-road bike facilities such as bicycle lanes.[53] One review of literature on transportation infrastructure and bicycle injuries and crashes found that on-road marked bike lanes consistently reduce injury rates, collision frequency, or crash rates by about 50 percent compared to unmodified roadways.[54]

Actions

◆ **Place marked crosswalks at intersections or mid-block, and create raised medians or intersection crossing islands.**
Pedestrian safety infrastructure, especially mid-block, promotes traffic safety.[55] However, safety may be limited without additional lights and signals.[56]

❖ **Create a network of bicycle anes, separated paths, and protected intersections.**
Cycling infrastructure is fundamental to cyclist safety and for promoting cycling as physical activity. However, there is unclear evidence about the ultimate safety of certain types and designs of

Sidewalks

Separated paths or bridges

Recreational trails

On-street bike lanes

Physically separated bike lanes

Protected intersections for cyclists

Prioritized signals

Crosswalks

Raised medians

Figure 28. Pedestrian and cyclist infrastructure examples

Seating

Public toilets

Drinking fountains

Garbage receptacles

Public art

Urban greening

Figure 29. Pedestrian amenities

cycling infrastructure, including separated cycle tracks without protected intersections.[57]

◆ **Provide pedestrian seating, public restrooms with universal design, and drinking fountains in public places.**
Recommended locations for these amenities include along sidewalks, in parks, at playgrounds, in schools, at transportation stops and stations, and near walkways and cycling paths. They can especially benefit children and aging populations.[58]

❖ **Beautify the public environment by providing strategically placed garbage and recycling receptacles, public art, and urban greening such as street trees, landscaping, green roofs, or walls.**
Though evidence on health outcomes is mixed, neighborhood maintenance and beautification programs are good to do. They may transform and rejuvenate public space[59] and shape perceptions of safety and neighborhood quality (related to social capital).[60] Street trees and green spaces promote urban cooling and comfort[61] and provide mental health benefits.

Connections

Walking and cycling bring multiple benefits to a very wide range of people. To understand this proposition better, go to:

- **Proposition 7:** Integrate universal design principles into neighborhood planning and design
- **Proposition 11:** Create a connected, "healthier" travel circulation pattern for pedestrians, bicyclists, and transit users—the vehicular pattern can be different
- **Proposition 12:** Increase access to a variety of locally relevant recreational facilities and green spaces
- **Proposition 14:** Adopt policies and planning practices to create safe neighborhood transportation options for all types of road users

To further investigate, look at:

- **Proposition 16:** Create publicly accessible neighborhood spaces, programs, and events to support healthy interactions and behaviors
- **Proposition 17:** Design the public realm to reduce street crime and fear of crime

Connection

Create opportunities for people to interact with each other in positive ways.

Whether through public spaces or community centers, neighborhood planning and design can support and supplement the common interests, family ties, and events that bring people together.

Social connections can increase one's sense of belonging in a community and the network of social support, and enhance informal control of antisocial activities.

How It works

Fundamental to health and well-being is the ability to connect to the people and resources needed to lead a healthy life. These connections can occur in many locations and across space, from the workplace to cyberspace; the neighborhood is one of these settings. However, not all connections promote health. A violent relationship or a peer group that encourages unhealthy eating or smoking are examples.

Evidence about Health

Social capital, social cohesion, and health—important connections

Social capital— the social connections among individuals or groups that facilitate collective action—has a number of forms:

- **Groups and networks:** Collections of individuals that promote and protect personal relationships, which improve welfare
- **Trust and solidarity:** Elements of interpersonal behavior that foster greater cohesion and more robust collective action
- **Collective action and cooperation:** The ability of people to work together toward resolving communal issues
- **Social cohesion and inclusion:** Connections that mitigate the risk of conflict and promote equitable access to the benefits of development by enhancing participation of the marginalized
- **Information and communication:** Breaking down of negative social capital and also enabling

of positive social capital by improving access to information[1]

These deal with perceptions of trust and reciprocity (cognitive social capital) and interpersonal networks and engagement (structural social capital). Social capital may involve strong bonds of family, friends, and close-knit communities or the more distant links between people who do not share as much in common.[2]

Given the variety of forms, researchers trying to identify the relationships between social capital and health- and wellness-related outcomes use a variety of measures, including trust of others, information dissemination, social interaction, and participation in group activities.[3]

In general, studies of the relationship between health and social capital focus on positive examples of the links between social capital and self-rated physical health, positive mental health, and overall life satisfaction outcomes (see Table 20). Participation in social activities and volunteering has been shown to have a positive relationship to physical and mental health, and sense of belonging.[4] Social engagement has been shown to be especially important for the health of older adults.[5] Other forms of social capital are also related to health. For example, an early article from 1987 by Rowe and Kahn focused on health, and older adults described strong social capital—in the form of support from family, friends, or community members—as a contributor to health. Older adults

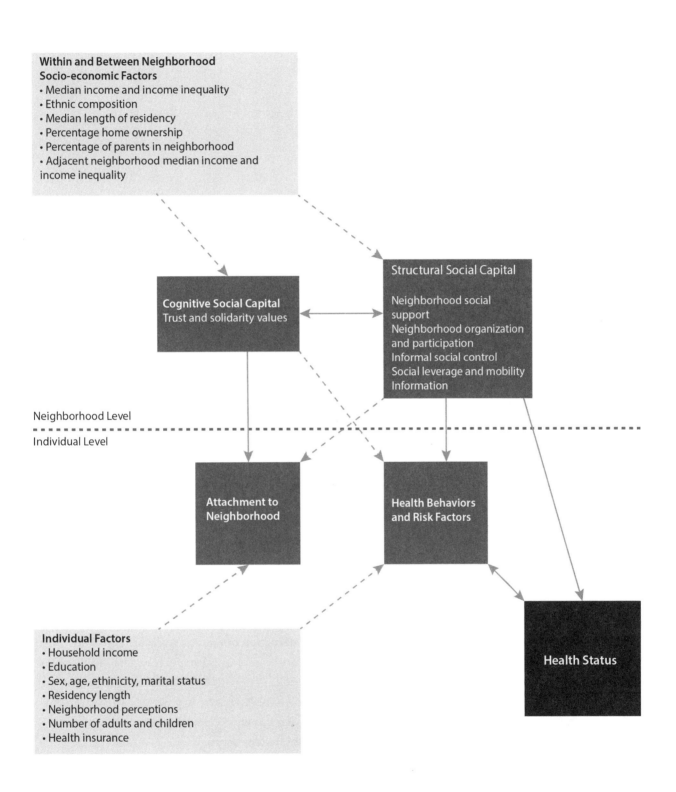

Figure 30. Relationship between neighborhoods and socioeconomic factors, social capital, and health status

Source: Adapted from Carpiano 2006, 169; Murayama et al. 2012, 179

Table 20. The positive and negative effects of social capital on health and wellness

Social capital description	Health and wellness impact
Higher levels of social support, close relationships, and interpersonal trust (a)	• Better self-rated health (physical) (b, c) • Better mental health, reduced mental disorders, reduced stress (d, e) • Increased life satisfaction and happiness (f, g)
Lack of social support, social isolation, low social capital, loneliness (h, i, j)	• Worse cardiac and all-cause mortality among patients diagnosed with coronary heart disease (k) • Increased risk of depressive symptoms during pregnancy (l) • Increased risk of depressive symptoms, in general (m) • Increased institutionalization in the elderly (l, n) • Negatively related to self-reported health (b, m, o) • Psychological and physiological stress (h)

Sources: (a) Kim et al. 2006; (b) D'Hombres et al. 2010, 56, 66; (c) Rocco and Suhrcke 2012, 13 (d) de Silva et al. 2006; (e) Lofors and Sundquist 2007; (f) Elgar et al. 2011; (g) Leyden et al. 2011; (h) Ellen et al. 2001, 394; (i) Lancaster et al. 2010, 5; (j) Resnick et al. 2011; (k) Barth et al. 2010, 229; (l) Luppa et al. 2009; (m) Murayama et al. 2012, 184; (n) Gao et al. 2012, 2; (o) Kawachi et al. 1999, 1187

with strong social support display signs of "less mortality, greater recovery from illness and injury, and better adherence to good health habits."[6]

This research typically argues that social capital can play a role in establishing group norms that promote healthy behaviors such as physical activity or healthy eating, increase awareness about health resources in the community, or provide individuals with social support needed to recover when they fall ill. On the other end of the spectrum, lower levels of social capital—such as a lack of social support, loneliness, or sense of isolation—can lead to negative self-rated reports of health, and physical and psychological stress (see Table 20). How social connections influence health is very complex because so much depends on the nature of the individuals and networks.[7] As noted earlier, not all social networks and norms promote healthy behavior—for example, they may have no effect or even promote negative outcomes such as stress or sedentary behavior.

Social capital and environments— links far less clear

Whether physical planning and design aspects of the built environment foster or hinder social capital is inconclusive, with studies on walkable neighborhoods, different scales of density, and urban form yielding mixed findings. That is there is no consistent evidence relating physical form to social capital. This is due to a number of reasons:

- Social capital is inherently social and not physical. In general, there are many places for people to make connections: at work, at home, at school, in faith communities, and in other groups with common interests.[8] Communication may be face to face but also via mail, telephone, or the Internet, or through scheduled or semi-scheduled activities found in settings like workplaces, sports groups, and committees. People certainly may meet each other casually at the dog park and start to chat over shared interests, or run into each other in the street having met at a school function. However, these kinds of place-based interactions are only part of a very large landscape of interaction.

- Even if it does seem that particular kinds of social connections are fostered by a place, from a research perspective it is hard to disentangle cultural influences and self-selection from the effect of place (i.e., people choose types of neighborhoods to reside in based on preference and are likely to become friends with neighbors who have also selected that neighborhood and may be socially similar.[9]

- People use spaces in ways not intended by designers or their patterns of use, not merely the space, are key. For example, there is an idea that places like coffee shops foster rich and uplifting dialogue. This may be true if a book club chooses

Table 21. Health and wellness factors—where social capital may have mixed or no effects

Health care access	• Social capital can increase health care access, but it depends on quality of relationship and norms or beliefs of the members within the network (a)
Mortality	• Literature has found positive (b, c), negative (d), and no effects (e) of social capital and death rates
Health behaviors	• Depends on the health behavior: for example, social capital may improve/increase physical activity, or diabetes control, but mixed results for smoking cessation • Also depends on culture of the community, social norms, informal social control, etc. (d, f, g, h, i, k)
Resilience to disasters	• Mixed results on withstanding heat stress; Causal pathways not clearly understood—but recent evidence suggests social capital may provide more resources to deal with disasters (k, l)
Buffering effects of poverty on health	• Social capital can buffer some of the negative effects of poverty on health (m, n, o, p) • It can also be harmful to health to those providing social support and practical assistance through burdening people's already stressful lives

Sources: (a) Derose and Varda 2009, 287; (b) Lochner et al. 2003; (c) Martikainen et al. 2003; (d)Murayama et al. 2012, 184; (e) van Hooijdonk et al. 2008; (f) Carpiano 2007; (g) Kim et al. 2006; (h) Long et al. 2010; (i) Meijer et al. 2012, 1204; (j) Poortinga 2006; (k) Kawachi et al. 2013, 183–184; (l) Romero-Lankao et al. 2012; (m) Kawachi et al. 2013, 16; (n) Mitchell and LaGory 2002; (o) Sapag et al. 2008; (p) Uphoff et al. 2013, 9

to meet at such a location or there are regulars there who foster a sense of sociability, but it would not be the case in a place where everyone is fully engaged with their smartphones (which may involve a great deal of social networking, just not related to the place). Or as another example, someone who is an avid gardener may meet people walking by as she works in her front yard, but someone who hires a lawn service would not.

Public spaces with outdoor furniture can facilitate social gathering.

While these are simple examples, they are played out with more complexity in other settings.

So what can be done?

There are some forms of neighborhood- and district-scale social connections that can be fostered by good planning. These include making sure that there are opportunities for civic engagement, informal gathering, recreation and physical activity, and coalescing around common interests. The following are examples:

- **Neighborhood organizations:** Resident associations, community gardeners, or other groups can be part and parcel of neighborhood development.
- **Spaces for meeting and gathering:** Cities can provide meeting rooms, community and senior centers, libraries, dog parks, playgrounds, community gardens, or wide walking paths with outdoor furniture (benches) and features that facilitate socializing. Some spaces that are private—extensions of the household such as restaurants, gyms, and private clubs—can also provide this kind of facility.
- **Programming of spaces for interaction:** While not specifically physical, spaces need to be able to accommodate programs that happen at specific times, such as community festivals, sports events, and club meetings.

The main takeaway is that different kinds of places support different kinds of connections and networks; however the effect of place may be weak or nonexistent depending on the form of social capital. To deal with this conundrum, the best strategy is to create a variety of different types of environments, institutional arrangements, and events, like those suggested earlier.

Connections

Having accessible health-related resources within a neighborhood, and connections to such resources outside, is a key challenge for places over the long term. To understand this proposition better, go to:

- **Proposition 7:** Integrate universal design principles into neighborhood planning and design

- **Proposition 9:** Create mixed use neighborhoods with a balance of activities that support good health
- **Principle 5. Access:** Provide options for getting around and increasing geographic access

To further investigate, look at:
- **Proposition 16:** Create publicly accessible neighborhood spaces, programs, and events to support healthy interactions and behaviors
- **Proposition 17:** Design the public realm to reduce street crime and fear of crime
- **Principle 8. Implementation:** Create diverse actions over time

Interactive spaces, like the basketball court pictured, can create opportunities for group activities.

Proposition 16: Create publicly accessible neighborhood spaces, programs, and events to support healthy interactions and behaviors

Neighborhoods and districts should have accessible, safe, and well-maintained public spaces for people to engage in healthy behaviors and interactions, if they are interested. Having a purpose to the space—a library, sports activities, or playground—greatly enhances its use.

How It Works

Public space is a key part of the physical landscape and much talked about. There can be areas—public or private—that enable strangers to enter at no cost or very low cost and offer opportunities to engage in social, political, and economic activities. Spaces like parks, street cafes, or civic plazas may be "generalized," meaning they are without any one core attraction and might be used by people with similar schedules.[10] Playgrounds, dog parks, libraries, and shopping areas are public spaces where strangers may cluster around shared interests.[11] Festivals, concerts, sporting events, farmers markets, and other programs can generate activity and populate publicly accessible spaces at different times of day to "increase use, safety, and a sense of place."[12]

As noted in Principle 6, not all social networks occur in a specific place. That is not to say public spaces are unimportant. They can provide a casual sense of belonging, hold activities and events, and may promote a sense of psychological well-being or allow certain forms of physical activity, as discussed in the previous propositions.[13]

Evidence about Health

Social support and interaction often come from family and friends in private spaces such as homes, organizations, and work sites. People with things in common are more likely to create social networks or gather around common interests.[14] Increasingly, social interaction is via personal communication (mail, phone, email, video chatting, and social media). These technologies have the potential to further complicate, and potentially dilute, the relationship between place, health, and social capital. As described in Principle 6, strong social capital is linked to positive health outcomes and vice versa (refer to Table 20).

Although the connections between public and shared spaces and health behaviors and outcomes may seem intuitive, there is limited research specifically linking them. A literature review of research on public open spaces and physical activity found mixed

General space for social connections (e.g. public community resources, "third spaces," public open space)

Specific programs and places to support shared interests (e.g. dog parks, children's playgrounds)

Community events and placemaking efforts to support social connections

Figure 31. Public spaces can host programs and events, or be generalized spaces that support social gathering and interaction

associations on levels of physical activity, which varied based on the proximity, size, and quality of the public space. Associations also differed because of varying methods and definitions used to conduct the studies being reviewed.[15] Further complicating matters, was that attributes of the same type of public open space might affect gender, age, and socioeconomic groups differently.[16] However, if there are no public spaces at all, there will still be some effect—at least on where activities happen. A US-based study of 436 older adults aged 65 and older found that those living in neighborhoods without parks and walking areas

Place-based social groups promote civic engagement and community affiliations.

engaged in less regular physical activities or social activities than those who did.[17]

Actions

◇ **Maximize flexibility of space for different users and activities, and at different times of the day, week, and year.**
Design choices, such as the selection and location of street furniture and lighting, can encourage the space to serve multiple purposes and be used at different times of day: "For example, a small plaza can be a great lunchtime spot on weekdays, a place for a flea market on Saturday mornings, and then the main stage for an annual festival."[18]

◆ **Provide maintenance and upkeep of the space and surrounding areas.**
The condition of the public space may influence its perceived safety.[19] Litter, graffiti, or other signs of neglect may deter users from visiting the area, whereas well-maintained features and amenities can signal and investment care for the space.[20]

◆ **Ensure spaces are highly accessible to pedestrians.**
Publicly accessible spaces should be linked to other areas via pathways and sightlines that draw users in from surrounding areas.[21] Ideally, neighborhood recreational green spaces will be located within easy walking distances (optimally between 0.25 and 0.5 miles, or 400 and 800

meters) from all residences.[22] Where possible, parks should be located adjacent to transit to increase accessibility, especially for those who do not drive or cannot walk long distances.[23]

◆ **Allow and promote programs and places for social activities and community affiliations, such as volunteering, religious or social organizations, community education, or parent-teacher associations.**
While not specifically about the physical place, such place-based social groups can alter the way neighborhoods and districts are used.

◆ **Encourage civic engagement related to neighborhood issues.**
Policy committees, community meetings, community groups, and planning workshops enable and empower community members to provide input on issues of interest to them, which can help foster a sense of belonging and enable residents to make a difference where they live— thereby potentially strengthening social capital.[24]

Connections

Having places to be with others is a fundamental part of neighborhoods and districts. To understand this proposition better, go to:

- **Principle 3. Vulnerability:** Plan and design for those with the most health vulnerabilities and fewest resources for making healthy choices
- **Proposition 9:** Create mixed use neighborhoods with a balance of activities that support good health
- **Principle 5. Access:** Provide options for getting around and increasing geographic access
- **Proposition 15:** Ensure adequate pedestrian and cycling infrastructure and amenities
- **Principle 6. Connection:** Create opportunities for people to interact with each other in positive ways

To further investigate, look at:

- **Proposition 17:** Design the public realm to reduce street crime and fear of crime

◆ Directly from research evidence   ❖ Informed by research   ◇ General good practice   **161**

Proposition 17: Design the public realm to reduce street crime and fear of crime

Design publicly accessible spaces, and adjacent sites and buildings, to provide natural surveillance of activities in the public realm as a way to improve real and perceived safety from criminal activity. Leverage social connections to improve this sense of safety.

How It Works

Many factors influence the relationships between neighborhood crime and violence (real or perceived), the built environment, and health.[25] Although crime and violence are perpetrated by individuals, it has long been thought that criminal behavior and the built environment affect each other. The condition of the built environment can potentially reduce actual and perceived crime behaviors, which is linked to a range of health issues. For example, vandalism or other criminal activity might be more likely to take place in neighborhoods with abandoned or vacant lots, rundown buildings, poor lighting, or limited pedestrian activity.[26]

Design Strategy Effectiveness

Design strategies, several of which fall under the concept of Crime Prevention Through Environmental Design (CPTED), attempt to improve neighborhood safety by improving natural surveillance and generating activity in the public realm (Table 22). In their literature review and synthesis of over 130 articles on theories and causal pathways of crime and health,

Lorenc et al. found that such design treatments can be effective in improving perceptions of crime.[27]

In terms of actual crime there is sufficient evidence that lighting strategies, which can be used to increase natural surveillance and to strategically brighten dark corners or high-risk areas, can be an effective crime prevention strategy in public spaces as well as a strategy to reduce fear of crime.[28] Welch and Farrington reviewed 13 US and UK studies on lighting and crime and found that "improved street lighting significantly reduces crime [and] is more effective in reducing crime in the United Kingdom than in the United States".[29] However, while these strategies represent generally good planning, it is unclear how effective these interventions are and whether CPTED actually reduces incidents of crime or prevents crime from occurring.[30]

Evidence about Health

There are a number of ways in which crime and other antisocial behavior (actual or perceived) can influence health:

Table 22. Strategies to reduce perceived and actual crime

Strategy	Examples
Good evidence	
Improved street lighting (a, b)	• Adding or increasing lighting in dark areas
Mixed evidence	
Demarcating public from private space (CPTED) (c, d)	• Signage • Fences • Pavement treatments • Landscaping
Improving visibility to increase surveillance (CPTED) (d)	• Lighting • Windows overlooking the street • Low wall/fences • Trees and shrubbery not too thick • Clear sight lines along route
Limiting points of entry to control access (CPTED) (e)	• Reduced routes through housing complexes • Concierges • Protective screens on buses • Street barriers
Activity support (f)	• Activity generation • Pedestrian traffic • Mixed use neighborhoods

Sources: (a) Schneider and Kitchen 2007, 199; (b) Welsh and Farrington 2008 (c) Politechnico di Milano et al. 2007, 36 (d) Cozens et al. 2005, 331–332; (e) Lorenc et al. 2012, 761; (f) Hand et al. 2012, 875
Note: Other strategies, such as alarms and surveillance cameras, are not neighborhood design and planning strategies.

- Obviously, if someone is a victim of a violent crime, there is a health effect—an injury or death.
- Neighborhood crime and violence, real or perceived, can cause or exacerbate depression, anxiety, stress and stress-disorders, and other mental health effects, especially among children and older adults.[31]

Ellen et al. reviewed evidence on health outcomes and neighborhoods effects, finding strong evidence that the level of neighborhood crime or violence influences health-related behaviors, mental health, and, to a lesser extent, birthweight. There was weak evidence that neighborhoods influenced the development of functional limitations, such as mobility problems, or other physical diseases.[32] They proposed that time was a key dimension in understanding the relationship between crime, health, and place with stressors accumulating over long periods in a process they call weathering, which they outline in more detail:

> This suggests to us that neighborhoods may primarily influence health in two ways: first, through relatively short-term influences on behaviors, attitudes, and healthcare utilization, thereby affecting health conditions that are most immediately responsive to such influences; and second, through a longer-term process of "weathering," whereby the accumulated stress, lower environmental quality, and limited resources of poorer communities, experienced over many years, erodes the health of residents in ways that make them more vulnerable to mortality from any given disease.[33]

In their review of 41 quantitative studies on the relationship between neighborhood crime and physical activity levels, Foster and Giles-Corti find insufficient evidence to conclude that crime-related safety concerns influence physical activity levels generally.[34] However, older people do seem to limit their outdoor physical activity when they fear crime, and this is also a problem, though less so, for women, low-income people, and some ethnic groups.[35]

Safety and social capital

One of the ways in which crime may relate to neighborhoods is through social capital. For some, positive perceptions of neighborhood safety are linked to a positive sense of community or sense of belonging and strong social capital. Places with strong social networks and shared values may have more control of antisocial behavior—for example, neighbors feeling they can tell youth to change uncivil behavior.[36] Stronger social cohesion and social networks can potentially increase perceptions of safety and the likelihood of neighbors or institutions providing information or help.[37]

Most research studies on safety and social connections are single-site or single-city studies and systematic reviews are not available which makes it hard to generalize. However, some studies are large. For example, Dallago et al. used a World Health Organization survey of health behavior, administered to 15 year old students in 13 countries to understand the perception of their neighborhood in terms of place attachment (the connection that people develop toward specific places), social capital, and safety.[38] Social capital was measured in terms of informal neighboring (saying hello in the street), trust of those nearby, and whether respondents could ask neighbors for help. The authors found that "despite cultural

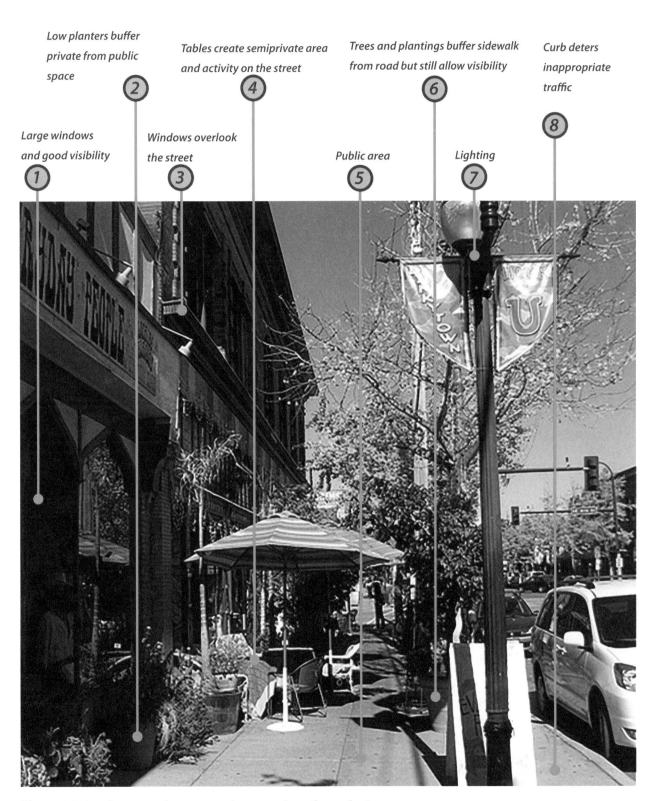

Figure 32. Implementation strategies to reduce fear of crime

Source: Ramsey et al. 2000; adapted from Steiner and Butler 2007, 274

and geographic differences, social capital had an important role in making students feel safer."[39]

Conflicts among guidelines for crime and other health-related topics

It is worth noting that there is debate on some planning concepts advocated in this book in relation to crime. Studies of burglary, for example, show links to increased street connectivity and permeability, particularly through gridiron street layouts, because residential and commercial areas are more at risk due to exposure to external traffic.[40] A summary of 12 studies on incidents of crime suggests that mixed use settings are more prone to crime compared to homogeneous land-use areas.[41] Connected pedestrian networks and mixed uses increase access to resources for health, however. Careful planning and design can maintain these benefits while minimizing safety concerns. It is also important to recognize the multitude of factors unrelated to the built environment that affect both perceived and actual crime, including socioeconomic factors, public disorder and incivility (loitering), and media reports.[42]

Actions

◆ **Provide adequate street lighting to enhance safety at night.**

Lighting should be used to increase visibility and the potential for positive surveillance in public and high-risk spaces, such as narrow passages, underground areas, and dark alleys at night.[43]

❖ **Delineate public and private property to manage activities in those spaces.**

Design elements such as signage, fences, surface treatments, and landscaping can delineate property types to signal ownership and risk of trespassing, which can aid in managing the activities that take place in those spaces.[44]

Blind corners and grade changes are problematic. Clear sight lines are important for pedestrian visibility and sense of safety.

❖ **Enhance visibility and sight lines to provide visual access to public spaces.**

While lighting is the only environmental feature absolutely supported by research in terms of deterring crime, clear sight lines are a related feature.[45] People need to be able to see others and see alternative paths so they can avoid problematic situations. Blind corners, grade changes, and vegetation at eye-level height can be particularly problematic.[46]

❖ **Avoid building places where people can be isolated or entrapped.**

Avoid entrapment spots (where people can be hemmed in with no escape) and movement predictors (where there is only one possible route, which is dangerous or not visible, and perpetrators can lie in wait).[47] Appropriate nearby activity and lighting can help and special care is needed for separated pedestrian and bicycle routes if used at night.

❖ **Maintain public space, abandoned properties, and vacant lots.**

In order to signal that there is investment, commitment, and attention to a given area, it is important to maintain public spaces and remove visual signs of decay, which may deter actual crime and perceptions of crime.[48] This can also prevent problems of isolation and vandalism.[49]

❖ **Mix land uses to promote diversified activities at different times of day.**

Co-locating commercial, residential, recreation land uses, and bicycle and pedestrian routes can generate different activities throughout the day, potentially increasing the vitality of the streets and natural surveillance of an area.[50]

Connections

Perceived and actual safety from crime can support healthy behaviors such as increased outdoor physical or recreational activities, increasing informal surveillance of the public realm. To understand this proposition better, go to:

- **Principle 3. Vulnerability:** Plan and design for those with the most health vulnerabilities and fewest resources for making healthy choices
- **Proposition 11:** Create a connected, "healthier" travel circulation pattern for pedestrians, bicyclists, and transit users—the vehicular pattern can be different
- **Proposition 14:** Adopt policies and planning practices to create safe neighborhood transportation options for all types of road users
- Proposition 15: Ensure adequate pedestrian and cyclist infrastructure and amenities

◆   Directly from research evidence   ❖   Informed by research   ◇   General good practice   **167**

Protection

Reduce harmful exposures at a neighborhood level through a combination of wider policies and regulations along with local actions.

Neighborhood- and district-level strategies to protect residents from harmful exposures (e.g. toxics, disasters, noise) require a comprehensive approach that is dependent on the particular hazard, geography, or demographics involved. Many strategies need to be coordinated across regions, rather than acting in a single district, and will not yield specific health benefits for some years.

How It Works

Planners and designers can try to limit health risks from harmful exposures at the neighborhood-scale—whether from toxics, disastrous events, or noise—by reducing these hazards at the source, buffering people from them, or mitigating them with technology or design.

However, it is important to recognize the inherent limitations in how much neighborhood-level planning and design interventions can do. There are two main variables to consider.

First, the largest issue is that many exposures are best controlled at scales other than a neighborhood or district (Figure 33). Business practices, technologies, household practices and preferences, and wider regulations are important. For example, outdoor air quality can be improved by regional and national regulations for industrial and vehicle emissions and indoor air quality by regulations about building materials and ventilation. Street layout and building siting can help provide ventilation without wind tunnels, but such neighborhood-level actions are just part of a very large picture. Similar points can be made about water quality, noise, the health effects of energy generation, such as respiratory problems, and health issues related to climate change, such as animal and insect-borne diseases, floods, and droughts.

Second, exposure influences health over different time periods. Health risks may be immediate, as in exposure to certain toxics or a disastrous storm. Alternatively, hazards might cause serious problems down the road such as long-term exposure to air pollution or chronic loud noises. Many aspects of healthy neighborhood planning aim to achieve health benefits or foster healthy behaviors and limit unhealthy exposures in the short term. Yet some strategies, while good planning in the here and now, do not achieve their full array of health benefits until fairly far into the future. This is particularly the case in three areas— water quality (low impact design to improve aquifer recharge over decades), new energy sources (relevant to health in terms of air pollution and long-term climate change), and better waste systems (with longer-term effects on exposures to chemicals).

The propositions that follow do not necessarily divide out the long- and short-term oriented actions. They do, however, focus on what can be done at the neighborhood level as opposed to other scales.

Further, the health effects and potential solutions of harmful exposures vary greatly, depending on the specific hazard or events, vulnerability to that hazard, exposure (proximity, or concentration or degree of the hazard), and time factors. That said, the neighborhood is an important part of people's daily experience and some actions at that level can be helpful in reducing risks in the short and long term.

Evidence about Health

Evidence about the prevalence of hazards, their health effects, and those groups that are most vulnerable indicates that while some deaths are attributable to harmful exposures, the hazards also cause a great deal of disease, disability, and disruption. Key hazards include:

- **Pollutants and chemicals:** Toxic chemicals, especially those that contribute to indoor and outdoor air pollution, are responsible for millions of deaths annually.[1] Contaminated drinking water, poor sanitation and hygiene are estimated to cause over 1.7 million deaths annually, particularly as a result of diarrheal disease.[2] Exposure to chemicals through waste disposal

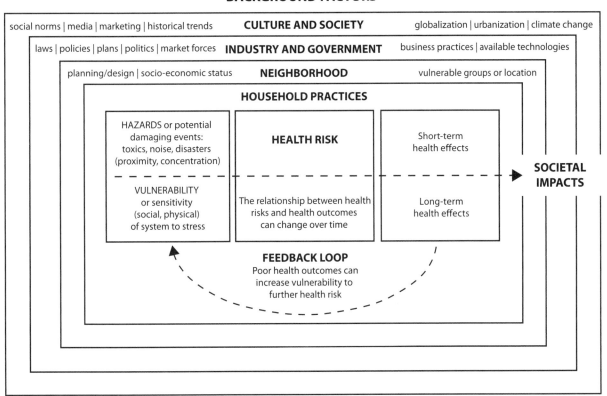

Figure 33. Health risks related to hazards, vulnerability, and exposure over time

The relationship between health risks and short- and long-term health outcomes is complex. It can change over time and vary based on numerous background factors, which influence the magnitude, vulnerability, and exposure to those risks.

Source: Developed by authors

and processing is linked to asthma, respiratory and heart disease, cancer, and low birth weight, though health risks vary based on proximity and waste management practices (Table 23).[3]

- **Natural disasters:** Natural disasters affect millions of people every year. Between 2002 and 2011, natural disasters killed on average over 100,000 people per year.[4] The rates of natural disasters are increasing, in part, due to climate change.[5]

- **Technological disasters:** Transportation, industrial, and other accidents, such as nuclear power plant accidents and mass communications crashes, are categorized as technological disasters.[6]

Between 2002 and 2012, technological disasters on average killed over 8,000 people and affected over 1.1 million people each year.[7]

- **Environmental noise:** Finally, environmental noise affects the health and quality of life of millions of people. For example, the World Health Organization estimates that in Europe alone "one in three individuals is annoyed during the daytime and one in five has disturbed sleep at night because of traffic noise."[8]

Identifying vulnerable groups can help planners decide which areas and groups should be prioritized for toxics, noise, and disaster mitigation measures.

Table 23. Global deaths from air pollutants, chemical exposure, and natural disasters

Hazards	Annual Global Deaths Due to Hazard/ Percent of Deaths Due to Hazard (g)
Indoor air pollutants (2012) (a)	4.3 million/7.8 of annual deaths%
Outdoor air pollutants (2012) (b)	3.7 million/ 6.7%
Chemicals (single chemicals, occupational exposures, and acute poisoning) (2004) (c)	1.3 million/2.6%
Contaminated drinking water and poor sanitation/diarrhea (2002) (d)	1.7 million/3.4%
Natural disasters (global annual average 2002–2011) (e)	107,000/ 0. 2%
Technological disasters (global annual average 2002–2012) (f)	8,735/0.02%

Indoor air pollution is the greatest environmental hazard to contribute to global deaths, followed by outdoor air pollution, other chemicals, and contaminated drinking water and poor sanitation. Global deaths by natural and technological disasters represent a smaller share of global deaths due to such hazards, but one that is increasing as a result of climate change.

Sources: (a) WHO 2012; (b) WHO 2014; (c) Prüss-Üstün et al. 2011, 6–7;(d) WHO 2015d; (e) Guha-Sapir et al. 2013, 1,3; (f) Guha-Sapir et al. 2015; (g) U.S. Census Bureau 2015

Connections

Reducing exposures often involves implementing policies or technologies that are not specific to neighborhood planning and design. However, there are some issues relevant to neighborhoods and districts. To understand this proposition better, go to:

- **Principle 3. Vulnerability:** Plan and design for those with the most health vulnerabilities and fewest resources for making healthy choices

- **Principle 4. Layout:** Foster multiple dimensions of health through overall neighborhood layout

To further investigate, look at:

- **Proposition 18:** Reduce pollutants and chemicals at the source, and separate people from toxins through buffers, technology, or design

- **Proposition 19:** Separate people and infrastructure from areas vulnerable to natural disasters, and build in resilience through technology or design

- **Proposition 20:** Reduce unwanted local noise exposure at the source, and separate people from noise through buffers, technology, or design

Despite contributing to millions of deaths annually, many interventions to prevent air pollution happen beyond the scale of the neighborhood.

Proposition 18: Reduce pollutants and chemicals at the source, and separate people from toxins through buffers, technology, or design

Preventing toxins from being released in the community is the most effective way to reduce human exposure to harmful chemicals. Other approaches include establishing greater distance between residential, commercial, and recreational sites and polluted areas, and better technologies and designs.

How It Works

Exposure to environmental toxins—or poisonous substances—can cause severe health effects ranging from respiratory infections to birth defects, cancer, and death.[9] However, not all environmental toxins are related to issues that are controllable by the planning and environmental design fields at the local scale. For example, much of what can be done about fossil fuels, water pollution, and waste management is not about neighborhood planning. Rather, it occurs at the building level, such as efficiency measures and ventilation upgrades, or at the policy level through regulations and financial incentives.

Evidence about Health

The links between exposure to toxic chemicals and health are well researched with many systematic reviews on the health risks of specific toxins and pollutant sources. Prüss-Üstün et al.'s systematic review of 95 articles between 1990 and 2009 found that "in total, 4.9 million deaths (8.3 percent of

total) and 86 million Disability-Adjusted Life Years (DALYs) (5.7 percent of total) were attributable to environmental exposure and management of selected chemicals in 2004."[10]

Air pollution

Dirty fossil fuels (oil, gasoline, coal, and natural gas) and biomass (wood, charcoal, dung, and crop residues) are major sources of toxins found in air pollution, along with greenhouse gas emissions. They cause a number of health effects, including chronic obstructive pulmonary disease, asthma; premature deaths; respiratory diseases; infections; allergies; headache, dizziness, and nausea from carbon monoxide; neurological impacts from leaded fuel; and lung cancer.[11] Neighborhood design can exacerbate or reduce existing air pollution through air circulation and dispersion patterns; the location of busy roadways and industrial and waste sites; and the presence or lack of vegetation.

Table 24. Neighborhood-scale sources and pathways of human exposure to toxins

Exposure	Sources of exposure	Neighborhood and district pathway example
Neighborhood-scale		
Drinking water	Ingestion of drinking water contaminated with toxic chemicals from industrial effluents, human dwellings, agricultural runoff, oil and mining wastes, or from natural sources	Runoff from lawns; sewerage overflow; local industrial waste
Food	Consumption of food contaminated with chemicals at toxic levels through agricultural practices, industrial processes, environmental contamination, and natural toxins	Local gardening in contaminated soil
Outdoor air	Inhalation of toxic gases and particles from vehicle and industrial emissions, or naturally occurring sources such as volcanic emission or forest fires	Vehicle emissions, industrial production
Soil	Ingestion (particularly for children) or inhalation of soil contaminated through industrial processes, agricultural processes, or inadequate household and industrial waste management	Children playing in contaminated soil
Not at the neighborhood scale		
Human to human	Fetal exposure to toxic chemicals during pregnancy (through placental barrier) or through consumption of contaminated breast milk	*
Indoor air	Inhalation of pollutants released during indoor combustion of solid fuels, tobacco smoking, or from construction materials and furnishings	*
Non-food consumer products	Exposure by ingestion, inhalation, or dermal exposure to toxic chemicals contained in toys, jewelry and decoration items, textiles, food containers, or consumer chemical products	*
Occupation exposure	Chronic or acute exposures through inhalation, skin absorption, or secondary ingestion of toxic chemicals or by-products of industrial processes such as agriculture, mining, or manufacturing	*

Source: Modified from Prüss-Üstün 2011, 3, used with permission of WHO Regional Office for Europe180

* Not at the neighborhood scale (e.g., consumer product, building. workplace)

Water pollution

Urban runoff and waste water from precipitation, discharges from construction, industrial systems, and combined sewer overflows often carry large amounts of contaminants.[12] Stormwater tends to have a higher content of heavy metals whereas wastewater is a large source of organic and nitrogenous pollution.[13] Additionally, because urban areas have a larger proportion of impervious surfaces than rural areas, rainwater and stormwater can cause flooding and runoff into sewers, streams, and bodies of water instead of flowing into the ground.[14]

Pollution from waste

Uncontrolled and improperly managed waste causes many health and environmental problems. Waste is often contaminated with chemicals, heavy metals, microbes, and fecal matter.[15] It can attract insects and rodents and pollutes drinking water, food, and soil. Residential proximity to hazardous waste sites, landfills, and old incinerators has been associated with many diseases and birth defects. However, harmful health effects from residential proximity to waste sites are likely contingent on how well these services and sites are managed and regulated—for example, uncontrolled dumps versus regulated and controlled landfills or incinerators.[16] Environmental pollution from uncontrolled urban waste is especially a health concern for pregnant women and children.[17] Ideally, where technology is available, waste can be turned into energy production.[18]

Actions

Many of the most effective actions are regulatory. Neighborhood planning and design interventions can help supplement more comprehensive policies and regulations.

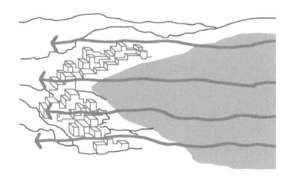

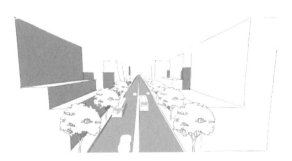

Figure 34. Urban planning and design actions to increase atmospheric dispersion of air pollution
Such actions include siting developments to take advantage of natural air flow and stepping back buildings to allow dispersion.
Source: Adapted from Whinston-Sprin 1986

Table 25. Neighborhood-scale strategies to reduce health risks from hazards

Type of strategy	Neighborhood and district examples
Reduce hazards at the source	• Neighborhood street patterns to capitalize on prevailing sun, shade, and wind patterns(a) • Trees and vegetation to lower energy use and promote urban cooling (a) • Coal, oil, and natural gas based fuels, reduced through household weatherization and energy-efficiency improvements • On-site renewable energy (solar, wind), district energy, smart-grids, or eco-districts • Water efficient policies, technologies, and landscaping to reduce water use (b) • Community waste reduced, reused, recycled and composted as much as possible (c) • Biomass power generation carefully designed to avoid air quality problems • Transportation and parking policies that promote walking and cycling (d)
Buffer people away from hazards	• Hazardous land uses zoned away from residents
Mitigate with technologies or design	• Centralized sanitation and sewer systems (separate stormwater and sanitation water) (e) • Water-sensitive urban design (to filter pollutants) (f) • Building improvements such as ventilated stoves, non-toxic, and low-toxic construction materials • (Clean) incinerators and well-managed landfills (g)

Sources: (a) Davoudi et al. 2009, 38, 39; Stone et al. 2010, 1427; (b) Bernstein 1997; Dixon et al. 2014; Hilaire et al. 2008; Kent et al. 2006; Postel 1997; Wang 2015; (c) Kemp et al. 2007, 85; Powrie and Dacombe 2006; Seadon 2006; Seadon 2010; U.S. EPA 2002; (d) Reiter and Kockelman 2015; (e) Benova et al. 2014; Dangour et al. 2013; Fink et al. 2011; Hunter et al. 2010; Schwarzenbach et al. 2010, 127; (f) Davis et al. 2009; Schueler 2000; Scholes et al. 2008; (g) Kemp et al. 2007; Powrie and Dacombe 2006; Seadon 2006; Seadon 2010; U.S. EPA 2002

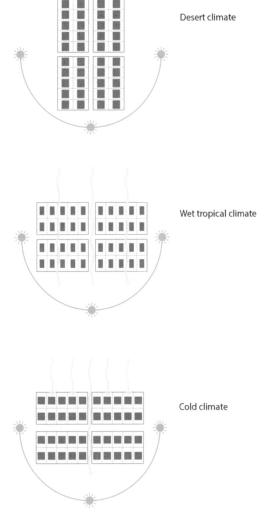

Desert climate

Wet tropical climate

Cold climate

Figure 35. Street patterns for renewable and efficient energy use

Street patterns and building orientation can take advantage of natural sun exposure to maximize heating and cooling.

Sources: Developed by authors

Figure 36. Various water-efficient technologies and landscaping approaches

Top: Xeriscaping—the use of native vegetation to landscape.

Bottom: Technology like graywater recycling reduces water use.

Sources: Developed by authors

Reduce toxics and pollutants at the source

◆ **Orient developments to best take advantage of sunlight and natural ventilation in order to reduce energy use and associated pollutants.**

Solar and wind orientation and vegetative cover of streets, lots, and buildings can greatly alter the temperature of structures, affecting energy use, greenhouse gas emissions, and human health and comfort.[19] Where trees are not practical due to water scarcity, other forms of shade should be used, such as awnings, overhanging roofs, and colonnades.[20]

◆ **Use and promote water efficient policies, technologies, and landscaping to reduce water use.**

Efficient water use can reduce wastewater runoff, thus minimizing groundwater contamination from toxics and ensuring that water sources can be naturally replenished.[21] Neighborhood strategies include water efficient technologies (high-efficiency irrigation systems, recycling gray water, smart metering), the watering of lawns and landscaping at restricted times or days, tiered pricing of water use (where higher rates of use get higher prices), and low-water-use landscaping (such as xeriscaping in desert climates).[22]

◇ **Use public interventions and educational campaigns to reduce waste and increase reuse, composting, and recycling.**

A comprehensive solid waste management program seeks primarily to prevent waste in the first place (reduce and reuse), then recycle and compost waste into new uses, and finally dispose

Table 26. Neighborhood interventions to reduce waste and increase reuse, composting, and recycling

Category	Examples
Prevent waste (reduce and reuse) (a–j)	• Funding for neighborhood pilot projects targeted to the needs, barriers, motivations, and norms of the community • Coordinating local activities, e.g. designated neighborhood freecycle location, organized neighborhood or block yard sales • Incorporating scrap dealers, waste pickers, scavengers into organized or formal co-operatives
Recycle and compost waste (b, f, h)	• Distributing composting bins, kitchen caddies, and biodegradable bags, advice leaflets, and information packs • Providing recycling and composting bins alongside all public community trash bins

Sources: (a) Barr 2007 (b) Bass et al. 1991 (c) Bulkeley and Gregson 2009 (d) Cox et al. 2010, 208 (e) Darnton et al. 2006 (f) Dixon et al. 2014, 267 (g) Ebreo and Vining 2001, 447 (h) Kurlan 2006 (i) Seadon 2006 (j) Seadon 2010

◆ Directly from research evidence ❖ Informed by research ◇ General good practice **179**

of waste safely through (clean) incinerators and well-designed landfills.[23]

Buffer people from toxics and pollutants

❖ **Separate incompatible uses from one another.**

Separating incompatible land uses, such as residential and industrial activities, can prevent chemicals from entering the water stream or can isolate residential areas from sources of pollution.

Table 27. Acceptable distances from harmful exposure to residential area to reduce negative health risks

Distance from Residences	Site Type
At least 2 km or 1.2 miles (a)	• Landfills
At least 3 km or 1.9 miles (a, b)	• Toxic waste site • Coal mining • Oil refineries
100–500 meters or up to 0.3 miles (c)	• Busy roads and factories
>3–5 km or 2–3 miles, and depending on a population size, 16–48 km or 10–30 miles (d, e)	• Nuclear power plant

Sources: (a) Porta et al. 2009, 8; (b) Brender et al. 2011, 38, 49; (c) Zhou and Levy 2007, 8; (d) U.S. NRC 2014; (e) Pearlman and Waite 1984, 16–18

Table 27 indicates preferable distances from toxic source to residential area to limit exposure and health risks.

Mitigate exposure to toxics and pollutants with technology

❖ **Separate stormwater and sanitary water in water treatment infrastructure, and create stormwater sedimentation tanks.**

Upgrading sewage treatment is one of the most important interventions for preventing health problems from microbes, parasites, and toxins.[24] It also can prevent overflows during storm events and can be used to recycle wastewater (graywater).[25]

◆ **Use water-sensitive urban design in areas vulnerable to stormwater runoff.**

Water-sensitive urban design strategies that collect runoff and allow it to penetrate the soil slowly have the greatest ability to remove pollutants (suspended solids, nutrients, hydrocarbons, heavy metals).[26] Examples include infiltration or bioretention basins; rain gardens; constructed wetlands; porous paving; soakaways; infiltration trenches and strips; direct roof drains to rain barrels, gardens, or yards; and riparian (vegetative) buffers beside streams and rivers.[27]

◆   Directly from research evidence   ❖   Informed by research   ◇   General good practice

Various design features allow stormwater to soak into the ground.

Infiltration basins can remove a large amount of pollutants from stormwater.

Figure 37. Water-sensitive urban design examples

Connections

Toxic exposures are a particular problem for children—though depending on the source, many other population groups may be affected. To understand this proposition better, go to:

- **Principle 3. Vulnerability:** Plan and design for those with the most health vulnerabilities and fewest resources for making healthy choices
- **Principle 4. Layout:** Foster multiple dimensions of health through overall neighborhood layout
- **Proposition 9:** Create mixed use neighborhoods with a balance of activities that support good health

Proposition 19: Separate people and infrastructure from areas vulnerable to natural disasters, and build in resilience through technology or design

People and infrastructure need to be separated from and resistant to potential hazards, since neighborhoods in close proximity to unstable soil, coastlines, and waterways have an increased vulnerability to natural disasters and drought as they occur more frequently over time.

How It Works

The Office of US Foreign Disaster Assistance (OFDA) and Center for Research on the Epidemiology of Disasters (CRED) identifies five categories of disasters:[28]

- **Natural** (including earthquakes, volcanoes, storms, floods, extreme temperatures, droughts, or wildfires)
- **Biological** (such as epidemics, insects, or animal stampedes)
- **Technological** (such as nuclear power plant accidents or mass communications crashes)
- **Economic** (such as a financial system collapse)
- **Terrorism**

Natural disasters are the most common type of disaster, affecting millions of people every year with the largest numbers of people affected by floods, droughts, and storms.[29] Extreme storms, floods, and droughts will be an ongoing, increasing concern for urban planning and design, due to climate change.[30]

Evidence about Health

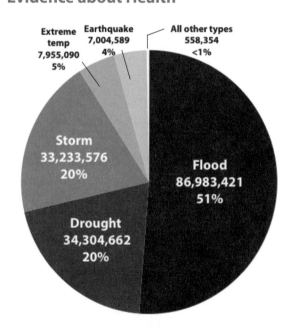

Figure 38. Average number of people affected by natural disaster disasters each year 2004–2014, by type

Source: EM-DAT International Disaster Database

According to OFDA/CRED data, from 2004 to 2014 on average over half of disaster victims worldwide were from floods, 20 percent from droughts, and 20 percent from storms (see Figure 38). The geographic distribution of disaster victims was concentrated in Asia and Africa, which together accounted for 95 percent of the global victims of natural disasters.[31] Formal and informal developments in close proximity to coastlines, waterways, or geological hazards have increased environmental vulnerability to floods, storms, sea-level rise, landslides, and unstable soils.[32] As Figure 39 shows, health risks from disasters occur directly, but they also happen indirectly through events such as the destruction of infrustructure.

Urban environments may be particularly vulnerable to natural disasters. Large populations living in cities and megacities mean

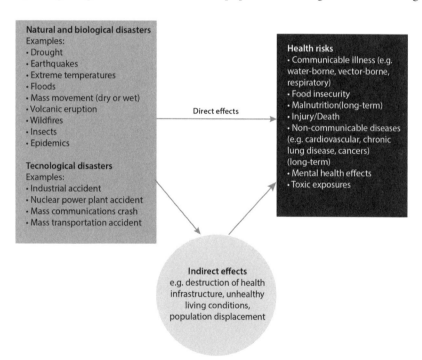

Figure 39. Disasters' effects on health risks

Sources: Based on, HAPI 2014m, 5–6; Alderman et al. 2012, 38–45; Bellos et al. 2010, 1; Bhutta et al. 2009, 45; Chaffee 2009, 50; Chan et al. 2009; Coleman 2006; Doocy et al. 2013a, 21; Doocy et al. 2013b; Guha-Sapir et al. 2013; Harville et al. 2010, 68, 84; Kimbrough et al. 2012; Maslow et al. 2012, 1186; McLaughlin et al. 2012, 1222; Norris 2002; Stanke et al. 2012; START 2012; UNSCEAR 2008, 15, 17; Uscher-Pines 2009, 2, 5.

Table 28. Neighborhood-scale strategies to reduce health risks from natural disasters

Buffer people away from hazards	• Use climactic and vulnerability information to inform urban planning and design, including location of development (a)
	• Limit development in areas vulnerable to disasters, such as floods or landslides (b)
Mitigate with technologies or design	• Landscape to mitigate disasters, for example vegetative buffers for flood prevention along waterways or climate appropriate landscaping (c)
	• Provide early warning systems and risk communications (d)
	• Incorporate water efficiency, such as low-flow technologies and water recycling
	• Use building and construction technologies to make buildings in areas vulnerable to disasters more resilient (e)

Source: (a) Godschalk 2003, 140; Romero-Lankao et al. 2012; Rosenthal et al. 2014; Berke and Smith 2009; Kidokoro et al. 2008, 19, 114; Schwab 2011, 49; (b) Berke and Smith 2009; Coppola 2011, 21, 26; Godschalk 2003, 141; (c) Stone et al. 2010; Adger et al. 2005, 1038; Berke and Smith 2009; Wamsler 2014, 130–133; (d) Adger et al. 2005, 1038; Chan et al. 2009, 55; Coppola 2011, 26; Kidokoro et al. 2008, 20; (e) Berke and Smith 2009; Coppola 2011, 21, 26; Kidokoro et al. 2008, 20

there are more concentrations of people who can be affected by hazards. Spatial segregation of the urban poor brings an increased likelihood of their residences being in a vulnerable area.[33] Women and children tend to have worse disaster health outcomes generally, and older adults face an increased risk of drowning in floods, death from earthquakes, and sensitivity to extreme temperatures (especially heat). Other vulnerable groups include low-income people and people in low-income countries, those with chronic diseases, and individuals in medically underserved communities, such as poor and rural communities.[34,35]

At the neighborhood level, planning can locate development away from likely natural hazards. Such efforts can also help mitigate problems such as

drought or floods with water sensitive designs and use neighborhood social networks for early warning.

Actions
Buffer people from disaster prone areas

◆ **Assess the potential health and environmental risks of development projects and plans from disasters and other hazards.**
Conduct an inventory of the current population, housing stock, infrastructure, urban climactic and vulnerability information, and existing or proposed hazards to identify sites and groups that are more at risk for health effects from disasters.[36]

◆ **Limit or relocate development in areas prone to floods, sea-level rise, and severe storms (e.g., hurricanes).**
Regulations or housing relocation programs can reduce future injuries, fatalities, and destruction by preventing residents from moving to disaster-prone areas or assist in relocating those already there.[37] While expensive, such programs will increase in numbers as public and insurance costs of disasters increase.

Mitigate disasters with technologies and techniques

❖ **Mitigate water-, heat-, and fire-related disasters with context-sensitive landscaping.**
Vegetation, xeriscaping, and other landscaping techniques can reduce risks from extreme heat, floods, wind, drought and other natural disasters.[38]

◆ **Enhance warning systems and risk communication between decision makers and residents with neighborhood-level actions.**
Warning systems can be "low-regret measures,"[39] with low costs and potentially high benefits, to alert the public to hazards, including heat events, floods, earthquakes, or storms.[40] The neighborhood-level implications have not been

explored but could include signage clearly indicating previous flood levels, for example.

❖ **Construct buildings to be more resilient against natural disasters.**
This may include better building insulation and material selection to protect against extreme heat or cold, harvesting of rain and groundwater and storage of water for droughts, or strengthening of building design and regulations to protect from floods, sea-level rise, earthquakes, or storms.[41]

Connections

Most places are vulnerable to some kinds of hazards, but making them more resilient can help, including making it easier for people to evacuate if necessary. To understand this proposition better, go to:

- **Proposition 4:** Understand that trade-offs are inherent in planning for health at all scales, and this is true of neighborhoods as well
- **Proposition 11:** Create a connected, "healthier" travel circulation pattern for pedestrians, bicyclists, and transit users—the vehicular pattern can be different
- **Proposition 12:** Increase access to a variety of locally relevant recreational facilities and green spaces
- **Principle 5. Access:** Provide options for getting around and increasing geographic access

Proposition 20: Reduce unwanted local noise exposure at the source, and separate people from noise through buffers, technology, or design

Planning and design interventions—along with policies, regulations, and new technologies—can reduce exposure to environmental noise, which can be especially burdensome in densely populated areas.

How It Works

Environmental noise exposure is not a life-threatening public health issue, but it is a problem increasing due to urbanization.[42] To some extent, environmental noise emitted from transportation, construction, manufacturing, and industrial activities and large gatherings, such as concerts, festivals, and sporting events—is an inherent part of urban life. But research consistently shows that environmental noise can affect overall quality of life, and planners should consider these effects:

- At the neighborhood scale, planners can identify areas at risk for excessive noise levels.
- Given the sensitivities of vulnerable populations to noise exposure (discussed later), special consideration should be taken to reduce environmental noise in areas that children and older adults frequent, including schools, playgrounds, parks, community and

Table 29. Health effects of environmental noise, based on location, duration, and noise level

Specific Environment	Health effect(s)	Noise dB(A)	Duration (hours)
Outdoors (a)	Annoyance	55+	16
Noise outside bedrooms (a, b)	Sleep disturbance; secondary effects: mental health impacts, increased risk of injury	45–60	8
Transportation noise: road traffic, aircraft noise (a, b, c, d)	Cardiovascular risks, children's cognition and memory problems	55–75	Long-term
Occupational noise (d)	Hypertension, heart disease, increased risk of heart attack	80–100	Long-term
Events/festivals (a)	Hearing impairment	100+	4

Sources: HAPI 2014d, 3, citing (a) Berglund et al. 1999; (b) Fritschi et al. 2011, 45; (c) Babisch 2006; (d) van Kempen et al. 2002, 314

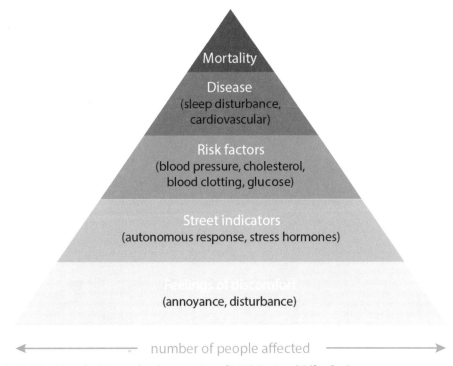

Mortality

Disease
(sleep disturbance,
cardiovascular)

Risk factors
(blood pressure, cholesterol,
blood clotting, glucose)

Street indicators
(autonomous response, stress hormones)

Feelings of discomfort
(annoyance, disturbance)

number of people affected

Sources: Babisch 2002, Fritschi et al. 2011, used with permission of WHO Regional Office for Europe

Figure 40. Health risks associated with environmental noise

senior centers, nursing homes, residential developments, and other facilities that cater to the young and old.[43]

- Planners can implement noise reduction measures by focusing on vehicular traffic flow and speeds. Vehicles produce more noise when they accelerate to higher speeds and produce breaking noises as they decelerate.

- Planners and designers can buffer residents from noise by taking building site and orientation into consideration.

- Technology or design strategies include barriers that block the line of sight from the noise source—such as buildings, walls, and geographic contours (hills)—create "sound shadows" that absorb, transmit, or reflect sound and force sound waves to travel a longer path, lowering perceptible noise levels.[44]

Evidence about Health

The health risks associated with noise exposure are greater once sound reaches 55 decibels (dB) during the night and 70 dB during the day, and over long durations. Table 29 summarizes these health risks in specific settings. Certain age cohorts, mainly children and older adults, are most vulnerable to the health risks posed by environmental noise. Short-term environmental noise can impair children's cognitive skills,[45] and older adults are more vulnerable to the cardiovascular effects of noise exposure than other age groups.[46] Reducing noise levels can provide short-term and immediate health benefits.

There is consensus that environmental noise from air and vehicular traffic at excessive levels is linked to cardiovascular disease.[47] However, less is known about the effect of other environmental noise sources such as rail, the duration and volume that pose the most risk for cardiovascular effects, the different health

Table 30. Neighborhood-scale strategies to reduce health risks from environmental noise

Reduce hazards at the source	• Analyze existing noise patterns to target interventions and inform plans (a)
	• Use strategies to slow traffic and reduce noise from cars (b)
Buffer people away from hazards	• Avoid putting flight paths and heavy traffic near residences and vice versa (c)
	• Consider site and building positioning to minimize noise exposure (d)
Mitigate with technologies or design	• Noise walls (e)
	• Quiet road pavements (b)
	• Building improvements (g)

Source: (a) Berglund et al. 1999, xviii; (b) Moudon 2009, 170; (c) Daigle 1999, 157; (d) FHWA 2011; (e) Daigle 1999, 137; (f) Dzhambov and Dimitrova 2014, 157; (g) WHO 1999, 77; Murphy and King 2015, 225; FHWA 2011

outcomes based on gender and age, and the long-term effects of chronic noise on children.[48]

Since environmental noise is concentrated in urban areas, it is often combined with air pollution and other exposures. Yet, according to the World Health Organization, "the health impacts of the combined exposure to noise, air pollutants, and chemicals are rarely considered in epidemiological studies. Combined exposures occur, for example, when people are exposed to road traffic where noise and air pollution co-exist."[49]

Actions

Neighborhood planning and design interventions can help supplement more comprehensive policies and regulations (Table 30).

Reduce noise at the source

◆ **Analyze existing noise patterns to target interventions and inform plans.**

Monitoring human exposure to noise and assessing the effectiveness of existing noise policies are important to understand the "soundscape" and determine the most effective interventions.[50] For example, England's Department for Environmental Food and Rural Affairs creates noise maps in order to inform noise action plans for large urban areas, transportation services, and industrial sites throughout the country (see Figure 41).[51]

◆ **Use strategies to slow traffic and reduce noise emitted from cars.**

Lowering traffic speeds in noise-sensitive areas, adopting "quiet" road pavements, or incorporating time restrictions on noisy activities can all reduce

◆ Directly from research evidence   ❖ Informed by research   ◇ General good practice

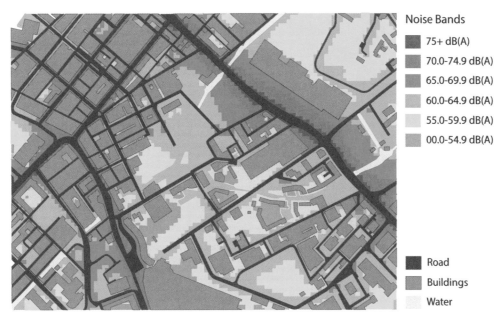

Noise Bands

■ 75+ dB(A)
■ 70.0-74.9 dB(A)
■ 65.0-69.9 dB(A)
■ 60.0-64.9 dB(A)
■ 55.0-59.9 dB(A)
■ 00.0-54.9 dB(A)

■ Road
■ Buildings
■ Water

Figure 41. Road noise mapping in central London, UK

The colors in this map represent the environmental noise transmitted in this London neighborhood, measured in decibels. The purple and red (or darker) bands indicate greater volumes, and perhaps not surprisingly, are located along a major roadway. The orange, yellow, and green clusters (lighter colors) indicate lower noise volumes and can be found along narrow side roads and between buildings.

Source: England's Department for Environmental Food and Rural Affairs (http://services.defra.gov.uk/wps/portal/noise).

noise.[52] The World Health Organization has documented that reducing truck speeds from 90 to 60 km/hr (56 to 37 mph), or car speeds from 140 to 100 km/hr (87 to 62 mph) on concrete roads can reduce maximum sound levels by 5 and 4 decibels, respectively.[53]

Buffering people from noise

◆ **Designate compatible land uses to separate noise sources from vulnerable groups and areas.**
Designating undeveloped land as open space or land near highways, railways or airports for light industrial or commercial purposes can create barriers between the noise sources and sensitive areas such as residential areas, schools, and hospitals.[54]

189

◆ **Consider site and building positioning to minimize noise exposure.**
Positioning of new development can minimize noise impacts by "capitalizing on the site's natural shape and contours."[55] Hong Kong has done a great deal of work in this area.

◆ **Optimize the layout of residential structures in relation to streets, businesses, and schools to buffer residents from exposure to environmental noise.**
Within buildings, room arrangement, window placement, and location of balconies and other features such as courtyards and balconies can help control exposure to environmental noise.[56] Urban green spaces and vegetation can reduce negative perceptions of noise.[57]

Mitigate noise with technology and techniques

◆ **Erect noise walls or fairly continuous buildings as a barrier between major roadways and sensitive land uses.**
Noise walls—in the form of berms or earth mounds, vertical walls, or a combination of both—can be an effective noise reduction strategy near highways, busy roads, railroads, and even airports, reducing sound, on average, by 5 to 12 decibels.[58]

Connections

Although it is virtually impossible to eliminate environmental noise, efforts can be taken to reduce the volume and frequency of unwanted noise and to separate people from noise sources. To understand this proposition better, go to:

- **Principle 3. Vulnerability:** Plan and design for those with the most health vulnerabilities and fewest resources for making healthy choices
- **Proposition 9:** Create mixed-use neighborhoods with a balance of activities that support good health
- **Proposition 10.** Provide enough density of population to support services for a healthy lifestyle
- **Proposition 14:** Adopt policies and planning practices to create safe neighborhood transportation options for all types of road-users

Noise walls along busy roads and highways can reduce sound significantly for nearby homes.

◆   Directly from research evidence   ❖   Informed by research   ◇   General good practice

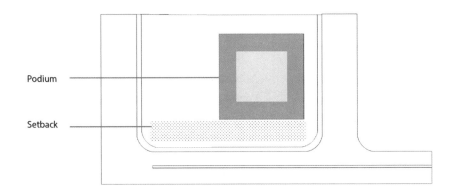

Podium

Setback

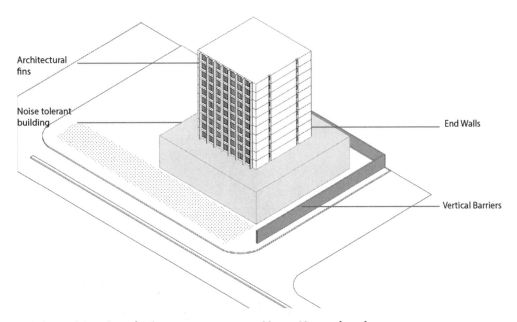

Architectural
fins

Noise tolerant
building

End Walls

Vertical Barriers

Figure 42. Noise mitigation design measures at a Hong Kong development

Site and building positioning, and architectural features can mitigate noise exposure from surrounding areas and within the development.

Source: Adapted from Government of Hong Kong Environmental Protection Department (EPD) 2015.

Implementation

Create diverse actions over time.

Places that make big changes in patterns of behavior, exposures, and connections—or that prevent large changes from happening—typically combine a range of different implementation approaches at the same time, and over time.

Table 31. Implementation approaches to build and maintain healthy neighborhoods and districts

Implementation approach	Examples
Built projects	• Private developments • Public sector infrastructure
Master plans at various scales (region, municipality, district, small area)	• District or neighborhood municipal plans
Regulations, codes, ordinances, and standards	• Ordinances for land-use zoning • New development controls • Tree and landscape protection
Policies, guidelines, performance criteria	• Design guidelines
Incentives and bonuses	• Providing extra resources for doing the right thing, for example allowing more housing units to be built if developers provide parks and trails
Commissions, boards, review processes, committees, associations	• Boards and committees reviewing proposals and existing places and suggesting changes to make them healthier
Programming	• How places are used—from festivals to book clubs
Pricing	• How much it costs—making it less expensive to do the healthy thing
Education and awareness-raising	• Books on healthy planning and design • Talks about options • Tours of existing healthy places

Several strategies can be implemented—alone or coordinated with other efforts—to create healthy neighborhoods.

Source: Table developed by authors

How It Works
Many ways to implement

Implementation involves taking specific actions to get something done. While it may be obvious that a place is created by constructing things, how those buildings and landscapes are designed, maintained, and used is typically a more complicated process. As Table 31 demonstrates, implementation can take a number of forms, alone or in combination with other actions. With so much information and guidance about making places healthier, why is it not a more common practice? Rather, implementation is always a difficult problem for projects at the urban scale. This involves a number of issues:

Complex setting: Whether a neighborhood is built from scratch or redeveloped, it is part of a set of complex physical, economic, social, regulatory, and ecological systems that have their own trajectories. A neighborhood or district needs to be part of these larger systems:

- Connecting to transportation and communication networks locally and regionally.
- Creating housing units that fit regulatory requirements and can sell to people who may want to resell later—that is, housing that can fit within the wider market.
- Providing open spaces for recreation and green infrastructure that are part of a larger network of such spaces.
- Operating businesses that are viable.

- Engaging with civic and governmental spaces and programs at varying geographies from schools, libraries, community centers, and faith communities to hospitals, garbage collection, and policing.

These other systems all have their own logics, and the district or neighborhood of interest may benefit or not. It is possible for neighborhood-level actions to have some influence outside the immediate area but unrealistic to think that influence can dramatically change the shape of these larger systems. Savvy implementation works out how to operate within this context, using its positive aspects and working around the negatives.

Multiple authors: Unlike a small building that may be on a single site with one client, one designer, and one builder, a large urban project or a plan for a district requires input from multiple people and organizations over years and even decades. Comprehensive coordination is difficult due to the nature of organizations—governments, private sector entities, and community groups—and their competing interests and internal divisions. This affects all attempts to improve urban areas, including work to make healthier places. It is vital to build alliances and to ensure that healthy placemaking is a long-lasting goal of organizations involved.

Multiple health dimensions: Large projects, which even at the neighborhood-scale is not very large in an urban setting, affect multiple dimensions of health.

Exemplary health places are often very small or do one thing well—it is very complicated to do more comprehensive work at a large scale.

However, it is rarer that they affect each and every dimension in a positive way for all population groups. Thus making a healthier place involves prioritizing important issues while engaging many different topics at once. This is why when healthy places are highlighted as exemplars, they are often very small or do one thing well—it is very complicated to do more comprehensive work at a large scale.

Different people, different effects: There is also a complicated relationship between people and place. Those with less education and fewer financial resources often have worse health outcomes because they may have fewer means to learn about or engage in healthy behaviors, particularly ones that are complicated or expensive or both. Older people and children also have additional health concerns and limitations. So the same place inhabited by different people will have different health outcomes. For example, a recreational facility with hilly terrain may be terrific for exercise for the able-bodied but unattractive to the frail who will need assistance walking.

Evolution over time: Neighborhoods and districts evolve over time and may have different strengths related to health at different periods. This means the best plan at one time may not be the best at another. Typical processes include:

- Physical aging of the buildings and infrastructure, requiring reinvestment (an opportunity for making them healthier, or not).
- Aging and mobility in the population, changing the demographic mix.
- Economic and demographic changes associated with redevelopment or the lack of it.
- Changes in the surrounding context.
- Cultural evolution and education changing how people live their lives and use the spaces.

196

Table 32. Evaluation topic checklist

Question	Considerations to evaluate	Yes	No	Maybe
Is the neighborhood or district connected to these larger systems?	• Local and regional transportation and communication networks	☐	☐	☐
	• Housing that both fits within regulatory requirements and the wider market	☐	☐	☐
	• A network of open spaces for recreation and green infrastructure	☐	☐	☐
	• Viable businesses	☐	☐	☐
	• Civic and governmental spaces and programs	☐	☐	☐
Does the project or a plan prioritize health issues, and engage many different topics at once?		☐	☐	☐
Does the project or a plan address how the plan or proposal may influence health outcomes among different types of people (e.g. older adults, low-income adults, children)?		☐	☐	☐
Is the project or a plan coordinated with multiple people and organizations?	• Government agencies	☐	☐	☐
	• Private sector entities	☐	☐	☐
	• Community groups	☐	☐	☐
Are the following changes over time addressed when evaluating the project or a plan?	• Physical aging of the buildings and infrastructure	☐	☐	☐
	• Aging and mobility of the population	☐	☐	☐
	• Economic and demographic changes associated with redevelopment or the lack of	☐	☐	☐
	• Changes in the surrounding context	☐	☐	☐
	• Cultural evolution and education changing how people live their lives and use spaces	☐	☐	☐

Implementation can take a number of forms, alone or in combination with other approaches. This checklist highlights key questions to consider when evaluating implementation appproaches being used.

Source: developed by authors

Actions

How can healthier places get implemented? Systematic evidence comes primarily from case studies and histories of specific projects and plans in Asia, Europe, the United States, and Australasia.[1] Overall they point to a number of key elements and actions for implementation over time:

◇ **Find a champion.**

At key points, particularly when there is innovation, someone needs to be a strong proponent and build coalitions. When a healthy place is part of a larger area that may not value

A place should serve more than one group and one purpose. This place combines mixed land use, handicapped parking, a taxi stand, shade, and seating.

health in the same way, there needs to be someone to push the health agenda forward.[2] This is not the hero who single-handedly puts everything in place but rather someone who can keep the process going forward because that person is politically powerful, such as a mayor. Or it may be someone who is in a good position to advocate for health allied with someone skilled at fostering collaborations between multiple public constituencies involved in deliberating about and using spaces. Without such a proponent, or team of proponents, there is often no voice for health.

◇ **Do more than one thing for more than one group.**

This has been a theme of this volume. Having a place that works for multiple people to further multiple aspects of well-being is important for health. It is also important for implementation, however, at least beyond a small single area with a short time frame. Examples like suburbanization—which provided houses for families, jobs for builders, a sense of possibility for society—demonstrate this. This is not to say that specialized environments are not possible, but they need to be seen to be more broadly useful. For example, an environment aimed at helping youth, such as a community center or specialized park, may help the wider community save money or disruption from vandalism or youth alienation.

Table 33. Monitoring types and potential sources of data

Type	Definition	Example data sources
Monitoring the broad process		
Process evaluation	How it was conducted	• Event logs—what happened, when, and with who • Surveys—behavior, satisfaction • Interviews with key participants
Output evaluation	Products of the process such as reports and modified decisions	• Archival records/analyses of documentation such as reports, minutes, etc. • Interviews with key participants
Monitoring various outcomes		
Basic outcome evaluation	Long-term inded and unintended effects on community and individuals	• Observations of behavior and environments • Surveys—behavior, satisfaction • Interviews with key participants • Indicators and standards (below)
Goal attainment	How well it achieved its aims	• Archival records/analyses of documentation such as reports to identify goals • Results from other evaluation types to assess attainment
Peer review	Whether it means processional standards	• Professional peer panel/blue ribbon committee review
Stakeholder evaluation	Satisfaction of key parties	• Surveys—satisfaction • Interviews with key participants • Participatory evaluation workshops such as identifying strengths, weaknesses, opportunities, and threats (SWOT); group interviews • Participatory observation exercises such as community tours, site observations
Standards	Assessing against indicators and standards	• Technical indicators for neighborhoods from available data such as census, property records, etc. • Technical indicators from wider municipal/county/regional level such as regularly collected health indicators • Participatory indicators from local engagement • Standards such as national regulations for water quality and air quality • Comparisons with peer locations such as park provision and accessibility

This framework provides a quick guide to key data sources or methods for monitoring and evaluating complex topics worthy of their own manuals. It should be noted that very few health statistics are available at a neighborhood level so such evaluations typically rely on other kinds of information.

Source: Adapted from Forsyth et al. 2010b; University of Kansas 2015b

◇ **Engage an institution that can shepherd the neighborhood over the long haul.**
Places take a long time to build. The infrastructure and programs that make places work well on multiple levels—from community centers to shopping centers—can be costly at first. They are maintained and rebuilt. Some institution needs to bear that cost with an eye on the long term. There needs to be an entity that cares, can see the bigger picture, and can provide funding—a government, a nonprofit organization with a dedicated revenue source such as property assessments, or a very large-scale developer that maintains substantial ownership.

◇ **Develop a process for monitoring, evolution, and change.**
Places evolve. Populations shift. Knowledge about health develops. There needs to be a way to make changes. It can be particularly tricky balancing an initial, presumably good plan with current needs. When is it watering down the vision and when it is being realistic? A monitoring and feedback process can help keep attention focused on important health issues (Table 33). A formative or diagnostic evaluation can be key to ongoing improvement.

◇ **Deal with the problems of success.**
A place that is clearly better, including a successful, healthy neighborhood, can become a victim of its own success. For example, a healthy neighborhood may become more expensive because people are attracted to it. A really healthy neighborhood will have in place mechanisms—in this case, substantial amounts of permanently affordable housing—to reduce these negative outcomes.

◇ **Implement some quick wins to get things going and build connections.**
Multifaceted plans for making neighborhoods and districts healthier have a lot of moving parts and likely a long list of actions. Some of the actions will be obvious priorities because they implement important goals. Others will be time sensitive—needing coordination with deadlines, other organizations, and the like. Whatever the priorities, it is important to head for at least some quick wins or low-hanging fruit. This involves having early successes to get support and allies. These help build momentum and may be inexpensive and reversible. For an existing place this might include events that start to use public space in new ways or the posting of uncomplicated signage. For a proposal, it may be establishing a collaboration and taking some initial steps.

Connections

Implementation of healthier places takes time and many different kinds of approaches. To understand this proposition better, go to:

- **Principle 2. Balance:** Make healthier places by balancing physical changes with other interventions to appeal to different kinds of people
- **Proposition 4:** Understand that trade-offs are inherent in planning for health at all scales, and this is true of neighborhoods as well
- **Proposition 5:** Appreciate that there is no ideal size for a healthy community, but different dimensions of health relate to different scales
- **Principle 3. Vulnerability:** Plan and design for those with the most health vulnerabilities and fewest resources for making healthy choices

Implementing a neighborhood or district plan or project requires imput from multiple people and organizations over the long term. In the short term it is vital to build alliances to ensure that healthy placemaking is a long lasting goal of the partners involved.

Conclusion

It is tempting to create a long-term plan and imagine that it is done. However, making the plan is just a beginning of a longer process of making a place healthier.

Most of the well-loved places in the world have gone through multiple versions over time via redevelopment, demolition, and rebuilding.

How It works

Plans need to be implemented over time, not just quick wins but more difficult long-term projects, collaborations, and programs:

- **Some activities have to wait.** Phasing is important. Most building needs a road system to be constructed first. A neighborhood or town center may be sparsely developed in an initial phase and then once the surrounding population grows can have additional activities filled in.
- **It is very hard to create a place that feels rich and real from scratch.** Most of the well-loved places in the world have gone through multiple revisions over time via redevelopment, demolition, and rebuilding.
- **The development itself is changing as it ages.** The physical place, even if built very well at first, will need maintenance and alterations, demographics will shift, the regional context will change because other places are evolving, and ideas about what is a good place will also evolve due to cultural shifts and new knowledge.
- **The world changes.** Technological innovations, or changes in regional infrastructure, may alter how people communicate and get around. There will likely be many changes in how places are used in coming years, with implications for creating healthy neighborhoods.
- **The main health issues may change.** A place initially created to reduce exposures to pollutants is addressing a very different kind of problem than one that will lead to healthy behaviors.

While it can be tempting to want to lock in the good ideas of today for the next 50 years and prevent short-sighted departures from the plan, this is not really possible.

How can a place be flexible or robust enough to respond to change over time?[1] There are a number of dimensions that can allow this:

- **Design with an eye for change.** For example, some owners of shopping malls create an underlying framework that will allow the parking lots to be redeveloped in a pattern of blocks and streets. Later, the area can be filled with housing and public spaces.
- **Do not overdesign and cut off options for reusing and repurposing later on.** It can be tempting to highly design spaces; however, that can make it hard for them to evolve. Ironically, making spaces too flexible can also make them difficult to reuse, such as the vast open plan offices that do not allow for privacy.
- **Make sure places work for multiple groups** This helps build support for the perspective of considering health.

- **Consider more than the physical space but also the process of building and using it over time.** A process of monitoring and feedback allows adjustment over time

Creating healthy neighborhoods is thus a complex process. This process is important, however, because health is key to quality of life and making a healthy place will have wider benefits. It is also important because neighborhoods and districts are vital building blocks of urban areas and the locations of daily life experience. Making good neighborhoods and districts does much to make good towns and cities over the long term.

Creating a healthy place is a complex process. Planning and designing places to work for multiple groups is one important step.

Appendix A: Actions checklist

◆ Directly from research evidence   ❖ Informed by research   ◇ General good practice

Principle 1. Importance: Examine how much health may matter in this place

Proposition 1: Figure out if there are good reasons for considering health

◇ Compile information from multiple sources, particularly where there might be controversy or different perspectives (see Table 3).

◇ Move forward in the book if there are any open questions relevant to health including large or irreversible changes, large physical areas or populations, existing concerns about health problems, and differential effects on vulnerable groups (see Table 2).

◇ Be cautious in moving forward if there seems to be no possibility of making changes.

Proposition 2: Identify an inital list of neighborhood-relevant health issues

◇ Identify an initial list of health issues balancing a need to focus on important topics with a need to understand links that are obvious (see Table 5).

◇ Consider the potential for differential effects on population subgroups such as children, older people, those with low incomes, with pre-existing conditions, and with other forms of marginalization (see Table 10).

◇ Use numerical indicators to aid this process of scoping as well as more qualitative assessments such as resident and professional perceptions.

Proposition 3: Figure out if anyone else cares

◇ Identify allies by figuring out who they are, understanding their roles and resources, and potentially making contact (see Table 7).

◇ Involve others in the project in a way that respects their time, capitalizes on their knowledge, and encourages joint ownership of a solution where that is needed.

◇ Identify strategies that aim to have multiple health benefits (e.g. physical activity options and mental health benefits from a park) in order to gain support and also make it more likely that a proposal will help at least one group.

Principle 2. Balance: Make healthier places by balancing physical changes with other interventions to appeal to different kinds of people

Proposition 4: Understand that trade-offs are inherent in planning for health at all scales and this is true of neighborhoods as well

◇ Understand that designing and planning a complete neighborhood involves engaging multiple needs and goals.

◇ Recognize and prioritize health trade-offs systematically (for example, Table 8).

◇ Identify actions beyond planning and design that can help foster a healthier place, mitigating some of the less than optimal characteristics in any design and planning approach.

Proposition 5: Appreciate that there is no ideal size for a healthy community, but different dimensions of health relate to different scales

◇ Consider how planning and design proposals are framed by scales beyond the neighborhood.

◇ Focus on good planning and design relevant to the size of a neighborhood or district.

Principle 3. Vulnerability: Plan and design for those with the most health vulnerabilities and fewest resources for making healthy choices

Proposition 6: Create a variety of housing options to promote housing choices within the neighborhood

◆ Directly from research evidence   ❖ Informed by research   ◇ General good practice

❖ Take a lifecourse approach to creating a housing mix (e.g. different building types, universal design features).

◆ Provide housing of high physical quality (see Table 12).

◆ Use strategies beyond size and density to protect affordability, particularly in high-cost areas (see Table 11).

Proposition 7: Integrate universal design principles into neighborhood planning and design

◇ Use the core universal design principles as a checklist for neighborhood planning, design, and redevelopment (see Tables 13 and 14).

Proposition 8: Increase choice, access, and exposure to high-quality, diverse, and healthy food options, especially in low-income areas

❖ Create a flexible neighborhood plan to make it possible to adjust to the geographically varied and evolving food retail landscape.

◆ Focus on providing access to lower cost sources of healthy food.

◇ Concentrate most food stores in locations where people already walk, cycle, and take transit.

◇ Carefully locate food retail and dining places including convenience stores, restaurants, food vendors, or public markets, considering both access and commercial viability.

◇ Use food-related activities to generate health benefits beyond nutrition (e.g. community gardens, buy local programs).

Principle 4. Layout: Foster multiple dimensions of health through overall neighborhood layout

Proposition 9: Create mixed use neighborhoods with a balance of activities that support good health

❖ Mix the right kinds of activities for daily life in a neighborhood or district.

◇ Consider specific uses carefully including how they ae spatially mixed and whether there are useful clusters of activities within the district (see Figure 17).

◆ Identify potentially problematic uses for special treatment (e.g. moving, buffering, as is explained in later sections) (see Table 27).

Proposition 10. Provide enough density of population to support services for a healthy lifestyle

◆ Create a critical mass of people to support daily services within walking, cycling, or transit distance (see Table 19).

◆ Focus on the very young, the old, and those who don't have cars, ensuring that neighborhoods and districts have centers that can be a focal point for activities and transportation, while avoiding congestion.

◆ Mitigate against noise and air pollution, and provide green space to support physical activity and mental health in very high-density areas.

Proposition 11: Create a connected, "healthier" travel circulation pattern for pedestrians, bicyclists, and transit users—the vehicular pattern can be different

◆ Provide multiple route options to encourage pedestrian and bicycle travel (see Figure 22).

◆ Connect cul-de-sacs to each other and to destinations (where possible) with pedestrian and bike paths.

❖ Minimize distances between destinations to avoid penalizing non-vehicular traffic.

❖ Deal with each kind of underlying pattern differently, moving toward healthier patterns where possible (see Table 16).

Proposition 12: Increase access to a variety of locally relevant recreational facilities and green spaces.

◆ Plan for a network of spaces with varied functions and users to achieve different, and hopefully multiple, health outcomes (see Table 17).

◆ Make the spaces physically and/or visually accessible to likely users, and in particular those with health vulnerabilities and a likelihood of using such spaces (e.g. the young and the old).

◆ Link spaces so that people can travel between them as parts of tours or loops for exercise and recreation.

◆ Plan spaces to allow for multiple uses and reduce problematic conflicts.

◆ Plan green spaces near buildings for increased mental wellbeing, improved cognition, reduced stress, and better healing.

Principle 5. Access: Provide options for getting around and increasing geographic access

Proposition 13: Coordinate land-use planning and urban design with transit to increase efficiency, access, and mobility

◆ Locate transit close to activity generators and the reverse (see Table 19).

◆ Prioritize and cluster transit, health, and social services near where vulnerable populations live.

◆ Co-locate transit stops with pedestrian and cyclist-friendly infrastructure and amenities.

❖ Ensure continuity across neighborhood and jurisdictional boundaries.

Proposition 14: Adopt policies and planning practices to create safe neighborhood transportation options for all types of road users

◆ Create speed limits appropriate for type of street.

❖ Provide a variety of street parking, but buffer from cyclist infrastructure.

◆ Retrofit problematically fast roads with a variety of traffic calming measures (see Table 27).

Proposition 15: Ensure adequate pedestrian and cyclist infrastructure and amenities

◆ Place marked crosswalks at intersections or mid-block, and create raised medians or intersection crossing islands.

❖ Create a network of bicycle-lanes, separated paths, and protected intersections.

◆ Provide pedestrian seating, public toilets with universal design, and drinking fountains in public places.

❖ Beautify the public environment by providing strategically placed garbage and recycling receptacles, public art, and urban greening such as street trees, landscaping, and green roofs or walls.

Principle 6. Connection: create opportunities for people to interact with each other in positive ways

Proposition 16: Create publicly accessible neighborhood spaces, programs, and events to support healthy interactions and behaviors

◇ Maximize flexibility of space for different users and activities, and at different times of day, week, and year.

◆ Provide maintenance and upkeep of the space and surrounding areas.

◆ Ensure spaces are highly accessible to pedestrians.

◆ Allow and promote programs and places for social activities and community affiliations such as volunteering, religious or social organizations, community education, or parent-teacher associations.

◆ Encourage civic engagement related to neighborhood issues.

Proposition 17: Design the public realm to reduce street crime and fear of crime

◆ Provide adequate street lighting to enhance safety at night.

❖ Delineate public and private property to manage activities in those spaces (see Table 22).

❖ Enhance visibility and sight lines to provide visual access to public spaces.

❖ Avoid building places where people can be isolated or entrapped.

❖ Maintain public space, abandoned properties, and vacant lots.

❖ Mix land uses to promote diversified activities at different times of day.

Principle 7. Protection: Reduce harmful exposures at a neighborhood level through a combination of wider policies and regulations along with local actions

Proposition 18: Reduce pollutants and chemicals at the source and separate people from toxins through buffers, technology, or design (see Table 25)

◆ Orient developments to best take advantage of sunlight and natural ventilation in order to reduce energy use and the associated pollutants (see Figure 34 and Figure 35).

◆ Use and promote water efficient policies, technologies, and landscaping to reduce water use (see Figure 36).

◇ Use public interventions and educational campaigns to reduce waste, increase reuse, composting, and recycling (see Table 26).

❖ Separate incompatible uses from one another (see Table 27).

❖ Separate stormwater and sanitary water in water treatment infrastructure, and create stormwater sedimentation tanks.

◆ Use water sensitive urban design (WSUD) in areas vulnerable to stormwater runoff (see Table 27).

Proposition 19: Separate people and infrastructure from areas vulnerable to natural disasters and build in resilience through technology or design

◆ Assess the potential health and environmental risks of development projects and plans from disasters, and other hazards.

◆ Limit or relocate development in areas prone to floods, sea-level rise, and severe storms.

◆ Mitigate water, heat-, and fire- related disasters with context-sensitive landscaping.

◆ Enhance warning systems and risk communication between decision-makers and residents with neighborhood-level actions.

❖ Construct buildings to be more resilient against natural disasters.

Proposition 20: Reduce unwanted local noise exposure at the source and separate people from noise through buffers, technology, or design

◆ Analyze existing noise patterns to target interventions and inform plans (see Table 29 and Figure 41).

◆ Use strategies to slow traffic and reduce noise emitted from cars (see Figure 27).

◆ Designate compatible land uses to separate noise sources from vulnerable groups and areas.

◆ Consider site and building positioning to minimize noise exposure (see Figure 42).

◆ Optimize the layout of residential structures in relation to streets, businesses, and schools to buffer residents from exposure to environmental noise.

◆ Erect noise walls, or fairly continuous buildings, as a barrier between major roadways and sensitive land-uses.

Principle 8. Implementation: Create diverse actions over time

◇ Find a champion.

◇ Do more than one thing for more than one group.

◇ Engage an institution that can shepherd the neighborhood over the long haul.

◇ Develop a process for monitoring evolution, and change.

◇ Deal with the problems of success.

◇ Implement some quick wins to get things going and build connections.

◆ Directly from research evidence   ❖ Informed by research   ◇ General good practice   **209**

Appendix B: Health topics by section

	Air quality	Climate/ Heat-related illnesses	Disasters
Introduction: Toward healthy neighborhoods	●	●	●
Principle 1. Importance			
Proposition 1: Reasons for considering health	●		
Proposition 2: Identify an initial list of neighborhood-relevant health issues	●	●	●
Proposition 3: Figure out if anyone else cares			
Principle 2. Balance			
Proposition 4: Trade-offs are inherent in planning for health	●		
Proposition 5: There is no ideal size for a healthy community	●		
Principle 3. Vulnerability	●	●	●
Proposition 6: Create a variety of housing options	●	●	
Proposition 7: Integrate universal design principles into planning and design			●
Proposition 8: Increase access and exposure to healthy food options			
Principle 4. Layout	●		
Proposition 9: Create mixed-use neighborhoods with a balance of activities	●		
Proposition 10: Provide enough density of population to support services	●		●
Proposition 11: Create a connected, "healthier" travel circulation pattern			
Proposition 12: Increase access to recreational facilities and green spaces	●	●	
Principle 5. Access	●		
Proposition 13: Coordinate land-use planning and urban design with transit			
Proposition 14: Create safer neighborhood transportation options for all road users	●		
Proposition 15: Ensure adequate pedestrian and cyclist infrastructure and amenities			
Principle 6. Connection		●	●
Proposition 16: Create public spaces, programs, and events to support interaction			
Proposition 17: Design the public realm to reduce street crime and fear of crime			
Principle 7. Protection	●	●	●
Proposition 18: Reduce pollutants at the source and separate people from toxins	●	●	
Proposition 19: Separate and build resilience in areas vulnerable to natural disasters		●	●
Proposition 20: Reduce unwated noise at the source and separate people from noise	●		
Principle 8. Implementation			
Conclusion			

Source: Developed by authors

Housing	Mental Health	Noise	Toxics	Water quality	Access to community resources	Social capital	Mobility/ Universal design	Access to healthy food	Physical activity	Safety
●	●	●	●	●	●	●	●	●	●	●
●								●		
●		●		●						●
●	●	●	●	●	●	●	●	●		●
	●								●	
●	●					●		●		
●		●		●	●	●	●	●	●	●
			●	●	●					
●	●	●	●	●	●	●			●	●
●	●	●	●	●	●	●	●	●		●
●					●	●			●	
	●				●	●		●		
		●			●	●				
●	●	●	●	●	●	●			●	●
●	●	●		●	●	●			●	●
					●			●	●	●
	●	●		●	●	●		●	●	●
	●	●		●	●	●		●	●	●
●					●			●	●	●
					●				●	●
	●					●	●		●	●
	●								●	●
					●	●			●	●
●						●	●		●	●
		●	●	●						
			●	●						
●			●							
	●	●								
●							●			

Notes

Introduction

1. UNDESA 2013, xvii.
2. For an exception see NSW Health 2009
3. WHO 2006, orig 1946
4. HAPI 2015a, 2015b, 2015c; Rowe et al. 2016; Asensio and Mah 2016
5. UNDESA 2014, 1
6. UNDESA 2014, 1
7. UN 2004, 70
8. Forsyth 2014
9. Krizek et al. 2009b; Ely et al. 2002; Pawson 2003; Hammersley 2005
10. Ellen et al. 2001, 391
11. Krizek et al. 2009b
12. Cranz 1982
13. Rosenzweig and Blackmar 1992
14. Crewe 2001
15. Forsyth 2015
16. Forsyth and Crewe 2009; Sykes et al. 1967
17. Johnson et al 1994, 2
18. Roby 2014
19. Roby 2014
20. Vogt 1993, 31
21. Forsyth 2005a
22. Park 2012
23. World Meteorological Organization 2015
24. World Meteorological Organization 2015
25. WHO 2006, orig1946
26. Hancock and Minkler 2005; Forsyth et al. 2010c
27. WHO 2001
28. National Center for Healthy Housing and the American Public Health Association 2013
29. CDC 2015
30. City of Portland 2013
31. Park 2012
32. Scott 2014
33. Johnson et al. 1994, 382
34. Banerjee and Baer 1984
35. Johnson et al 1994, 442
36. FAO 2015
37. Park 2012
38. *Oxford English Dictionary* 2015
39. Vogt 1993; Forsyth et al. 2012s; Lytle 2009
40. Park 2012
41. Johnson et al. 1994, 528
42. World Meteorological Organization 2015
43. Vogt 1993, 221
44. World Bank 2015
45. Murayama et al. 2012
46. WHO 2016
47. Booth et al. 2012
48. National Geographic 2015
49. Lytle 2009; Forsyth et al. 2012
50. Park 2012, emphasis added
51. U.S. CDC 2015
52. U.S. CDC 2015
53. Park 2012

Principle 1

1. Forsyth et al 2010c; Kemm 2013
2. Hancock and Minkler 2005, 139; Orians et al. 2009
3. WHO 2001
4. This section draws on the Health and Places Initiative suite of health assessments (HAPI 2015a; 2015b; 2015c; 2015d; 2015e, 2015f). These in turn drew on earlier work by Design for Health (Design for Health 2007c; 2008a; 2008c; 2009; Krizek et al. 2009b; Slotterback et al. 2011; Forsyth et al 2010b; 2010c) as well as the wider literature on health impact assessment, particularly comprehensive reviews, HIA guidebooks, and process-oriented healthy places guidebooks (Scott-Samuel et al. 2001; Harris et al. 2007; Kemm 2013; U.S. EPA 2013; Ison 2013; NSW Health 2009). These overviews provide alternative examples of approaches to screening and scoping—all fairly similar but some more general and others applied to specific kinds of projects and plans. The strength of the HAPI tools is that they are aimed at the neighborhood scale and can deal with existing places as well as proposals and plans.
5. UCL Institute of Health Equity 2014
6. HAPI 2015d; 2015e; 2015f
7. Mindell et al. 2006

8. Gaber and Gaber 2007; Krizek et al. 2009b
9. Harris et al. 2007; Kemm 2013
10. Slotterback et al. 2011, 151
11. Orians et al. 2009
12. Forsyth et al. 2010b; 2010c; Kemm 2013
13. Design for Health 2008b, 4; Grootaert and van Bastelaer 2001, 9
14. Slotterback et al. 2011
15. UCL Institute of Health Equity 2014
16. Forsyth 2015a

Principle 2

1. Pucher et al. 2010; Forsyth and Krizek 2010; Forsyth 2005b
2. Forsyth 2005b; 2012
3. DiMento and Ellis 2013
4. Rees et al. 2014; Oka 2011
5. Pucher et al. (2010, s117)
6. Pucher et al. 2010, s122; Pucher and Buehler 2008
7. Pucher and Buehler 2008, 498
8. Pucher and Buehler 2008, 498
9. Pucher and Buehler 2008, 512, 521, 522
10. Forsyth 2015a
11. Wells et al. 2007; Sobal and Wansink 2007; Swinburn et al. 2011
12. Crewe and Forsyth 2011
13. Forsyth and Krizek 2011; Forsyth 2015b
14. Crewe and Forsyth 2011
15. Lynch 1981; Camagni et al. 2013
16. Gill and Goh 2009; Capello and Camagni 2000
17. Camagni et al. 2013
18. Brower 2000; Jacobs 1961
19. Banerjee and Baer 1984
20. Perry 1929; 1939, 53, 117
21. Forsyth 2005b, 123–4
22. Alexander et al. 1977, 71
23. Alexander 1965

Principle 3

1. This major review included 13 substantial task groups and a senior advisory panel working with the UCL Institute of Health Equity 2014
2. Gibson et al. 2011, 182
3. National Center for Healthy Housing and the American Public Health Association 2014
4. Thompson and Thomas 2015
5. Thompson and Thomas 2015, 208
6. Thompson and Thomas 2015, 211
7. Evans 2003, 537
8. Evans 2003, 537
9. Gibson et al. 2011, 183
10. UN 2004, 70; Morrow-Jones and Wenning 2005
11. WHO 2007, 30; AARP 2006, 43
12. Evans et al. 2003
13. Evans et al. 2003, 381; WHO 2007, 30
14. Cohen and Wardrip 2011, 1; Jacobs 2011, S118
15. Tsai 2015,14
16. Lubell et al. 2010, 6
17. Cohen and Wardrip 2011, 8; Cutts et. al 2011, 1508; Evans 2003, 538
18. Miller et al. 2011, S48
19. Gibson et al. 2011, 181
20. Gibson et al. 2011, 183
21. HAPI 2014c
22. Mace 1985, 147
23. Kose 1998, 44; EIDD 2004, 1; HAPI 2014c, 3
24. Grimble et al. 2010, 1
25. Skiba and Zuger 2009, 23–24; Van Cauwenberg et al. 2011, 467; WHO 2007
26. HAPI 2014c, 5; Boslaugh and Andresen 2006, 4; U.S. CDC 2009; WHO 2013
27. White et al 2010, 640
28. Maisel 2010, 3–4; HAPI 2014c
29. Gray et al. 2012, 87
30. STAQC 2005, 10
31. Swinburn et al. 2011, 804–805
32. Black et al. 2014; Aggarwal et al.2012; Drewnowski et al. 2012
33. Black et al. 2014; Beaulac et al. 2009; Fleischhacker et al. 2011
34. Black et al. 2014, 229
35. Swinburn et al. 2011, 807
36. Cannuscio et al. 2013, 606
37. Drewnowski et al. 2012, e77

38. Aggarwal et al. 2012, e37533

39. Drewnowski 2010, 1181

40. Foord 2010, 49; Grant 2002, 76, 78

Principle 4

1. McCormack and Shiell 2011, 1; Ewing and Cervero 2010

2. Ewing and Cervero 2010, 265

3. Ding et al. 2011, 448

4. Foord 2010, 49, 59

5. Foord 2010, 59

6. Foord 2010, 59

7. Mansfield et al. 2015; Schweitzer and Zhou 2010

8. Brabec et al. 2002; Barbosa et al. 2012; Burton and Pitt 2002

9. Schneider and Kitchen, 2007, 52; Browning et al. 2010, 335–337

10. Foord 2010, 59

11. Suzuki et al. 2013, 152

12. Douglas et al. 2008; Kidokoro et al. 2008, 4, 18, 100–101, 107; Pelling 2003; Wamsler 2014, 21–23, 82, 86

13. Levine et al. 2012, 157

14. Forsyth and Krizek 2010, 434

15. Alexander 1965

16. Lovegrove and Sayed 2006b, 73, 80

17. Ewing and Cervero 2010, 276

18. Rosso et al. 2011, 1, 7

19. Van Cauwenberg et al. 2011; Van Stralen et al. 2009

20. Marshall and Garrick 2011a, 769

21. Lovegrove and Sayed 2006b, 73, 80

22. Wei and Lovegrove 2012

23. Wei and Lovegrove 2012

24. Ding 2011; McGrath 2015; Sallis and Glanz 2006

25. Lovegrove and Sayed 2006a, 620

26. Lovegrove and Sayed 2006b

27. Wei and Lovegrove 2012

28. Wei and Lovegrove 2012, 147

29. Sykes et al. 1967

30. Harnick 2006, 57

31. Again this is an area of much research and interpretation: Appleton 1975; Kaplan and Kaplan 1989; Heerwagen and Gregory 2008; Orians 1986; Orians and Heerwagen 1992; Wilson 1984; Forsyth and Musacchio 2005; Tveit et al. 2007; Zube and Pitt 1981; Kellert et al. 2008, 12–13, 146–147

32. Barton and Pretty 2010

33. There are many excellent sources in this area including: Peacock et al.2007; Alcock et al. 2014; Blumenthal et al. 1999; Bowler et al. 2010b; Brown et al. 2013; Cimprich and Ronis 2003; Coon et al. 2011; Davis 2004; Dijkstra et al. 2006; Grahn and Stigsdotter 2010; Hartig 2003; Hull and Michael 1995; Kellert et al. 2008, 87–106; Maller et al. 2005; Orsega-Smith et al. 2004, Park et al. 2008; Tsunetsugu et al. 2005; Ulrich 1999; Ulrich 1984; Van den Berg et al. 2007; Biederman and Vessel 2006; Fjeld et al. 1998; Hartig et al. 1991; Heerwagen and Orians 2002; Heerwagen 2009; Isenberg and Quisenberry 2002; Lohr et al. 1996; Shibata and Suzuki 2002; Tennessen and Cimprich 1995; Wells 2000; Wells and Rollings 2012

34. Bowler et al. 2010b, 1, 9

35. Coon et al., 2011

36. Chalfont and Rodiek 2005; Kuo and Taylor 2004; Mooney and Nicell 1992; Rappe 2005; Taylor et al. 2001; Taylor and Kuo 2009; Ulrich 2002

37. Bauman et al. 2011; Lovasi et al. 2009

38. Ding et al. 2011; Rosso et al. 2011; Van Cauwenberg et al. 2011; Wendel-Vos et al. 2007, 425

39. Christian et al. 2015, 30

40. Forsyth and Musacchio 2005, 3–5

41. Christian et al. 2015, 33

42. Harnick 2006, 57

43. Greenways, Inc. 1992, 53–54

44. Forrest and Kearns 2001, 2140; ULI 2015, 63

Principle 5

1. Litman 2014, 14

2. Lynott et al. 2009, 3, 32

3. Zavestoski and Ageyman 2015

4. Curtis et al. 2009, 4

5. Curtis et al. 2009, 5

6. Curtis et al. 2009, 4

7. Ewing and Cervero 2001, 100; Guerra and Cervero 2011

8. Curtis et al. 2009, 4

9. Visser et al. 2014, 15

10. Lynott et al. 2009, 3, 32

11. Lindholm 2010, 6211

12. Wisetjindawat 2010, 13

13. BC Ministries of Health Services and Planning 2002, 5; Fortney et al. 2011; Michigan Department of Community Health 2014, 2; USHHS 1993

14. Wei and Lovegrove 2012

15. Faulkner et al. 2009; Wanner et al. 2012, 493; Yang et al. 2010, 7

16. WHO 2013b

17. Guerra and Cervero 2011, 287

18. Taylor and Fink 2013, 21

19. Several reviews that provide walking distance thresholds to transit: Agrawal and Schimek 2007; Alshalalfah and Shalaby 2007; Olszewski and Wibowo 2005

20. Black et al. 2001; Ewing et al. 2004; Timperio et al. 2004; Timperio et al. 2006

21. Martens 2004, 281; Pucher and Buehler 2008; Iacono et al. 2008, 8, 13

22. Chung 1997; Morral and Bloger 1996

23. Shoup 2005; Mukhija and Shoup 2006; Taylor and Fink 2013, 20; TCRP 1998

24. Hamer 2010

25. Suzuki et al. 2013, 149

26. See Curtis et al. 2009, 15; Guerra and Cervero 2011, 286; Taylor and Fink 2013, 23

27. Studies on the relationship of transit access and proximity to physical activity include: Bauman et al. 2012, Forsyth and Krizek 2010; McCormack and Shiell 2011; Owen et al. 2004; Sallis et al. 2009; Sugiyama et al. 2012. Research that focuses on these connections among the older adult population includes: Cunningham and Michael 2004; Moran et al. 2014, Rosso et al. 2011, Van Cauwenberg et al. 2011

28. Skiba and Zuger 2009, 26; Centre for Accessible Environments 2012, 22; Green 2013, S125; White et al. 2010, 639; University of Kansas 2013

29. Curtis et al. 2009, 153–169; Suzuki et al. 2013, 19

30. Dittmar and Ohland 2004, 24; Suzuki et al. 2013, 16–17

31.   WHO 2015a

32. Ewing and Dumbaugh 2009, 347

33. CEDR 2008, 100; Donnell et al. 2009, 80; Rosen and Sander 2009

34. Donnell et al. 2009, 7

35. Litman and Fitzroy 2015, 11–21

36. CEDR 2008, 112

37. Morrison et al. 2003, 329

38. Bunn et al 2003, 2

39. Positive evidence associated with slower traffic speeds and increased children's physical activity can be found in: Ding et al. 2011; Davison and Lawson 2006; Giles-Corti et al. 2009; McGrath et al. 2015; Sallis and Glanz 2006. Positive evidence for able-bodied adults:: Casagrande et al. 2009; Duncan et al. 2005; Forsyth and Krizek 2010; Frost et al. 2010. Research that found no relationship for able-bodied adults includes: McCormack and Shiell 2011; Saelens and Handy 2008; Sugiyama et al. 2012; Trost et al. 2002; Wendel-Vos et al. 2007. Research with mixed results: Humpel et al. 2002; Owen et al. 2004. Reviews that found no connection for older adults include: Cunningham and Michael 2004; Rosso et al. 2011; Van Cauwenberg et al. 2011 or mixed evidence Van Stralen et al. 2009.

40. FHWA 2012; WHO 2008

41. Ewing and Dumbaugh 2009, 347

42. Sugiyama et al. 2012; Van Cauwenberg et al. 2011

43. The systematic reviews and qualitative evidence referred to include: Bauman et al. 2012; Ding et al. 2011; Frost et al. 2010; McCormack and Shiell 2011; Wendel-Vos et al. 2007; Van Cauwenberg et al. 2011; Van Holle et al. 2012.

44. Casagrande et al. 2009; Duncan et al. 2005; Frost et al. 2010; Owen et al. 2004; Sallis et al. 2009; Sugiyama et al. 2012; Van Holle et al. 2012; Wendel-Vos et al. 2007. Others less conclusive: Forsyth and Krizek 2010; McCormack and Shiell 2011; Trost et al. 2002

45. Ding et al. 2011 (some mixed or uncertain evidence); Davison and Lawson 2006; Giles-Corti et al. 2009; McGrath et al. 2015; Sallis and Glanz 2006 ; Clarke et al. 2008; Rimmer et al. 2004, 421; University of Kansas 2013; WHO 2007, 12–14

46. Ding et al. 2011; Davison and Lawson 2006; Forsyth and Krizek 2010; Giles-Corti et al. 2009; Sallis and Glanz 2006

47. Davison and Lawson 2006; Forsyth and Krizek 2010, 436–437; Giles-Corti et al. 2009; Moran et al. 2014; McGrath et al. 2015; Van Cauwenberg et al.2011

48. Forsyth and Krizek 2010, 437; See also Humpel et al. 2002; McCormack and Shiell 2011; Sallis et al. 2009; Moran et al. 2014

49. WHO 2013b, 14

50. FHWA 2014

51. Forsyth and Krizek 2010, 437

52. Forsyth and Krizek 2010, 437

53. Forsyth and Krizek 2010

54. Reynolds et al. 2009, 14

55. FHWA 2014

56. FHWA 2005; Koepsell et al. 2002

57. Forsyth and Krizek 2010; Monsere et al. 2014; Falbo 2014

58. Jasper and Bartram 2012; Park et al. 2012; Skiba and Zuger 2009, 23–24; Preiser and Smith 2011, 20.4; ULI 2015, 60; van Cauwenberg et al. 2011, 467; WHO 2007, 13, 16–18, 25

59. Fleming 2007; Sharp et al. 2005

60. Baum and Palmer 2002, 351; Bjornstrom and Ralson 2014

61. Bowler et al., 2010a; Mills et al. 2010

Principle 6

1. World Bank 2015

2. Murayama et al. 2012

3. Grootaert and van Bastelaer 2001, 9; Kawachi et al. 2013, 3

4. Cheung 2011, 199; Fried et al. 2004, 64; Kawachi et al. 2013, 227; Sirven and Debrand 2012

5. Gao et al. 2012, 2; Resnick et al. 2011, 6; Rowe and Kahn 1987, 146

6. Rowe and Kahn 1987, 147

7. Design for Health 2008b, 4; Grootaert and van Bastelaer 2001, 9

8. Jackman 2001; Kawachi et al. 2013

9. Kawachi et al. 2013, 9

10. Ewing and Bartholomew 2013, 75

11. Forsyth 2000, 127; Lee et al. 2009

12. Jacobson and Forsyth 2008, 76

13. Frumkin 2003, 1453

14. Forrest and Kearns 2001, 2140

15. Koohsari et al. 2015, 75

16. Koohsari et al. 2015, 80

17. White et al. 2010, 369

18. Jacobson and Forsyth 2008, 78

19. Koohsari et al. 2015, 80

20. Cozens et al. 2005, 337–338

21. Ewing and Bartholomew 2013, 76

22. Forsyth and Krizek 2010, 431, 434–435, 441

23. Forsyth and Musacchio 2005, 145

24. Baum et al. 2011, 53; Forrest and Kearns 2001, 2140

25. Lorenc et al. 2012, 758

26. Branas et al. 2011, 1296; Lorenc et al. 2012, 762

27. Lorenc et al. 2012, 762

28. Welsh and Farrington 2008, 3; Schneider and Kitchen, 2007, 199

29. Welsh and Farrington 2008, 3

30. Cozens et al. 2005, 343

31. Ellen et al. 2001, 394, 397; Foster and Giles-Corti, 2008; Lorenc et al. 2012

32. Ellen et al. 2001, 404

33. Ellen et al. 2001, 392

34. Foster and Giles-Corti 2008, 249

35. Foster and Giles-Corti 2008; Lorenc et al. 2012

36. Sampson et al. 1997; Subramanian et al. 2003

37. Dallgo 2009, 149

38. Dallago et al. 2009, 152

39. Dallago et al. 2009, 155

40. Schneider and Kitchen, 2007, 47

41. Schneider and Kitchen, 2007, 52

42. Lorenc et. al. 2012

43. Jacobson and Forsyth 2008, 78; Politechnico di Milano et al. 2007, 35

44. Politechnico di Milano et al. 2007, 36

45. Gobster 2002, 151; Design for Health 2007c

46. Saraiva and Pinho 2011, 222

47. Saraiva and Pinho 2011, 222

48. Sampson and Raudenbush 2001, 5

49. Saraiva and Pinho 2011

50. Politechnico di Milano et al. 2007, 29

Principle 7

1. Prüss- Üstün et al. 2011, 6–7

2. WHO 2015d

3. Brender et al. 2011, S37, 49,; Porta et al. 2009, 1, 8

4. Guha-Sapir et al. 2013, 1, 3

5. IPCC 2012 5–7

6. Guha-Sapir et al. 2015; HAPI 2014m, 3

7. Guha-Sapir et al. 2015

8. Fritschi et al. 2011, vii

9. Prüss-Üstün et al. 2011, 1, 4

10. Prüss-Üstün 2011, 1

11. D'Amato et al. 2010, 95–97; Laumbach and Kipen 2012, 6, 10; Pascal et al. 2013; Perez-Padilla et al. 2010,1080–1082; Samet 2010, 321– 324; WHO 2014; Zhang et al. 2010, 1111

12. Barbosa et al. 2012; Burton and Pitt 2002; Wang 2015

13. Barbosa et al. 2012; Gasperi et al. 2010, Hvitved-Jacobsen et al. 2010

14. Brabec et al. 2002; Goonetilleke et al. 2005; Jacobson 2011

15. Research on waste and harmful hazards includes: Arukwe et al. 2012; Parkinson et al. 2010, 277; Prüss-Üstün 2011, 3; Schwarzenbach et al. 2010, 114, 127; Schueler, T.R. 2000. Studies on pathways to human exposure include: Parkinson et al. in Vlahov et al. (ed.) 2010, 277; Prüss-Üstün 2011, 3; Schwarzenbach et al. 2010, 114, 127. Studies on health and proximity waste include: Brender et al. 2011, 49; Mattiello et al. 2013; Porta et al. 2009

16. Mattiello et al. 2013, 731

17. Brender et al. 2011, S38, S49; Mattiello et al. 2013; Porta et al. 2009, 4, 6–7; Prüss-Üstün et al. 2011, 5; Sepúlveda et al. 2010, 36

18. Brown 2014, 104–110; Seadon 2010

19. Davoudi et al. 2009, 38, 39; Stone et al. 2010, 1427

20. Davoudi et al. 2009, 39

21. Engelman and LeRoy 1993; Postel 1997

22. Bernstein 1997; Dixon et al. 2014; Hilaire et al. 2008; Kent et al. 2006; Postel 1997; Wang 2015

23. Kemp et al. 2007, 85; Powrie and Dacombe 2006; Seadon 2006; Seadon 2010; U.S. EPA 2002

24. Benova et al. 2014; Dangour et al. 2013; Fink et al. 2011; Hunter et al. 2010, Schwarzenbach et al. 2010, 127

25. Barbosa et al. 2012, 6793; Capodaglio 2005; Haller et al. 2007; Tchobanoglous, et al. 2002; Wang 2015

26. Davis et al. 2009; Schueler 2000; Scholes et al. 2008

27. Austin 2014, 154–172; Burke 2009; Dixon et al. 2014; Kaufman and Wurtz 1997; Kronaveter et al. 2001; Scholes et al. 2008

28. Expanded from Guha-Sapir et al. 2013, 7

29. Guha-Sapir et al. 2013, 1, 3

30. IPCC 2012 5–7

31. Guha-Sapir et al. 2013, 2

32. The following studies focus on development vulnerable to disasters: Adger et al. 2005, 1036; Douglas et al. 2008; Joffe et al.

2013; Kidokoro et al. 2008, 4, 18, 100–101, 107; Pelling 2003; Wamsler 2014, 21–23, 82, 86

33. Adger et al. 2005, 1036; Douglas et al. 2008; Galea et al. 2006; Gaspirini 2014, 2–3, 68–69; Joffee et al. 2013, 2; Kidokoro et al. 2008, 4, 18, 100–101, 107; Pelling 2003; Wamsler 2014, 21–23, 82, 86

34. Davis et al. 2010, 1, 2,7; Norris et al. 2002, 236

35. Much research has been conducted on the health outcomes associated with disasters for women and children: Alderman et al. 2012, 38, 45; Basu 2009; Basu and Samet 2002; et al. 2009, 55, 57; Curriero et al. 2002, 85; Doocy et al. 2013a; Doocy et al. 2013b; Hajat and Kosatky 2009; Kovats and Hajat 2008; Reid et al. 2009; Romero-Lanko et al. 2012; Rosenthal et al. 2014; Shea and the Committee on Environmental Health 2007.

36. Godschalk 2003, 140; Romero-Lankao et al. 2012; Rosenthal et al. 2014; Berke and Smith 2009; Kidokoro et al. 2008, 19, 114; Schwab 2011, 49

37. Berke and Smith 2009; Coppola 2011, 21, 26; Godschalk 2003, 141

38. Stone et al. 2010; Adger et al. 2005, 1038; Berke and Smith 2009; Wamsler 2014, 130–133

39. IPCC 2012, 14

40. Adger et al. 2005, 1038; Chan et al. 2009, 55; Coppola 2011, 26; Kidokoro et al. 2008, 20

41. Berke and Smith 2009; Coppola 2011, 21, 26; Kidokoro et al. 2008, 20

42. Murphy and King 2015, 52

43. Berglund et al. 1999, xviii

44. FHWA 2001, 6

45. Babisch 2006; Fritschi et al. 2011, 45; van Kempen et al. 2002, 314; Berglund et al. 1999

46. van Kamp and Davies 2013, 158

47. Babisch 2006, 1; Babisch 2011, 201; Davies and van Kamp 2012, 287; Stansfeld and Crombie 2011, 229; van Kempen et al. 2002, 307

48. WHO 2011c, 16, 201; Davies and van Kamp 2012, 287; Fritschi et al. 2011, 103; Huss et al. 2010, 829; Gan et al. 2012, 898

49. Fritschi et al. 2011,103

50. Berglund et al. 1999, xviii

51. http://services.defra.gov.uk/wps/portal/noise; Note: Map is of central London, postal code E1. Darker areas are higher noise levels, e.g. 75+ dB(A), while lighter areas are below 55 dB(A).
52. Moudon 2009, 170
53. WHO 1999, 72
54. Daigle 1999, 157
55. FHWA 2011
56. WHO 1999, 77; Murphy and King 2015, 225; FWHA 2011
57. Dzhambov and Dimitrova 2014, 157
58. Daigle 1999, 137

Principle 8

1. Project types include new towns (Forsyth 1999, 2005b), transportation systems or elements (Altshuler 1965; Pucher and Buehler 2008), and land-use plans (Krizek et al. 2009b).
2. Krizek et al. 2009b

Conclusion

1. Bentley et al. 1985

References

AARP Public Policy Institute (AARP). 2006. *State of 50+ America: 2006*. Washington, D.C.: AARP.

Adger, W. Neil, Terry P. Hughes, Carl Folke, Stephen R. Carpenter, and Johan Rockström. 2005. "Social-ecological resilience to coastal disasters." *Science* 309, 5737: 1036–1039.

Aggarwal, Anju, Pablo Monsivais, and Adam Drewnowski. 2012. "Nutrient intakes linked to better health outcomes are associated with higher diet costs in the U.S." *PLoS ONE 7*, 5: e37533–e37533.

Agrawal, Asha Weinstein, and Paul Schimek. 2007. "Extent and correlates of walking in the USA." *Transportation Research Part D: Transport and Environment* 12, 8: 548–563.

Alcock, Ian, Mathew P. White, Benedict W. Wheeler, Lora E. Fleming, and Michael H. Depledge. 2014. "Longitudinal effects on mental health of moving to greener and less green urban areas." *Environmental Science & Technology* 48, 2: 1247–1255.

Alderman, Katarzyna, Lyle R. Turner, and Shilu Tong. 2012. "Floods and human health: a systematic review." *Environment International* 47: 37–47.

Alexander, Christopher, Sara Ishikawa, and Murray Silverstein. 1977. *A Pattern Language: Towns, Buildings, Construction*. New York: Oxford University Press.

Alexander, Christopher. 1965. "A city is not a tree." *Architectural Forum* 122, 1: 58–62.

Alshalalfah, B. W., and Amer S. Shalaby. 2007. "Case study: relationship of walk access distance to transit with service, travel, and personal characteristics." *Journal of Urban Planning and Development*, 133, 2: 114–118.

Altshuler, Alan. 1965. *The City Planning Process*. Ithaca, N.Y.: Cornell University Press.

American Planning Association. 2007. *Planning and Urban Design Standards*. Hoboken, N.J.: John Wiley & Sons.

Appleton, Jay. 1975. *The Experience of Landscape*. New York: Wiley.

Arukwe, Augustine, Trine Eggen, Monika Möder. 2012. "Solid waste deposits as a significant source of contaminants of emerging concern to the aquatic and terrestrial environments—A developing country case study from Owerri, Nigeria. "*Science of the Total Environment* 438: 94–102.

Austin, Gary. 2014. *Green Infrastructure for Landscape Planning: Integrating Human and Natural Systems*. London: Routlege.

Asensio-Villoria, Leire and David Mah, eds. 2016. *Lifestyled: Health and Place*. Berlin, Germany: Jovis.

Babisch, Wolfgang. 2002. "The noise/stress concept, risk assessment and research needs." *Noise & Health* 4, 16:1–11.

Babisch, Wolfgang. 2006. "Transportation noise and cardiovascular risk: updated review and synthesis of epidemiological studies indicate that the evidence has increased." *Noise & Health* 8: 1–29.

Babisch, Wolfgang. 2011. "Cardiovascular effects of noise." *Noise & Health* 13,52: 201–204.

Babisch, Wolfgang, Gabriele Wölke, Joachim Heinrich, and Wolfgang Straff. 2014. "Road traffic noise and hypertension–accounting for the location of rooms." *Environmental Research* 133: 380–387.

Banerjee, Tridib, and William Baer. 1984. *Beyond the Neighborhood Unit: Residential Environments and Public Policy*. New York: Plenum Press.

Barbosa, A. E., J. N. Fernandes, and L. M. David. 2012. "Key issues for sustainable urban stormwater management." *Water Research* 46, 20: 6787–6798.

Barr, Stewart. 2007. "Factors influencing environmental attitudes and behaviors a UK case study of household waste management." *Environment and Behavior* 39, 4: 435–473.

Barth, Jurgen, Sarah Schneider, and Roland von Kanel. 2010. "Lack of social support in the etiology and the prognosis of coronary heart disease: a systematic review and meta-analysis." *Psychosomatic Medicine* 72: 229–238.

Barton, Hugh, Marcus Grant, and Richard Guise. 2010. *Shaping Neighborhoods: For Local Health and Global Sustainability*. 2nd ed. London: Routledge.

Barton, Jo, and Jules Pretty. 2010. "What is the best dose of nature and green exercise for improving mental health? A multi-study analysis." *Environmental Science and Technology* 44, 10: 3947–55.

Bass, Ellen S., Rebecca L. Calderon, and Mary Ellen Khan. 1990. "Household hazardous waste: a review of public attitudes and disposal problems." *Journal of Environmental Health* 52, 6: 358–361.

Basu, Rupa, and Jonathan M. Samet. 2002. "Relation between elevated ambient temperature and mortality:

a review of the epidemiologic evidence." *Epidemiologic Reviews* 24, 2: 190–202.

Basu, Rupa. 2009. "High ambient temperature and mortality: a review of epidemiologic studies from 2001 to 2008." *Environmental Health* 8:40–53.

Baum, Fran, and Catherine Palmer. 2002. " 'Opportunity structures': urban landscape, social capital and health promotion in Australia." *Health Promotion International* 17, 4: 351–361.

Bauman, Adrian E., Rodrigo S. Reis, James F. Sallis, Jonathan C. Wells, Ruth J.F. Loos, and Brian W. Martin. 2012. "Correlates of physical activity: why are some people physically active and others not?" *Lancet* 380: 258–271.

Bauman, Adrian, Guansheng Ma, Frances Cuevas, Zainal Omar, Temo Waqanivalu, Philayrath Phongsavan, Kieren Keke, Anjana Bhushant. 2011. "Cross-national comparisons of socioeconomic differences in the prevalence of leisure-time and occupational physical activity, and active commuting in six Asia-Pacific countries." *Journal of Epidemiology and Community Health* 65: 35–43.

Beaulac, Julie, Elizabeth Kristjansson, Steven Cummins. 2009. "A systematic review of food deserts, 1966–2007." *Preventing Chronic Disease* 6, 3: 1–10.

Bellos, Anna, Kim Mulholland, Katherine L. O'Brien Shamim A. Qazi, Michelle Gayer, and Francesco Checchi. 2010. "The burden of acute respiratory infections in crisis-affected populations: a systematic review." *Conflict and Health* 4, 1: 3–15.

Benova, Lenka, Oliver Cumming, and Oona M.R. Campbell. 2014. "Systematic review and meta-analysis: association between water and sanitation environment and maternal mortality." *Tropical Medicine and International Health* 19, 4: 368–387.

Bentley, Ian, Alan Alcock, Paul Murrain, Sue McGlynn, and Graham Smith. 1985. *Responsive Environments: A Manual for Designers.* London: The Architectural Press.

Berglund, Birgitta, Thomas Lindvall, and Dietrich H. Schwela, eds. 1999. *Guidelines for Community Noise.* Geneva: World Health Organization.

Berke, Philip, and Gavin Smith. 2009. "Hazard mitigation, planning, and disaster resiliency: challenges and strategic choices for the 21st century." In *Building Safer Communities: Risk Governance, Spatial Planning and Responses to Natural Hazards*, ed. Urbano Fra Paleo, 1–20. Amsterdam: Ios Press.

Bernstein, J.D. 1997. "Economic Instruments." In *Water Pollution Control – A Guide to the Use of Water Quality Management Principles,* ed. Richard Helmer and

Ivanildo Hespanhol, 157–178. Geneva: World Health Organization/ UNEP.

Bhutta, Zulfiqar A., Fauzia A. Bawany, Asher Feroze, Arjumand Rizvi, Samman J. Thapa, and Mahesh Patel. 2009. "Effects of the crises on child nutrition and health in East Asia and the Pacific." *Global Social Policy* 9, 1: 119–143.

Biederman, Irving, and Edward Vessel. 2006. "Perceptual pleasure and the brain." *American Scientist* 94, 1: 249–255.

Bjornstrom, Eileen E.S., and Margaret L. Ralston. 2014. "Neighborhood built environment, perceived danger, and perceived social cohesion." *Environment and Behavior* 46, 6: 718–744.

Black, Christina, Graham Moon, and Janis Baird. 2014. "Dietary inequalities: What is the evidence for the effect of the neighborhood food environment?" *Health and Place* 27: 229–242.

Black, Colin, Alan Collins, and Martin Snell. 2001 "Encouraging walking: the case of journey-to school trips in compact urban areas." *Urban Studies* 38, 7: 1121–1141.

Blumenthal, James A., Michael A. Babyak, Kathleen Moore, W. Edward Craighead, Steve Herman,Parinda Khatri, Robert Waugh, Melissa Napolitano, Leslie M. Forman, Mark Appelbaum, P. Murali Doraiswamy, K. Ranga Krishnan. 1999. "Effects of exercise training on older patients with major depression." *Archives of Internal Medicine* 159, 19: 2349–356.

Booth, Andrew, Diana Papaioannou, Anthea Sutton. 2012. *Systematic Approaches to the Successful Literature Review.* Los Angeles: Sage.

Boslaugh, Sarah E., and Elena M. Andresen. 2006. "Correlates of physical activity for adults with disability." *Preventing Chronic Disease* 3, 3: A78. Online resource. www.ncbi.nlm.nih.gov/pmc/articles/PMC1636710.

Bowler, Diana E., Lisette Buyung-Ali, Teri M. Knight, and Andrew S. Pullin. 2010a. "Urban greening to cool towns and cities: a systematic review of the empirical evidence." *Landscape and Urban Planning* 97: 147–155.

Bowler, Diana E., Lisette M. Buyung-Ali, Teri M. Knight, and Andrew S. Pullin. 2010b. "A systematic review of evidence for the added benefits to health of exposure to natural environments." *BMC Public Health* 10, 1: 456.

Brabec, Elizabeth, Stacey Schulte, and Paul l. Richards. 2002. "Impervious surfaces and water quality: a review of current literature and its implications for watershed planning." *Journal of Planning Literature* 16: 499–514.

Bramley, Glen, and Sinead Power. 2009. "Urban form and social sustainability: the role of density and housing type." *Environment and Planning B: Planning and Design,* 39: 30–48.

Branas, Charles C., Rose A. Cheney, John M. MacDonald, Vicky W. Tam, Tara D. Jackson, and Thomas R. Ten Have. 2011. "A difference-in-differences analysis of health, safety, and greening vacant urban space." *American Journal of Epidemiology* 174, 11: 1296–1306.

Brender, Jean D., Juliana A. Maantay, and Jayajit Chakraborty. 2011. "Residential proximity to environmental hazards and adverse health outcomes." *American Journal of Public Health* 101, S1: S37–52.

British Columbia Ministries of Health Services and Health Planning. 2002. *Standards of Accessibility and Guidelines for Provision of Sustainable Acute Care Services by Health Authorities.* www.health.gov.bc.ca/library/publications/year/2002/acute_accessibility.pdf.

Brower, Sidney. 2000. *Good Neighborhoods: A Study of In-Town and Suburban Residential Environments.* Westport, Conn.: Praeger.

Brown, Daniel K., Jo L. Barton, and Valerie F. Gladwell. 2013. "Viewing nature scenes positively affects recovery of autonomic function following acute-mental stress." *Environmental Science & Technology* 47: 5562–5569.

Brown, Hillary. 2014. *Next Generation Infrastructure.* Washington, D.C.: Island Press.

Browning, Christopher R., Reginald A. Byron, Catherine A. Calder, Lauren J. Krivo, Mei-Po Kwan, Jae-Yong Lee, and Ruth D. Peterson. 2010. "Commercial density, residential concentration, and crime: Land use patterns and violence in neighborhood context." *Journal of Research in Crime and Delinquency* 47, 3: 329–357.

Bulkeley, H., and N. Gregson. 2009. "Crossing the threshold: municipal waste policy and household waste generation." *Environment and Planning* 41, 4: 929-945.

Bunn, Frances, Timothy Collier, Chris Frost, Katharine Ker, Rebecca Steinbach, Ian Roberts, and Reinhard Wentz. 2003. "Area-wide traffic calming for preventing traffic related injuries." *Cochrane Database of Systematic Reviews.* 1: CD003110. Online resource.

Burke, David. 2009. "Water systems for urban improvements." *Blue: Water Energy and Waste* vol 1: 53–69. http://issuu.com/grimshawarchitects/docs/blue_01.

Burton, G. Allen, and Robert Pitt. 2002. *Stormwater Effects Handbook: A Toolbox for Watershed Managers, Scientists, and Engineers.* Boca Raton, Fla.: Lewis.

Camagni, Roberto, Roberta Capello, Andrea Araglui. 2013. "One or infinite optimal city sizes? In search of an equilibrium size for cities." *Annals of Regional Science* 51: 309–341.

Cannuscio, Carolyn C., Karyn Tappe, Amy Hillier Alison Buttenheim, Allison Karpyn, and Karen Glanz. 2013. "Urban food environments and residents' shopping behaviors." *American Journal of Preventive Medicine* 45, 5: 606–614.

Capello, Roberta, and Roberto Camagni. 2000. "Beyond optimal city size: an evaluation of alternative growth patterns." *Urban Studies* 37, 9: 1479–1496.

Capodaglio, A. G. 2005. "Improving sewage treatment plant performance in wet weather." In *Enhancing Urban Environment by Environmental Upgrading and Restoration,* ed. Jiri Marsalek, Daniel Sztruhar, Mario Guilianelli, and Ben Urbonas, 175–185. Dortrecht, Netherlands: Springer Science + Media.

Carpiano, Richard. 2006. "Toward a neighborhood resource-based theory of social capital for health: Can Bourdieu and sociology help?" *Social Science & Medicine* 62, 1: 165–175.

Casagrande, Sarah Stark, Melicia C. Whitt-Glover, Kristie J. Lancaster, Angela M. Odoms-Young, and Tiffany L. Gary. 2009. "Built environment and health behaviors among African Americans: a systematic review." *American Journal of Preventive Medicine* 36, 2: 174–181.

Centre for Accessible Environments. 2012. *Designing for Accessibility.* 2012 ed. London: RIBA.

Chaffee, Mary. 2009. "Willingness of health care personnel to work in a disaster: an integrative review of the literature." *Disaster Medicine and Public Health Preparedness* 3, 1: 42–56.

Chalfont, Garuth Eliot, and Susan Rodiek. 2005. "Building edge: an ecological approach to research and design of environments for people with dementia." *Alzheimer's Care Today* 6, 4: 341.

Chan, Emily YY, Yu Gao, and Sian M. Griffiths. 2009. "Literature review of health impact post-earthquakes in China 1906–2007." *Journal of Public Health* 32: 52–61.

Chatman, Daniel G., Robert Cervero, Emily Moylan, Ian Carlton, Dana Weissman, Joe Zissman, Erick Guerra, Jin Murakami, Paolo Ikezoe, Donald Emerson, Daniel Tischler, Daniel Means, Sandra Winkler, Kevin Sheu, and Sun Young. 2014. *Making Effective Fixed-Guideway Transit Investments: Indicators of Success.* Washington, D.C.: Transportation Research Board.

Cheung, Chau-Kiu. 2011. Children's sense of belonging and parental social capital derived from school. *The Journal of Genetic Psychology* 172, 2: 199–208.

Christian, Hayley, Stephen R. Zubrick, Sarah Foster, Billie Giles-Corti, Fiona Bull, Lisa Wood, Matthew Knuiman, Sally Brinkman, Stephen Houghton, and Bryan Boruff. 2015. "The influence of the neighborhood physical environment on early child health and development: a review and call for research." *Health & Place* 33: 25–36.

Chung, Kyusuk. 1997. "Estimating the effects of employment, development level, and parking availability on CTA rapid transit ridership: from 1976 to 1995 in Chicago." In *Metropolitan Conference on Public Transportation Research, 1997 Proceedings.* Chicago: University of Illinois.

Cimprich, Bernadine, and David L. Ronis. 2003. "An environmental intervention to restore attention in women with newly diagnosed breast cancer." *Cancer Nursing* 26, 4: 284.

City of Portland. 2013. *My Portland Plan: What Makes a Neighborhood Complete? Portland Plan.* Online resource. www.portlandonline.com/portlandplan/?a=437441&.

Clarke, Philippa, Jennifer A. Ailshire, Michael Bader, Jeffrey D. Morenoff, and James S. House. 2008. "Mobility disability and the urban built environment." *American Journal of Epidemiology* 168, 5: 506–513.

Cohen, Rebecca, and Keith Wardrip. 2011. "*Should I Stay or Should I Go? Exploring the Effects of Housing Instability and Mobility on Children.*" Washington, D.C.: Center for Housing Policy. http://nhc.org/media/files/HsgInstablityandMobility.pdf.

Coleman, Les. 2006. "Frequency of man-made disasters in the 20th century." *Journal of Contingencies and Crisis Management* 14, 1: 3–11.

Community Planning.net. 2016. *Community Planning Methods.* www.communityplanning.net/methods/methods_a-z.php.

Conference of European Directors of Roads (CEDR). 2008. *Best Practice For Cost-Effective Road Safety Infrastructure Investments.* Brussels, Belgium: CEDR's Secretariat General. www.cedr.fr/home/fileadmin/user_upload/Publications/2008/e_Road_Safety_Investments_Report.pdf.

Coon, J., Kate Boddy, Ken Stein, Rebecca Whear, Joanne Barton, and Michael H. Depledge. 2011. "Does participating in physical activity in outdoor natural environments have a greater effect on physical and mental wellbeing than physical activity indoors? A systematic review." *Environmental Science and Technology* 45: 1761–1772.

Coppola, Damon P. 2011. *Introduction to International Disaster Management,* 2nd ed. Burlington, Mass.: Elsevier.

Cox, Jayne, Sara Giorgi, Veronica Sharp, Kit Strange, David C. Wilson, and Nick Blakey. 2010. "Household waste prevention—a review of evidence." *Waste Management & Research* 28, 3: 193–219.

Cozens, Paul Michael, Greg Saville, and David Hillier. 2005. "Crime prevention through environmental design (CPTED): a review and modern bibliography." *Property Management* 23, 5: 328–356.

Cozens, Paul, and David Hillier. 2008. "The shape of things to come: new urbanism, the grid and the cul-de-sac." *International Planning Studies* 13, 1: 51–73.

Cranz, Galen. 1982. *The Politics of Park Design.* Cambridge Mass.: MIT Press.

Crewe, Katherine, and Ann Forsyth. 2011. "Compactness and connection in environmental design: insights from ecoburbs and ecocities for design with nature." *Environment and Planning-Part B* 38, 2: 267–288.

Crewe, Katherine. 2001. "The quality of participatory design: The effects of citizen input on the design of the Boston Southwest Corridor. *"Journal of the American Planning Association* 67, 4: 437–465.

Cunningham, Grazia O., and Yvonne L. Michael. 2004. Concepts guiding the study of the impact of the built environment on physical activity for older adults: a review of the literature. *American Journal of Health Promotion* 18, 6: 435–443.

Curriero, Frank C., Karlyn Heiner, Jonathan Samet, Scott Zeger, Lisa Strug, and Jonathan Patz. 2002. "Temperature and mortality in 11 cities of the eastern United States." *American Journal of Epidemiology* 155, 1: 80–87.

Curtis, Carey, John L. Renne, and Luca Bertolini, eds. 2009. *Transit Oriented Development: Making it Happen.* Farnham, England: Ashgate.

Cutts, Diana Becker, Alan F. Meyers, Maureen M. Black, Patrick H. Casey, Mariana Chilton, John T. Cook, Joni Geppert, Stephanie Ettinger de Cuba, Timothy Heeren, Sharon Coleman, Ruth Rose-Jacobs, and Deborah A. Frank. 2011. "US housing insecurity and the health of very young children." *American Journal of Public Health* 101, 8: 1508–1514.

D'Amato, Gennaro, L. Cecchi, M D'Amato, and G. Liccardi. 2010. "Urban air pollution and climate change as environmental risk factors of respiratory allergy: an update." *Journal of Investigational Allergology and Clinical Immunology* 20, 2: 95–102.

Daigle, Gilles. 1999. *Technical Assessment of the Effectiveness of Noise Walls*. Christchurch, New Zealand: International Institute of Noise Control.

Dallago, Lorenza, Douglas D. Perkins, Massimo Santinello, Will Boyce, Michal Molcho, and Antony Morgan. 2009. "Adolescent place attachment, social capital, and perceived safety: a comparison of 13 countries." *American Journal of Community Psychology* 44, 1–2:148–160.

Dallat, Mary Anne T., Isabelle Soerjomataram, Ruth Hunter, Mark A. Tully, Karen J. Cairns, and Frank Kee. 2014. "Urban greenways have the potential to increase physical activity levels cost-effectively." *The European Journal of Public Health* 24, 2: 190–195.

Dangour, Alan D., Louise Watson, Oliver Cumming, Sophie Boisson, Yan Che, Yael Velleman, Sue Cavill, Elizabeth Allen, and Ricardo Uauy. 2013. "Interventions to improve water quality and supply, sanitation and hygiene practices, and their effects on the nutritional status of children (Review)." *Cochrane Database of Systematic Reviews* 8(CD009382): 1465–1858.

Darnton, A., J. Elster Jones, K. Lucas, and M. Brooks. 2006. Influencing changes in behaviour: existing evidence to inform environmental leadership—review of theories and models (SD14002). London: Defra. http://randd.defra.gov.uk/Default.aspx?Menu=Menu&Module=More&Location=None&Completed=0&ProjectID=13984#RelatedDocuments.

Davies, Hugh, and Irene Van Kamp. 2012. "Noise and cardiovascular disease: a review of the literature 2008–2011." *Noise & Health* 14:287–291.

Davis, Allen P., William F. Hunt, Robert G. Traver, and Michael Clar. 2009. "Bioretention technology: overview of current practice and future needs." *Journal of Environmental Engineering* 135, 3: 109–117.

Davis, Jennifer R., Scoby Wilson, Amy Brock-Martin, Saundra Glover, and Erik R Svendsen. 2010. The impact of disasters on populations with health and health care disparities. *Disaster Medicine and Public Health Preparedness* 4, 1: 30–38.

Davis, John. 2004. *Psychological Benefits of Nature Experiences: An Outline of Research and Theory*. Boulder, Colo.: Naropa University. www.wildernessguidescouncil.org/sites/default/files/psychological_benefits_of_nature_experiences.pdf.

Davison, Kirsten K., and Catherine T. Lawson. 2006. "Do attributes in the physical environment influence children's physical activity? A review of the literature." *International Journal of Behavioral Nutrition and Physical Activity* 3, 1: 19.

Davoudi, Simin, Jenny Crawford, and Abid Mehmood, eds. 2009. *Planning for Climate Change: Strategies for Mitigation and Adaptation for Spatial Planners*. London: Earthscan.

de Nazelle, Audrey, Mark J. Nieuwenhuijsen, Josep M. Antó, Michael Brauer, David Briggs, Charlotte Braun-Fahrlander, Nick Cavill, Ashley Cooper, Hélène Desqueyroux, Scott Fruin, Gerard Hoek, Luc Int Panis, Nicole Janssen, Michael Jerrett, Michael Joffe, Zorana Jovanovic Andersen, Elise van Kempen, Simon Kingham, Nadine Kubesch, Kevin M. Leyden, Julian Marshall, Jaume Matamala, Giorgos Mellios, Michelle Mendez, Hala Nassif, David Ogilvie, Rosana Peiró, Katherine Pérez, Ari Rabl, Martina Ragettli, Daniel Rodríguez, David Rojas, Pablo Ruiz, James F. Sallis, Jeroen Terwoert, Jean-François Toussaint, Jouni Tuomisto, Moniek Zuurbier, and Erik Lebret. 2011. "Improving health through policies that promote active travel: A review of evidence to support integrated health impact assessment." *Environment International* 37, 4: 766–77.

De Silva, Mary J., Sharon R. Huttly, Trudy Harpham, and Michael G. Kenward. 2006. "Social capital and mental health: a comparative analysis of four low income countries." *Social Science and Medicine* 64: 5–20.

Department for Environment Food and Rural Affairs (Defra). 2015. Noise Mapping England Website. Online resource. http://services.defra.gov.uk/wps/portal/noise.

Design for Health. 2007a. *Key Questions: Accessibility*. Version 1.0. http://designforhealth.net/wp-content/uploads/2012/02/BCBS_KQAccessibility_071607.pdf.

Design for Health. 2007b. *Planning Information Sheet: Considering Safety through Comprehensive Planning and Ordinances*. Version 2.0. http://www.ca-ilg.org/sites/main/files/file-attachments/resources__bcbs_issafety_082807.pdf.

Design for Health. 2007c. *Preliminary Checklist*. Version 4.0. http://designforhealth.net/hia/hia-preliminary-checklist.

Design for Health. 2008a. *Health Impact Assessment Threshold Analysis*. Version 4.0. http://designforhealth.net/hia/hia-threshold-analysis.

Design for Health. 2008b. *Planning Information Sheet: Building Social Capital with Comprehensive Planning and Ordinances*. Version 1.2. http://designforhealth.net/wp-content/uploads/2012/12/BCBS_SocCap_0408.pdf.

Design for Health. 2008c. *Rapid Health Impact Assessment Toolkit.* Version 3.0. http://designforhealth.net/hia/hia-rapid-assessment.

Design for Health. 2009. Comprehensive Plan Review Checklists. http://designforhealth.net/resources/legacy/checklists.

D'Hombres, Béatrice, Lorenzo Rocco, Marc Suhrcke, and Martin McKee. 2010. "Does social capital determine health? Evidence from eight transition countries." *Health Economics* 9: 56–74.

Dijkstra, Karin, Marcel Pieterse, and Ad Pruyn. 2006. "Physical environmental stimuli that turn health care facilities into healing environments through psychologically mediated effects: systematic review." *Journal of Advanced Nursing* 56, 2: 166–181.

DiMento, Joseph, and Cliff Ellis. 2013. *Changing Lanes: Visions and Histories of Urban Freeways.* Cambridge, Mass.: MIT Press.

Dimitriou, Harry T., and Ralph Gakenheimer, eds. 2011. *Urban Transport in the Developing World: A Handbook of Policy and Practice.* Cheltenham, U.K.: Edward Elgar Publishing.

Ding, Ding, James F. Sallis, Jacqueline Kerr, Suzanna Lee, and Dori Rosenberg. 2011. "Neighborhood environment and physical activity among youth: a review." *American Journal of Preventative Medicine* 41, 4: 442–455.

Dittmar, Hank, and Gloria Ohland, eds. 2004. *The New Transit Town: Best Practices in Transit-Oriented Development.* Washington, D.C.: Island Press.

Dixon, Tim, Malcolm Eames, Judith Britnell, Georgia Butina Watson, and Miriam Hunt. 2014a. "Urban retrofitting: identifying disruptive and sustaining technologies using performative and foresight techniques." *Technological Forecasting and Social Change* 89: 131–144.

Dixon, Tim, Malcolm Eames, Miriam Hunt, and Simon Lannon. 2014b. *Urban Retrofitting for Sustainability: Mapping the Transition to 2050.* London: Routledge.

Doerksen, Shawna E., Robert W. Motl, and Edward McAuley. 2007. "Environmental correlates of physical activity in multiple sclerosis: a cross-sectional study." *International Journal of Behavioral Nutrition and Physical Activity* 4,1: 49.

Donnell, Eric T., Scott C. Hines, Kevin M. Mahoney, Richard J. Porter, Hugh McGee. 2009. *Speed Concepts: Informational Guide.* Washington, D.C.: Federal Highway Administration. http://safety.fhwa.dot.gov/speedmgt/ref_mats/fhwasa10001.

Doocy, Shannon, Amy Daniels, Anna Dick, and Thomas D. Kirsch. 2013a. "The human impact of tsunamis: a historical review of events 1900–2009 and systematic literature review." *PLoS Currents* 16, 5 Online resource. doi: 10.1371/currents.dis.40f3c5cf61110a0fef2f9a25908cd795.

Doocy, Shannon, Amy Daniels, Catherine Packer, Anna Dick, and Thomas D. Kirsch. 2013b. "The human impact of earthquakes: a historical review of events 1980–2009 and systematic literature review." *PLoS Currents* 16:5. Online resource. doi: 10.1371/currents.dis.67bd14fe457f1db0b5433a8ee20fb833.

Douglas, Ian, Kurshid Alam, MaryAnne Maghenda, Yasmin Mcdonnell, Louise McLean, and Jack Campbell. 2008. "Unjust waters: climate change, flooding and the urban poor in Africa." *Environment and Urbanization* 20, 1: 187–205.

Drewnowski, Adam, Anju Aggarwal, Philip M. Hurvitz, Pablo Monsivais, and Anne V. Moudon. 2012. "Obesity and supermarket access: proximity or price?" *American Journal of Public Health* 102, 8: e74-e80.

Drewnowski, Adam. 2010. "The cost of U.S. foods as related to their nutritive value." *American Journal of Clinical Nutrition* 92: 1181–1188.

Duncan, Mitch J., John C. Spence, and W. Kerry Mummery. 2005. "Perceived environment and physical activity: a meta-analysis of selected environmental characteristics." *International Journal of Behavioral Nutrition and Physical Activity* 2:11. Online resource. doi:10.1186/1479-5868-2-11.

Dzhambov, Angel Mario, and Donka Dimitrova Dimitrova. 2014. "Urban green spaces' effectiveness as a psychological buffer for the negative health impact of noise pollution: a systematic review." *Noise and Health* 16, 70: 157.

Ebreo, Angela, and Joanne Vining. 2001. "How similar are recycling and waste reduction? Future orientation and reasons for reducing waste as predictors of self-reported behavior." *Environment and Behavior* 33, 3: 424–448.

Elgar, Frank J., Christopher G. Davis, Michael J. Wohl, Stephen J. Trites, John M. Zelenski, and Michael S. Martin. 2011. "Social capital, health and life satisfaction in 50 countries." *Health and Place* 17: 1044–1053.

Ellen, Ingrid, Tod Mijanovich and Keri-Nicole Dillman. 2001. "Neighborhood effects on health: exploring the links and assessing the evidence." *Journal of Urban Affairs* 23, 3–4: 391–408.

Ely, John W., Jerome A. Osheroff, Mark H. Ebell, M. Lee Chambliss, Daniel C. Vinson, James J. Stevermer, and Eric A. Pifer. 2002. "Obstacles to answering doctors' questions about patient care with evidence: qualitative study." *British Medical Journal* 324: 710–717.

Engelman, Robert, and Pamela LeRoy. 1993. *Sustaining Water: Population and the Future of Renewable Water Supplies*. Washington, D.C.: Population and Environment Program, Population Action International.

European Institute for Design and Disability (EIDD). 2004. *The EIDD Stockholm Declaration*. Stockholm: European Institute for Design and Disability. Online resource. http://dfaeurope.eu/what-is-dfa/dfa-documents/the-eidd-stockholm-declaration-2004.

Evans, Gary W. 2003. "The built environment and mental health." *Journal of Urban Health* 80, 4: 536–555.

Evans, Gary W., Nancy M. Wells, and Annie Moch. 2003. "Housing and mental health: a review of the evidence and a methodological and conceptual critique." *Journal of Social Issues* 59, 3: 475–500.

Ewing, Reid, and Eric Dumbaugh. 2009. "The built environment and traffic safety: a review of empirical evidence." *Journal of Planning Literature* 23, 4: 347–367.

Ewing, Reid, and Keith Bartholomew. 2013. *Pedestrian- and Transit-Oriented Design*. Washington, D.C.: Urban Land Institute.

Ewing, Reid, and Robert Cervero. 2010. "Travel and the built environment: a meta-analysis." *Journal of the American Planning Association* 76, 3: 265–294.

Ewing, Reid, and Robert Cervero. 2001. "Travel and the built environment: a synthesis." *Transportation Research Record* 1780: 87–114.

Ewing, Reid, William Schroeer, and William Greene. 2004. "School location and student travel analysis of factors affecting mode choice." *Transportation Research Record* 1895: 55–63.

Falbo, Nick. 2014. "*Protected Intersections for Bicyclists.*" Vimeo video, 5:58. Online resource. www.protectedintersection.com/wp-content/uploads/2014/02/Falbo_ProtectedIntersection_Transcript1.pdf.

Faulkner, Guy E.J., Ron N. Buliung, Parminder K. Flora, and Caroline Fusco. 2009. "Active school transport, physical activity levels and body weight of children and youth: A systematic review." *Preventive Medicine* 48: 3–8.

Federal Highway Administration (FHWA). 2005. *Safety Effects of Marked Versus Unmarked Crosswalks at Uncontrolled Locations*. McClean, Va.: U.S. Department of Transportation. www.fhwa.dot.gov/publications/research/safety/04100/04100.pdf.

Federal Highway Administration (FHWA). 2012. *Methods and Practices for Setting Speed Limits: An Informational Report (FHWA-SA-12-004)*. Washington, D.C.: Federal Highway Administration. http://safety.fhwa.dot.gov/speedmgt/ref_mats/fhwasa12004/fhwasa12004.pdf.

Federal Highway Administration (FHWA). 2014. *Proven Safety Countermeasures: Medians and Pedestrian Crossing Islands in Urban and Suburban Areas (FHWA-SA-12-011)*. McClean, Va.: U.S. Department of Transportation. http://safety.fhwa.dot.gov/proven-countermeasures/fhwa_sa_12_011.pdf.

Federal Highway Administration (FWHA). 2001. *Keeping the Noise Down: Highway Traffic Noise Barriers*. Washington, D.C.: Federal Highway Administration. www.fhwa.dot.gov/environment/noise/noise_barriers/design_construction/keepdown.pdf.

Federal Highway Administration (FWHA). 2011. *The Audible Landscape*. Online resource. U.S. Department of Transportation. www.fhwa.dot.gov/environment/noise/noise_compatible_planning/federal_approach/audible_landscape/al04.cfm.

Fink, Gunther, Isabel Gunther, and Kenneth Hill. 2011. The effect of water and sanitation on child health: evidence from the demographic and health surveys 1986–2007. *International Journal of Epidemiology* 40: 1196–1204.

Flink, Charles A., and Robert M. Searns. 1993. *Greenways: A Guide to Planning, Design, and Development*. Washington, D.C.: Island Press.

Fjeld, Tove, Bo Veiersted, Leiv Sandvik, Geir Riise, and Finn Levy. 1998. The effect of indoor foliage plants on health and discomfort symptoms among office workers. *Indoor and Built Environment* 7, 4: 204–209.

Fleischhacker, S. E., K.R Evenson, D.A. Rodriguez, and A.S. Ammerman. 2011. A systematic review of fast food access studies. *Obesity* 12: e460–e71.

Fleming, Ronald Lee. 2007. *The Art of Placemaking: Interpreting Community Thorough Public Art and Urban Design*. London: Merrel.

Food and Agriculture Organization (FAO). 2015. 1.3. *Definition of Policy*. Online resource. www.fao.org/wairdocs/ilri/x5547e/x5547e05.htm.

Foord, Jo. 2010. "Mixed-use tradeoffs: how to live and work in a compact city neighbourhood." *Built Environment* 36, 1: 47–62

Forrest, Ray, and Ade Kearns. 2001. "Social cohesion, social capital and the neighbourhood." *Urban Studies* 38, 12: 2125–2143.

Forsyth, Ann. 2005a. "Density." In *Encyclopedia of the City*, ed. R. Caves. New York: Routledge.

Forsyth, Ann. 2005b. *Reforming Suburbia: The Planned Communities of Irvine, Columbia, and The Woodlands.* Berkeley: University of California Press.

Forsyth, Ann. 2012. "Defining suburbs." *Journal of Planning Literature* 27, 3: 270–281.

Forsyth, Ann. 2014. "Global suburbs and the transition century: physical suburbs in the long term." *Urban Design International* 19, 4: 259–273.

Forsyth, Ann. 2015a. "Holistic Planning." *Harvard Design Magazine* 40: 7.

Forsyth Ann. 2015b. "What is a Walkable Place? The Walkability Debate in Urban Design." *Urban Design International* 20, 4: 274-292.

Forsyth, Ann, and Laura Musacchio. 2005. *Designing Small Parks: A Manual for Addressing Social and Ecological Concerns.* Hoboken, N.J.: Wiley.

Forsyth, Ann, and Katherine Crewe. 2009. "New visions for suburbia: reassessing aesthetics and place-making in modernism, imageability, and new urbanism." *Journal of Urban Design* 14, 4: 415–438.

Forsyth, Ann, and Krizek, Kevin. 2010. "Promoting walking and bicycling: assessing the evidence to assist planners. "*Built Environment* 36, 4: 429–446.

Forsyth, Ann, and Krizek, Kevin. 2011. "Urban design: is there a distinctive view from the bicycle?" *Journal of Urban Design* 16, 4: 531–549.

Forsyth, Ann, Leslie Lytle, and David Van Riper. 2010a. "Finding food: issues and challenges in using Geographic Information Systems to measure food access." *Journal of Transport and Land Use* 3, 1: 43–65.

Forsyth Ann, Carissa Schively Slotterback, and Kevin Krizek. 2010b. "Health impact assessments in planning: development and testing of the design for health HIA tools." *Environmental Impact Assessment Review* 30: 42–51.

Forsyth Ann, Carissa Schively Slotterback, and Kevin Krizek. 2010c. "Health impact assessment for planners: What tools are useful?" *Journal of Planning Literature* 24, 3: 231–245.

Forsyth Ann, David Van Riper, Nciole Larson, Melanie Wall, Dianne Neumark-Sztainer. 2012. "Creating a replicable, cross-platform buffering technique:

The sausage network buffer for measuring food and physical activity built environments." *International Journal of Health Geographics* 11:14. Online only: www.ij-healthgeographics.com/content/11/1/14.

Forsyth Ann, Charles Brennan, Nelida Escobedo, and Margaret Scott. 2015. *Revitalizing Places: Improving Housing and Neighborhoods from Block to Metropolis.* Cambridge, Mass.: Harvard Graduate School of Design.

Fortney, John C., James F. Burgess, Hayden B. Bosworth, Brenda M. Booth, and Peter J. Kaboli. 2011. "A re-conceptualization of access for 21st century health care." *Journal of General Internal Medicine* 26, 2: 639–647.

Foster, Sarah, and Billie Giles-Corti. 2008. "The built environment, neighborhood crime and constrained physical activity: an exploration of inconsistent findings." *Preventive Medicine* 47, 3: 241–251.

Frank, Lawrence Frank, and Chris Hawkins. 2008. *Giving Pedestrians an Edge—Using Street Layout to Influence Transportation Choice.* Ottawa: Canada Mortgage and Housing Corporation. www.cmhc-schl.gc.ca/odpub/pdf/66086.pdf.

Fried, Linda P., Michelle C. Carlson, Marc Freedman, Kevin D. Frick, Thomas A. Glass, Joel Hill, Sylvia McGil, George W. Rebok, Teresa Seeman, James Tielsch, Barbara A. Wasik, and Scott Zeger. 2004. "A social model for health promotion for an aging population: initial evidence on the experience corps model." *Journal of Urban Health* 81,1:64–78.

Fritschi, Lin, Lex Brown, Rokho Kim, Dietrich Schwela, and Stelios Kephalopolous, eds. 2011. *Burden of Disease From Environmental Noise: Quantification of Healthy Life Years Lost in Europe.* Geneva: World Health Organization. www.who.int/quantifyingehimpacts/publications/e94888/en/.

Frost, Stephanie S., R. Turner Goins, Rebecca H. Hunter, Steven P. Hooker, Lucinda L. Bryant, Judy Kruger, and Delores Pluto. 2010. "Effects of the built environment on physical activity of adults living in rural settings." *American Journal of Health Promotion* 24, 4: 267–283.

Frumkin, Howard. 2003. "Healthy places: exploring the evidence." *American Journal of Public Health* 93, 9: 1451–1456.

Gaber, John, and Sharon Gaber. 2007. *Qualitative Analysis for Planning and Policy: Beyond the Numbers.* Chicago: APA Planners Press.

Galea, Sandro, Craig Hadley, and Sasha Rudenstine. 2006. "Social context and the health consequences of disasters." *American Journal of Disaster Medicine* 1, 1: 37–47.

Gan, Wen Qi, Hugh W. Davies, Mieke Koehoorn, and Michael Brauer. 2012. "Association of long-term exposure to community noise and traffic-related air pollution with coronary heart disease mortality." *American Journal of Epidemiology* 175, 9: 898-906.

Gao, Qin, Daniel Ebert, Xing Chen and Yao Ding. 2012. "Design of a mobile social community platform for older Chinese people in urban areas." *Human Factors and Ergonomics in Manufacturing and Service Industries* 25, 1: 66–89.

Gasparini, Paolo, Gaetano Manfredi, Domenico Asprone, eds. 2014. *Resilience and Sustainability in Relation to Natural Disasters: A Challenge for Future Cities.* Heidelberg, Germany: Springer.

Gasperi, Johnny, Marie-Christine Gromaire, M. Kafi, R. Moilleron, and Ghassan Chebbo. 2010. "Contributions of wastewater, runoff and sewer deposit erosion to wet weather pollutant loads in combined sewer systems." *Water Research* 44, 20: 5875–5886.

Gibson, Marcia, Mark Petticrew, Clare Bambra, Amanda J. Sowden, Kath E. Wright, and Margaret Whitehead. 2011. "Housing and health inequalities: a synthesis of systematic reviews of interventions aimed at different pathways linking housing and health." *Health & Place* 17, 1: 175–184.

Giles-Corti, Billie, Sally F. Kelty, Stephen R. Zubrick, and Karen P. Villanueva. 2009. "Encouraging walking for transport and physical activity in children and adolescents. How important is the built environment?" *Sports Medicine* 39, 12: 995–1009.

Gill, Indermit, and Chor-Ching Goh. 2009. "Scale economies and cities." *The World Bank Research Observer* 25: 235–262.

Gobster, Paul H. 2002. "Managing urban parks for a racially and ethnically diverse clientele." *Leisure Sciences*, 24: 143–59.

Godschalk, D.R. 2003. "Urban hazard mitigation: Creating resilient cities." *Natural Hazards Review* 4, 3: 136–143.

Google Earth Pro. 2015. New York. Map. 1:2,000.

Goonetilleke, Ashantha, Evan Thomas, Simon Ginn, and Dale Gilbert. 2005. "Understanding the role of land use in urban stormwater quality management." *Journal of Environmental management* 74, 1: 31–42.

Government of Hong Kong's Environmental Protection Department (EPD). 2015. *Innovative Noise Mitigation Designs and Measures.* Online resource. www.epd.gov.hk/epd/Innovative/greeny/eng/index.html.

Grahn, P., and U.K. Stigsdotter. 2010. "The relation between perceived sensory dimensions of urban green space and stress restoration." *Landscape and Urban Planning* 94, 3–4: 264–275.

Grant, Jill. 2002. "Mixed use in theory and practice: Canadian experience with implementing a planning principle." *Journal of the American Planning Association* 68, 1: 71–84.

Gray, Jennifer A., Jennifer L. Zimmerman, and James H. Rimmer. 2012. "Built environment instruments for walkability, bikeability, and recreation: Disability and universal design relevant?" *Disability and Health Journal* 5: 87–101.

Green, Geoff. 2012. "Age-friendly cities of Europe." *Journal of Urban Health: Bulletin of the New York Academy of Medicine* 90,1: S116–S128.

Green, Geoff. 2013. "Age-friendly cities of Europe." *Journal of Urban Health* 90, 1: 116–128.

Grimble, Michael, Gary S. Danford, and David M. Schoell. 2010. *Design Resources: DR-12. The Effectiveness of Universal Design: Case Study Demonstrations.* Buffalo, N.Y.: University of Buffalo, Center for Inclusive Design and Environmental Access. http://udeworld.com/documents/designresources/pdfs/TheEffectivenessofUniversalDesignCaseStudyDemonstrations.pdf.

Grootaert, Christiaan, and Thierry van Bastelaer. 2001. *Understanding and Measuring Social Capital: A Synthesis of Findings And Recommendations from the Social Capital Initiative.* Washington, D.C.: The World Bank Social Development Department. http://siteresources.worldbank.org/INTSOCIALCAPITAL/Resources/Social-Capital-Initiative-Working-Paper-Series/SCI-WPS-24.pdf.

Grootaert, Christiaan, and Thierry Van Bastelaer. 2002. *The Role of Social Capital in Development: An Empirical Assessment.* New York: Cambridge University Press.

Guerra, Erick, and Robert Cervero. 2011. "Cost of a ride: the effects of densities on fixed-guideway transit ridership and costs." *Journal of the American Planning Association* 77, 3: 267–290.

Guha-Sapir Debby, Ph. Hoyois, Regina Below. 2015. *EM-DAT: The CRED/OFDA International Disaster Database.* Online resource. Brussels: Université Catholique de Louvain. www.emdat.be/database.

Guha-Sapir, Debby, Femke Vos, Regina Below, and Sylvain Ponserre. 2013. *Annual Disaster Statistical Review 2012: The Numbers and Trends.* Brussels: CRED. www.cred.be/sites/default/files/ADSR_2012.pdf.

Hajat, Shakoor, and Tom Kosatky. 2009. "Heat-related mortality: a review and exploration of heterogeneity." *Journal Epidemiology Community Health* 64:753–760.

Haller, Laurence, Guy Hutton, and Jamie Bartram. 2007. "Estimating the costs and health benefits of water and sanitation improvements at global level." *Journal of Water and Health* 5, 4: 467–480.

Hamer, Paul. 2010. "Analysing the effectiveness of park and ride as a generator of public transport mode shift." *Road & Transport Research* 19, 1: 51–61.

Hammersley, Martyn. 2005. "Is the evidence-based practice movement doing more good than harm? reflections on Iain Chalmers' case for research-based policy making and practice." *Evidence and Policy* 1, 1, 85–100.

Hancock, Trevor, and Meredith Minkler. 2005. "Community Health Assessment or Healthy Community Assessment: Whose Community? Whose Health? Whose Assessment?" In *Community Organizing and Community Building for Health*, ed. Meredith Minkler, 138–157. Piscataway, N.J.: Rutgers University Press.

Hand, Carri, Mary Law, Steven Hanna, Susan Elliott, and Mary Ann McColl. 2012. "Neighbourhood influences on participation in activities among older adults with chronic health conditions." *Health & Place* 18, 4: 869–876.

Harnick, Peter. 2006. "The excellent city park system: what makes it great and how to get there." In *The Humane Metropolis: People and Nature in the Twenty-first Century City,* ed. Rutherford, H. Platt, 47–60. Amherst: University of Massachusetts Press.

Harris, P., Harris-Roxas, B., Harris, E., & Kemp, L. 2007. *Health Impact Assessment: A Practical Guide.* Sydney: Centre for Health Equity Training, Research and Evaluation (CHETRE). http://hiaconnect.edu.au/wp-content/ uploads/2012/05/Health_Impact_Assessment_A_ Practical_Guide.pdf.

Hartig, Terry, Gary W. Evans, Larry D. Jamner, Deborah S. Davis, and Tommy Gärling. 2003. "Tracking restoration in natural and urban field settings." *Journal of Environmental Psychology* 23: 109–123.

Hartig, Terry, Marlis Mang, and Gary W. Evans. 1991. "Restorative effects of natural environment experiences." *Environment and Behavior* 23, 1: 3–26.

Harville, E. W., Xu Xiong, and Pierre Buekens. 2010. "Disasters and perinatal health: a systematic review." *Obstetrical and Gynecological Survey* 65, 11: 7–1.

Health and Places Initiative (HAPI). 2014o. *Health and Places Initiative Research Brief Series.* Cambridge, Mass.: Harvard Graduate School of Design. http://research.gsd.harvard.edu/hapi/research/research-briefs.

Health and Places Initiative (HAPI). 2014a. *Food Options, Health and Place. A Research Brief.* Version 1.0. Cambridge, Mass.: Harvard Graduate School of Design. http://research.gsd.harvard.edu/hapi/research/research-briefs/food-options.

Health and Places Initiative (HAPI). 2014b. *Housing, Health, and Place. A Research Brief.* Version 1.0. Cambridge, Mass.: Harvard Graduate School of Design. http://research.gsd.harvard.edu/hapi/research/research-briefs/housing.

Health and Places Initiative (HAPI). 2014c. *Mobility, Universal Design, Health, and Place. A Research Brief.* Version 1.0. Cambridge, Mass.: Harvard Graduate School of Design. http://research.gsd.harvard.edu/hapi/research/research-briefs/mobility-and-universal-design.

Health and Places Initiative (HAPI). 2014d. *Noise, Health, and Place. A Research Brief.* Version 1.0. Cambridge, Mass.: Harvard Graduate School of Design. http://research.gsd.harvard.edu/hapi/research/research-briefs/noise.

Health and Places Initiative (HAPI). 2014e. *Social Capital, Health, and Place. A Research Brief.* Version 1.0. Cambridge, Mass.: Harvard Graduate School of Design. http://research.gsd.harvard.edu/hapi/research/research-briefs/social-capital.

Health and Places Initiative (HAPI). 2014f. *Toxics, Health, and Place. A Research Brief.* Version 1.0. Cambridge, Mass.: Harvard Graduate School of Design. http://research.gsd.harvard.edu/hapi/research/research-briefs/toxics.

Health and Places Initiative (HAPI). 2014g. *Access to Community Resources, Health, and Place. A Research Brief.* Version 1.0. Cambridge, Mass.: Harvard Graduate School of Design. http://research.gsd.harvard.edu/hapi/research/research-briefs/accessibility.

Health and Places Initiative (HAPI). 2014h. *Mental Health, Health, and Place. A Research Brief.* Version 1.0. Cambridge, Mass.: Harvard Graduate School of Design. http://research.gsd.harvard.edu/hapi/research/research-briefs/mental-health.

Health and Places Initiative (HAPI). 2014i. *Physical Activity, Health, and Place. A Research Brief.* Version 1.0. Cambridge, Mass.: Harvard Graduate School of Design. http://research.gsd.harvard.edu/hapi/research/research-briefs/physical-activity.

Health and Places Initiative (HAPI). 2014j. *Physiology and Psychology of Aging, Health, and Place. A Research Brief.* Version 1.0. Cambridge, Mass.: Harvard Graduate School of Design. http://research.gsd.harvard.edu/hapi/physiology-and-psychology-of-aging.

Health and Places Initiative (HAPI). 2014k. *Water Quality, Health, and Place. A Research Brief.* Version 1.0. Cambridge, Mass.: Harvard Graduate School of Design. http://research.gsd.harvard.edu/hapi/research/research-briefs/water-quality.

Health and Place Initiative (HAPI). 2014l. *Air Quality, Health, and Place. A Research Brief.* Version 1.0. Cambridge, Mass.: Harvard Graduate School of Design. http://research.gsd.harvard.edu/hapi/research/research-briefs/air-quality.

Health and Place Initiative (HAPI). 2014m. *Disasters, Health, and Place. A Research Brief.* Version 1.0. Cambridge, Mass.: Harvard Graduate School of Design. http://research.gsd.harvard.edu/hapi/research/research-briefs/disasters.

Health and Place Initiative (HAPI). 2014n. *Safety, Health, and Place. A Research Brief.* Version 1.0. Cambridge, Mass.: Harvard Graduate School of Design. http://research.gsd.harvard.edu/hapi/research/research-briefs/safety.

Health and Places Initiative (HAPI). 2015a. *Health Assessment Tool 1. Screening Survey of Health in Place (SSHIP).* Version 1.2. Cambridge, Mass.: Harvard Graduate School of Design. http://research.gsd.harvard.edu/hapi/research/health-impact-assessment-tools.

Health and Places Initiative (HAPI). 2015b *Health Assessment Tool 2. Health Opportunity Checklist (HOC).* Version 1.2. Cambridge, Mass.: Harvard Graduate School of Design. http://research.gsd.harvard.edu/hapi/research/health-impact-assessment-tools.

Health and Places Initiative (HAPI). 2015c. *Health Assessment Tool 3. HAPI Health Assessment Workshop.* Version 1.2. Cambridge, Mass.: Harvard Graduate School of Design. http://research.gsd.harvard.edu/hapi/research/health-impact-assessment-tools.

Health and Places Initiative (HAPI). 2015d. *How to Guide: Health Assessment Tool 1. Screening Survey of Health in Place (SSHIP).* Version 1.1. Cambridge, Mass.: Harvard Graduate School of Design. http://research.gsd.harvard.edu/hapi/research/health-impact-assessment-tools.

Health and Places Initiative (HAPI). 2015e. *How to Guide: Health Assessment Tool 2: Health Opportunity Checklist (HOC).* Version 1.2. Cambridge, Mass.: Harvard Graduate School of Design.

http://research.gsd.harvard.edu/hapi/research/health-impact-assessment-tools.

Health and Places Initiative (HAPI). 2015f. *How to Guide: Health Assessment Tool 3: HAPI Health Assessment Workshop.* Version 1.2. Cambridge, Mass.: Harvard Graduate School of Design. http://research.gsd.harvard.edu/hapi/research/health-impact-assessment-tools.http://research.gsd.harvard.edu/hapi/research/health-impact-assessment-tools.

Heerwagen, Judith. 2009. Biophilia, health and well-being. In *Restorative Commons: Creating Health and Well-being through Urban Landscapes,* ed. Lindsay Campbell and Anne Wiesen, 39–57. Newtown Square, Pa.: U.S. Department of Agriculture, Forest Service, Northern Research Station. www.nrs.fs.fed.us/pubs/gtr/gtr_nrs-p-39r.pdf.

Heerwagen, Judith ,and Bert Gregory. 2011. "Biophilia and Sensory Aesthetics." In *Biophilic Design: The Theory, Science and Practice of Bringing Buildings to Life*, ed. Stephen R. Kellert, Judith Heerwagen, and Martin Mador, 227–241. San Francisco: John Wiley & Sons.

Heerwagen, Judith H., and Gordon H. Orians. 2002. "The ecological world of children." In *Children and Nature: Psychological, Sociocultural, and Evolutionary Investigations*, ed. P.H.J. Kahn and S.R. Kellert, 29–64. Cambridge, Mass.: MIT Press.

Hilaire, Rolston St, Michael A. Arnold, Don C. Wilkerson, Dale A. Devitt, Brian H. Hurd, Bruce J. Lesikar, Virginia I. Lohr, Chris A. Martin, Garry V. McDonald, Robert L. Morris, Dennis R. Pittenger, David A. Shaw, David F. Zoldoske. 2008. "Efficient water use in residential urban landscapes." *HortScience* 43, 7: 2081–2092.

Hitchins, Jane, Lidia Morawska, R. Wolff, and Dale Gilbert. 2000. "Concentrations of submicrometre particles from vehicle emissions near a major road." *Atmospheric Environment* 34, 1: 51–59.

Hull, R.B., and Sean E. Michael. 1995. "Nature-based recreation, mood change, and stress restoration." *Leisure Sciences* 17, 1: 1–14.

Humpel, Nancy, Neville Owen, and Eva Leslie. 2002. "Environmental factors associated with adults' participation in physical activity: a review." *American Journal of Preventative Medicine* 22, 3: 188–199.

Hunter, Paul R., Alan M. MacDonald, and Richard C. Carter. 2010. "Water supply and health." *PLoS Med* 7, 11: e1000361. Online resource. doi:10.1371/journal.pmed.1000361.

Huss, Anke, Adrian Spoerri, Matthias Egger, Martin Röösli, and Swiss National Cohort Study Group. 2010. "Aircraft noise, air pollution, and mortality from myocardial infarction." *Epidemiology* 21, 6 : 829–836.

Hvitved-Jacobsen, Thorkild, Jes Vollertsen, and Asbjorn Haaning Nielsen. 2010. *Urban and Highway Stormwater Pollution: Concepts and Engineering.* Boca Raton, Fla.: CRC Press.

Iacono, Michael, Kevin Krizek, and Ahmed El-Geneidy. 2008. *Access to Destinations: How Close is Close Enough? Estimating Accurate Distance Decay Functions for Multiple Modes and Different Purposes.* St. Paul: Minnesota Department of Transportation.

Intergovernmental Panel on Climate Change (IPCC). 2012. "Summary for Policymakers." In *Managing the Risks of Extreme Events and Disasters to Advance Climate Change Adaptation,* ed. Christopher B. Field, Vicente Barros, Thomas F. Stocker, Qin Dahe, David Jon Dokken, Gian-Kasper Plattner, Kristie L. Ebi, Simon K. Allen, Michael D. Mastrandrea, Melinda Tignor, Katharine J. Mach, Pauline M. Midgley, 1–19. Cambridge, U.K.: Cambridge University Press.

Isenberg, Joan Packer, and Nancy Quisenberry. 2002. "A position paper of the Association for Childhood Education International PLAY: Essential for all Children." *Childhood Education* 79, 1: 33–39.

Ison, E. 2013. "Health impact assessment in a network of European cities." *Journal of Urban Health* 90, 1s1: 105–115.

Jackman, R.W. 2001. "Social capital." In *International Encyclopedia of Social and Behavioral Sciences*, ed. Neil J. Smelser, Paul B. Baltes,14216–14219. Amsterdam: Elsevier.

Jacobs, David E. 2011. "Environmental health disparities in housing." *American Journal of Public Health* 101, S1: S115–S122.

Jacobs, Jane. 1961. *The Death and Life of Great American Cities.* NY: Vintage Books.

Jacobson, Carol R. 2011. "Identification and quantification of the hydrological impacts of imperviousness in urban catchments: a review." *Journal of Environmental Management* 92, 6: 1438–1448.

Jacobson, Justin, and Ann Forsyth. 2008. "Seven American TODs: good practices for urban design in transit-oriented development projects." *Journal of Transport and Land Use* 1, 2: 51–88.

Jasper, Christian, Thanh-Tam Le, and Jamie Bartram. 2012. "Water and sanitation in schools: a systematic review of the health and educational outcomes." *International Journal of Environmental Research and Public Health* 9, 8: 2772–87.

Joffe, Helene, Tiziana Rossetto, and John Adams eds. 2013. *Cities at Risk: Living with Perils in the 21st Century. Advances in Natural and Technological Hazards Research* Vol. 33 Dortrecht: Springer Science & Business Media.

Johnson, Ron, Derek Gregory, and David Smith, eds. 1994. *The Dictionary of Human Geography.* Oxford: Blackwell Reference.

Kaplan, Rachel, and Stephen Kaplan. 1989. *The Experience of Nature: A Psychological Perspective.* Cambridge, U.K.: Cambridge University Press.

Kaufman, Martin M., and Matthew Wurtz. 1997. Hydraulic and economic benefits of downspout diversion. *Journal of the American Water Resources Association* 6,3: 491–497.

Kawachi, Ichiro, Bruce P. Kennedy, and Roberta Glass. 1999. "Social capital and self-rated health: a contextual analysis."*American Journal of Public Health* 89, 8: 1187–1193.

Kawachi, Ichiro, Soshi Takao, and S.V. Subramanian, eds. 2013. *Global Perspectives on Social Capital and Health.* New York: Springer.

Kellert, Stephen R., Judith Heerwagen, and Martin Mador, eds. 2011. *Biophilic Design: The Theory, Science and Practice of Bringing Buildings to Life.* San Francisco: John Wiley & Sons.

Kemm, John. 2013. *Health Impact Assessment: Past Achievement, Current Understanding, and Future Progress.* Oxford: Oxford University Press.

Kemp, René, Derk Loorbach, and Jan Rotmans. 2007. "Transition management as a model for managing processes of co-evolution towards sustainable development." *International Journal of Sustainable Development & World Ecology* 14, 1: 78–9.

Kidokoro, Tetsuo, Junichiro Okata, Shuichi Matsumura, and Norihisa Shima, eds. 2008. *Vulnerable Cities: Realities, Innovations, and Strategies. cSUR-UT: Library for Sustainable Urban Regeneration.* Vol. 8. Hicom, Japan: Springer Science & Business Media.

Kim, D., S.V. Subramanian, and I. Kawachi. 2006. "Bonding versus bridging social capital and their associations with self rated health: a multilevel analysis of 40 US communities." *Journal of Epidemiology and Community Health* 60: 116–122.

Kimbrough, William, Vanessa Saliba, Maysoon Dahab, Christopher Haskew, and Francesco Checchi. 2012. "The burden of tuberculosis in crisis-affected populations: a systematic review. "*The Lancet Infectious Diseases* 12, 12: 950–965.

Koepsell, Thomas, Lon McCloskey, Marsha Wolf, Anne Vernez Moudon, David Buchner, Jess Kraus, and Matthew Patterson. 2002. "Crosswalk markers and the risk of pedestrian-motor vehicle collisions in older pedestrians." *Journal of the American Medical Association* 288, 17: 2136–2143.

Koohsari, Mohammad Javad, Suzanne Mavoa, Karen Villianueva, Takemi Sugiyama, Hannah Badland, Andrew T. Kaczynski, Neville Owen, and Billie Giles-Corti. 2015. "Public open space, physical activity, urban design and public health: concepts, methods and research agenda." *Health & Place* 33: 75–82.

Kose, Satoshi. 1998. "From barrier-free to universal design: an international perspective." *Assistive Technology* 10, 1: 44–50.

Kovats, R. Sari, and Shakoor Hajat. 2008. "Heat stress and public health: a critical review." *The Annual Review of Public Health* 29:41–55.

Krieger, Martin. 2011. *Urban Tomographies*. Philadelphia: Penn Press.

Krizek, Kevin, Ann Forsyth, and Clarissa Shively Slotterback. 2009b. "Is there a role for evidence-based practice in urban planning and policy?" *Journal of Planning Theory and Practice* 10, 4: 455–474.

Krizek, Kevin, Ann Forsyth, and Laura Baum. 2009a. *Walking and Cycling International Literature Review*. Melbourne, Australia: Victoria Department of Transport.

Kronaveter, Lea, Uri Shamir, and Avner Kessler. 2001. "Water-sensitive urban planning: modeling on-site infiltration." *Journal of Water Resources Planning and Management* 127, 2: 78–88.

Kuo, Frances E., and Andrea Faber Taylor. 2004. "A potential natural treatment for Attention-Deficit/Hyperactivity Disorder: evidence from a national study." *American Journal of Public Health* 94, 9: 1580.

Kurian, Joseph. 2006. "Stakeholder participation for sustainable waste management." *Habitat International* 30, 4: 863–871.

Lancaster, Christie A., Katherine J. Gold, Heather A. Flynn, Harim Yoo, Sheila M. Marcus, and Matthew M. Davis. 2010. "Risk factors for depressive symptoms during pregnancy: A systematic review." *American Journal of Obstetric Gynecology* 202, 1: 5–14.

Laumbach, Robert, and Howard Kipen. 2012. "Respiratory health effects of air pollution: update on biomass smoke and traffic pollution." *Clinical Reviews in Allergy and Immunology* 129: 3–11.

Lee, Hyung-Sook, Mardelle Shepley, and Chang-Shan Huang. 2009. "Evaluation of off-leash dog parks in Texas and Florida: A study of use patterns, user satisfaction, and perception." *Landscape and Urban Planning* 92, 3: 314–324.

Levine, Jonathan, Joe Grengs, Qingyun Shen, and Qing Shen. 2012. "Does accessibility require density or speed? a comparison of fast versus close in getting where you want to go in U.S. metropolitan regions." *Journal of the American Planning Association* 78, 2: 157–172.

Leyden, Kevin M., Abraham Goldberg, and Philip Michelbach. 2011. "Understanding the pursuit of happiness in ten major cities." *Urban Affairs Review* 47, 6: 861–888.

Li, Yue, Jennifer Anna Hsu, and Geoff Fernie. 2012. "Aging and the use of pedestrian facilities in winter—the need for improved design and better technology." *Journal of Urban Health: Bulletin of the New York Academy of Medicine* 90, 4: 602–617.

Lindholm, Maria. 2010. "A sustainable perspective on urban freight transport: factors affecting local authorities in the planning procedures." *Procedia-Social and Behavioral Sciences* 2, 3: 6205–6216.

Litman, Todd. 2014. *Evaluating Complete Streets: The Value of Designing Roads for Diverse Modes, Users and Activities*. Victoria, B.C.: Victoria Transport Policy Institute. www.vtpi.org/compstr.pdf.

Litman, Todd, and Steven Fitzroy. 2015. *Safe Travels: Evaluating Mobility Management Traffic Safety Impacts*. Victoria, B.C.: Victoria Transport Policy Institute. www.vtpi.org/safetrav.pdf.

Lofors, Jonas, and Kristina Sundquist. 2007. "Low-linking social capital as a predictor of mental disorders: a cohort study of 4.5 million Swedes." *Social Science & Medicine* 64:21–34.

Lohr, Virginia I., Caroline H. Pearson-Mims, and Georgia K. Goodwin. 1996. "Interior plants may improve worker productivity and reduce stress in a windowless environment." *Journal of Environmental Horticulture* 14, 97–100.

Lorenc, Theo, Stephen Clayton, David Neary, Margaret Whitehead, Mark Petticrew, Hilary Thomson, Steven Cummins, Amanda Sowden, and Adrisan Renton. 2012. "Crime, fear of crime, environment, and mental health and wellbeing: mapping review of theories and causal pathways." *Health & Place* 18, 4: 757–765.

Lovasi, Gina S., Malo A. Hutson, Monica Guerra, and Kathryn M. Neckerman. 2009. "Built environments and obesity in disadvantaged populations." *Epidemiologic Reviews* 31: 7–20.

Lovegrove, Gordon R., and Tarek Sayed. 2006a. "Macro-level collision prediction models for evaluating neighbourhood traffic safety." *Canadian Journal of Civil Engineering* 33, 5:609–621.

Lovegrove, Gordon R., and Tarek Sayed. 2006b. "Using macro-level collision prediction models in road safety planning applications." *Transportation Research Record* 1950: 73–82.

Lubell, Jeffery, Rebecca Morley, M. Ashe, and L. Merola. 2010. *Housing and Health: New Opportunities for Dialogue and Action.* Columbia, Md.: National Center for Healthy Housing. www.changelabsolutions.org/sites/default/files/Health%20%20Housing%20New%20Opportunities_final.pdf.

Lubell, Jeffery. 2014. "Filling the Void between Homeownership and Rental Housing: A Case for Expanding the Use of Shared Equity Homeownership." In *Homeownership Built to Last*, ed. Eric Belsky, Christopher Hebert, and Jennifer Molinsky, 203–230. Washington, D.C.: Brookings Institution Press.

Luppa, Melanie, Tobias Luck, Siegfried Weyerer, Hans-Helmut König, Elmar Brähler, and Steffi G. Riedel-Heller. 2009. "Prediction of institutionalization in the elderly: a systematic review." *Age and Ageing*: afp202. Online resource. doi:10.1186/1479-5868-4-49.

Lynch, Kevin. 1981. *Good City Form.* Cambridge, Mass.: MIT Press.

Lynott, Jana, Jessica Haase, Kristin Nelson, Amanda Taylor, Hannah Twaddell, Jared Ulmer, Barbara McCann, and Edward R. Stollof. 2009. *Planning Complete Streets for an Aging America.* Washington, D.C.: AARP Public Policy Institute. http://assets.aarp.org/rgcenter/ppi/liv-com/2009-12-streets.pdf.

Lytle, Leslie A. 2009. "Measuring the food environment: state of the science." *American Journal of Preventive Medicine* 36, 4S:S134–S144.

Mace, Ron. 1985. "Universal design, barrier-free environments for everyone." *Designers West* 33, 1: 147–152.

Maisel, Jordana. 2010. *Design Resources: DR-05 Levels in Inclusive Housing.* Buffalo, N.Y.: University of Buffalo, Center for Inclusive Design and Environmental Access. www.udeworld.com/documents/designresources/pdfs/LevelsofInclusiveHousing.pdf.

Maller, Cecily, Mardie Townsend, Anita Pryor, Peter Brown, and Lawrence St. Leger. 2005. "Healthy nature healthy people: contact with nature as an upstream health promotion intervention for populations." *Health Promotion International* 21, 1: 45–54.

Maller, Cecily, Mardie Townsend, Lawrence St. Leger, Claire Henderson-Wilson, Anita Pryor, Lauren Prosser, and Megan Moore. 2009. "Healthy parks, healthy people: the health benefits of contact with nature in a park context." *The George Wright Forum* 26,2: 51–83. http://search.proquest.com.ezp-prod1.hul.harvard.edu/docview/198432908?accountid=11311

Mang, Hong Anh. 2013. "Stakeholders' perceptions on the design and feasibility of the fused grid street network pattern." MLA thesis, University of Texas, Arlington.

Mansfield, Theodore, Daniel Rodriguez, Joseph Huegy, and Jacqueline Gobson. 2015. "The effects of urban form on ambient air pollution and public health risk: a case study in Raleigh, North Carolina." *Risk Analysis* 35, 5: 901–918.

Marquardt, Gesine. 2011. "Wayfinding for people with dementia: a review of the role of architectural design." *HERD: Health Environments Research & Design Journal* 4, 2: 75–90.

Marshall, Stephen. 2005. *Streets & Patterns: The Structure of Urban Geometry.* New York: Spon Press.

Marshall, Wesley Earl, and Norman W. Garrick. 2011. "Does street network design affect traffic safety?" *Accident Analysis & Prevention* 43, 3: 769–781.

Martens, Karel. 2004. "The bicycle as a feedering mode: experiences from three European countries." *Transportation Research Part D: Transport and Environment* 9, 4: 281–294.

Maslow, Carey B., Stephen M. Friedman, Parul S. Pillai, Joan Reibman, Kenneth I. Berger, Roberta Goldring, Steven D. Stellman, and Mark Farfel. 2012. "Chronic and acute exposures to the world trade center disaster and lower respiratory symptoms: area residents and workers." *American Journal of Public Health* 102, 6: 1186–1194.

Massachusetts Institute of Technology. 2011. *The Density Atlas.* Online resource. http://densityatlas.org/casestudies.

Mattiello, Amalia, Paolo Chiodini, Elvira Bianco, Nunzia Forgione, Incoronata Flammia, Ciro Gallo, Renato Pizzuti, and Salvatore Panico. 2013. "Health effects associated with the disposal of solid waste in landfills and incinerators in populations living in surrounding areas: a systematic review." *International Journal of Public Health* 58, 5: 725–735.

McCormack, Gavin R., and Alan Shiell. 2011. "In search of causality: a systematic review of the relationship between the built environment and physical activity among adults." *International Journal of Behavioral Nutrition and Physical Activity* 8: 125. Online resource. doi:10.1186/1479-5868-8-125.

McGrath, Leslie J., Will G. Hopkins, and Erica A. Hinckson. 2015. "Associations of objectively measured built-environment attributes with youth moderate-vigorous physical activity: a systematic review and meta-analysis." *Sports Medicine* 45,6: 841–865.

McLaughlin, P.D., B. Jones, and M.M. Maher. 2012. "An update on radioactive release and exposures after the Fukushima Dai-ichi nuclear disaster." *The British Journal of Radiology* 85: 1222–1225.

Michigan Department of Community Health. 2014. *Certificate of Need Review Standards for Hospital Beds.* www.michigan.gov/documents/mdch/HB_Standards_399445_7.pdf.

Miller, Wilhelmine D., Craig E. Pollack, and David R. Williams. 2011. "Healthy homes and communities: putting the pieces together." *American Journal of Preventive Medicine* 40, 1: S48–S57

Mills, G., H. Cleugh, R. Emmanuel, W. Endlicher, E. Erell, G. McGranahan, E. Ng, A. Nickson, J. Rosenthal, and K. Steemer. 2010. "Climate information for improved planning and management of mega cities (needs perspective)." *Procedia Environmental Sciences* 1: 228–246.

Mindell, J., J.P. Biddulph, A. Boaz, A. Boltong, S. Curtis, M. Joffe, K. Lock, and L. Taylor. 2006. *A Guide to Reviewing Evidence for use in Health Impact Assessment.* London: London Health Observatory. www.lho.org.uk/ Download/Public/10846/1/Reviewing%20EvidenceFinal%20v6.4_230806.pdf.

Monsere, Christopher M., Nick Foster, Jennifer Dill, and Nathan McNeil. 2014. *User Behavior and Perceptions at Intersections with Turning and Mixing Zones on Protected Bike Lanes.* Paper submitted for presentation at the Transportation Research Board 94th Annual Meeting, Washington, D.C., November 11–15, 2015. http://docs.trb.org/prp/15-1178.pdf.

Mooney, Patrick, and P. Lenore Nicell. 1992. "The importance of exterior environment for Alzheimer residents: effective care and risk management." *Health care Management Forum* 5, 2: 23–29.

Moran, Mika, Jelle Van Cauwenberg, Rachel Hercky-Linnewiel, Ester Cerin, Benedicte Deforche, and Pnina Plaut. 2014. "Understanding the relationships between the physical environment and physical activity in older adults: a systematic review of qualitative studies." *International Journal of Behavioral Nutrition and Physical Activity* 11. Online resource. doi: 10.1186/1479-5868-11-79.

Morrall, John, and Dan Bolger. 1996. "The relationship between downtown parking supply and transit use." *Ite Journal-Institute of Transportation Engineers* 66, 2: 32–36.

Morrison, David S., Mark Petticrew, and Hilary Thomson. 2003. "What are the most effective ways of improving population health through transport interventions? Evidence from systematic reviews." *Journal of Epidemiology and Community Health* 57, 5: 327–333.

Morrow-Jones, Hazel, and Mary Wenning. 2005. "The housing ladder, the housing life-cycle, and the housing life-course: upward and downward movement among repeat home-buyers in a U.S. metropolitan housing market." *Urban Studies* 42, 10: 1739–1754.

Moudon, Anne Vernez. 2009. "Real noise from the urban environment: how ambient community noise affects health and what can be done about it." *American Journal of Preventative Medicine* 39, 2: 167–171.

Mukhija, Vinit, and Donald Shoup. 2006. "Quantity versus quality in off-street parking requirements." *Journal of the American Planning Association* 72, 3: 296–308.

Murayama, Hiroshi, Yoshinori Fujiwara, and Ichiro Kawachi. 2012. "Social capital and health: a review of prospective multilevel studies." *Journal of Epidemiology* 22, 3: 179–187.

Murphy, Enda, and Eoin King. 2015. *Environmental Noise Pollution: Noise Mapping, Public Health, and Policy.* Burlington, Mass.: Elsevier.

Nasar, Jack L., and Jennifer Evans-Cowley, eds. 2007. *Universal Design and Visitability: From Accessibility to Zoning.* Columbus, Ohio: National Endowment for the Arts and John Glenn School of Public Affairs.

National Center for Healthy Housing and the American Public Health Association. 2014. *National Healthy Housing Standard.* Columbia, Md.: National Center for Healthy Housing. www.nchh.org/Portals/0/Contents/NHHS_Full_Doc.pdf.

National Consortium for the Study of Terrorism and Responses to Terrorism (START). 2012. *Global Terrorism Database.* Online resource. www.start.umd.edu/gtd.

National Geographic. 2015. *Style Manual.* Online resource. http://stylemanual.ngs.org.

Neuman, Michael. 2005. "The compact city fallacy." *Journal of Planning Education and Research* 25: 11–26.

Norris, Fran H., Matthew J. Friedman, Patricia J. Watson, Christopher M. Byrne, Eolia Diaz, and Krzysztof Kaniasty. 2002. "60,000 disaster victims speak: part I. An empirical review of the empirical literature, 1981–2001." *Psychiatry* 65, 3: 207–239.

NSW Health. 2009. *Healthy Urban Development Checklist.* Sydney, Australia: NSW Department of Health. www.health.nsw.gov.au/urbanhealth/Publications/healthy-urban-dev-check.pdf.

OECD. 2011. *How's Life? Measuring Well-being*. Paris: OECD Publishing. Online resource. http://dx.doi. org/10.1787/9789264121164-en.

Oka, Masayoshi. 2011. "Toward designing and environment to promote physical activity." *Landscape Journal* 30: 2–11.

Olszewski, Piotr, and Sony Wibowo. 2005. "Using equivalent walking distance to assess pedestrian accessibility to transit stations in Singapore." *Transportation Research Record* 1927: 38–45.

Orians, Carlyn, Shyanika Rose, Brian Hubbard, John Sarisky, Letitia Reason, Tiffiny Bernichon, Edward Liebow, Bradley Skarpness, and Sharunda Buchanan. 2009. "Strengthening the Capacity of Local Health Agencies through Community-Based Assessment and Planning." *Public Health Reports* 124: 875-882.

Orians, Gordon H. 1986. "An ecological and evolutionary approach to landscape aesthetics." In *Meanings and Values in Landscape,* ed. E.C. Penning-Rowsell and D. Lwenthal, 3–25. London: Allen and Unwin.

Orians, Gordon H., and Judith H. Heerwagen. 1992. "Evolved responses to landscapes." In *The Adapted Mind,* ed. J. Barkow, J. Toobey, and L. Cosmides, 555–579. New York: Oxford University Press.

Orsega-Smith, Elizabeth, Andrew J. Mowen, Laura L. Payne, and Geoffrey Godbey. 2004. "The interaction of stress and park use on psycho-physiological health in older adults." Journal of Leisure Research 36, 2: 232–257.

Owen, Neville, Nancy Humpel, Eva Leslie, Adrian Bauman, and James F. Sallis. 2004. "Understanding environmental influences on walking: review and research agenda." *American Journal of Preventive Medicine* 27, 1: 67–76.

Oxford English Dictionary. 2015. www.oed.com.

Park, Bum-Jin, Yuko Tsunetsugu, Hideki Ishii, Suguru Furuhashi, Hideki Hirano, Takahide Kagawa, and Yoshifumi Miyazaki. 2008. "Physiological effects of Shinrin-yoku (taking in the atmosphere of the forest) in a mixed forest in Shinano Town, Japan." *Scandinavian Journal of Forest Research* 23: 278–283.

Park, Chris. 2012. *A Dictionary of Environment and Conservation*. 1st ed. Online resource. Oxford University Press. DOI: 10.1093/acref/9780198609957.001.0001.

Park, Sohyun, Bettylou Sherry, Holly Wethington, and Liping Pan. 2012. "Use of parks or playgrounds: reported access to drinking water fountains among U.S. adults, 2009." *Journal of Public Health* 34, 1: 65–72.

Parkinson, Jonathan, Martin Mulenga, and Gordon McGranahan. 2010. "Provision of Water and Sanitation Services." In *Urban Health: Global Perspectives*, ed. Vlahov, David, Jo Ivey Boufford, Clarence Pearson, and Laurie Norris, 267–282. San Francisco: Wiley.

Participation Compass. 2016. Website. http://participationcompass.org.

Pascal, Mathilde, Laurence Pascal, Marie-Laure Bidono, Amandine Cochet, Hélène Sarter, Morgane Stempfelet, and Vérène Wagner. 2013. "A review of the epidemiological methods used to investigate the health impacts of air pollution around major industrial areas." *Journal of Environmental and Public Health* 2013:1–17. Online resource. http://dx.doi. org/10.1155/2013/737926.

Passini, Romedi. 1996. "Wayfinding design: logic, application and some thoughts on universality." *Design Studies* 17: 319–331.

Pawson, Ray. 2003. "*Assessing the Quality of Evidence in Evidence-Based Policy: Why, How and When.*" *Working Paper No. 1.* ESRC Research Methods Programme. Manchester, U.K.: University of Manchester. www. ccsr.ac.uk/methods.

Peacock, J., R. Hine, and J. Pretty. 2007. *Ecotherapy: The Green Agenda for Mental Health*. London: Mind.

Pearlman, Kenneth, and Nancy Waite. 1984. "Controlling land use and population growth near nuclear power plants." *Washington University Journal of Urban and Contemporary Law*. 27: 9–69.

Pelling, Mark. 2003. *The Vulnerability of Cities. Natural Disaster and Social Resilience*. London: Earthscan.

Perez-Padilla, R., A. Schilmann, and H. Riojas-Rodriguez. 2010. "Respiratory health effects of indoor air pollution." *The International Journal of Tuberculosis and Lung Disease* 14, 9: 1079–1086.

Perry, Clarence. 1929. "The neighborhood unit, a scheme of arrangement for the family-life community." In *Neighborhood and Community Planning Regional Survey, Volume VII*. New York: Regional Plan of New York and its Environs.

Perry, Clarence. 1939. *Housing for the Machine Age*. New York: Russell Sage Foundation.

Politechnico di Milano, DiAP, IAU île-de-France & Regione Emilia Romagna. 2007. *Planning Urban Design and Management for Crime Prevention Handbook. AGIS- Action SAFEPOLIS*. Brussels: European Commission Directorate-General Justice, Freedom and Security. www.veilig-ontwerp-beheer. nl/publicaties/handbook-planning-urban-de-

sign-and-management-for-crime-prevention/
at_download/file.

Porta, Daniela, Simona Milani, Antonio Lazzarino, Carlo Perucci, and Francesco Forastiere. 2009. "Systematic review of epidemiological studies on health effects associated with management of solid waste." *Environmental Health* 8, 1: 60.

Postel, Sandra. 1997. *Last oasis: facing water scarcity*. New York: WW Norton.

Powrie, William, and Paul Dacombe. 2006. "Sustainable waste management—what and how?" *Proceedings of the ICE-Waste and Resource Management* 159, 3: 101–116.

Preiser, Wolfgang F. E. and Korydon H. Smith, eds. 2011. *Universal Design Handbook*. 2nd ed. New York: McGraw Hill.

Prüss-Üstün, Annette, Carolyn Vickers, Pascal Haefliger, and Roberto Bertollini. 2011. "Knowns and unknowns on burden of disease due to chemicals: A systematic review." *Environmental Health* 10, 9. Online resource. doi:10.1186/1476-069X-10-9.

Pucher, John, and Ralph Buehler. 2008. "Making cycling irresistible: lessons from the Netherlands, Denmark, and Germany." *Transport Reviews*, 28: 495–528.

Pucher, John, Jennifer Dill, and Susan Handy. 2010. "Infrastructure, programs, and policies to increase bicycling: an international review." *Preventive Medicine* 50: S106–25.

Pushkarev, Boris, and Jeffrey M. Zupan. 1977. *Public Transportation and Land Use Policy*. Bloomington: Indiana University Press. documents/evaluating-complete-streets-projects.pdf.

Ramsey, Charles George, Sleeper, Harold Reeve, Hoke, John Ray, and American Institute of Architects. 2000. *Ramsey/Sleeper Architectural Graphic Standards*. 10th ed. New York: John Wiley & Sons.

Rappe, Erja. 2005. *T"he Influence of a Green Environment and Horticultural Activities on the Subjective Well-Being of the Elderly Living in Long-Term Care."* PhD dissertation, University of Helsinki. www.thl.fi/attachments/arkkinen/Rappe_vaitoskirja.pdf.

Rees, Vaughan W., Robyn R. Keske, Kevin Blaine, David Aronstein, Ediss Gandelman, Vilma Lora, Clara Savage, and Alan C. Geller. 2014. "Factors influencing adoption of and adherence to indoor smoking bans among health disparity communities." *American Journal of Public Health*104, 10: 1928–34.

Regional Plan Association. 1976. *Where Transit Works: Urban Densities for Public Transportation*. New York: Regional Plan Association.

Reid, Colleen E., Marie S. O'Neill, Carina J. Gronlund, Shannon J. Brines, Daniel G. Brown, Ana V. Diez-Roux, and Joel Schwartz. 2009. "Mapping community determinates of heat vulnerability." *Environmental Health Perspectives* 117, 11: 1730–1736.

Reiter, Matthew S., and Kara M. Kockelman. 2015. "The Problem of Cold Starts: A Closer Look at Mobile Source Emissions Levels." In *Proceedings of the Annual Meeting of the TRB (January*, vol. 19, p. 20. www.caee.utexas.edu/prof/kockelman/public_html/TRB15coldstarts.pdf.

Resnick, Barbara, Lisa P. Gwyther, and Karen A. Roberto. 2011. *Resilience in Aging: Concepts, Research, and Outcomes*. New York, NY: Springer.

Reynolds, C., Anne Harris, Kay Teschke, Peter A. Cripton, and Meghan Winters. 2009. "The impact of transportation infrastructure on bicycling injuries and crashes: a review of the literature." *Environmental Health* 8. Online resource. doi:10.1186/1476-069X-8-47.

Rimmer, James H., Barth Riley, Edward Wang, Amy Rauworth, and Janine Jurkowski. 2004. "Physical activity participation among persons with disabilities: barriers and facilitators." *American Journal of Preventive Medicine* 26: 419–425.

Roby, Helen. 2014. *A Supplementary Dictionary of Transport Studies*. Online resource. Oxford University Press. Online resource. doi: 10.1093/acref/9780191765094.001.0001.

Rocco, Lorenzo, and Marc Suhrcke. 2012. *Is Social Capital Good for Health?: A European Perspective*. Copenhagen: WHO Regional Office for Europe.

Rodrigue, Jean-Paul, Claude Comtois, and Brian Slack. 2006. *The Geography of Transport Systems*. London: Routledge.

Romero-Lankao, Patricia, Hua Qin, and Katie Dickinson. 2012. "Urban vulnerability to temperature-related hazards: a meta-analysis and meta-knowledge approach." *Global Environmental Change* 22: 670–683.

Rosen, Erik, and Ulrich Sander. 2009. "Pedestrian fatality risk as a function of car impact speed." *Accident Analysis and Prevention* 41: 536–542.

Rosenthal, Joyce Klein, Patrick L. Kinney, and Kristina B. Metzger. 2014. "Intra-urban vulnerability to heat-related mortality in New York City, 1997–2006." *Health & Place* 30: 45–60.

Rosenzweig, Roy, and Elizabeth Blackmar. 1992. *The Park and the People*. Ithaca, N.Y.: Cornell University Press.

Rosso, Andrea L., Amy H. Auchincloss, and Yvonne L. Michael. 2011. "The urban built environment and mobility in older adults: a comprehensive review." *Journal of Aging Research* 1: 1–10.

Rowe, Peter, Ann Forsyth, and Har Ye Kan. 2016. *China's Urban Communities: Concepts, Contexts, and Well-being.* Berlin: Birkhauser.

Rowe, John W., and Robert L. Kahn. 1997. "Human aging: usual and successful." *Science* 237, 4811: 143–149.

Rowe, John, and Robert Kahn. 1987. "uman aging: usual and successful." *Science* 237,4811: 143–149.

Sacramento Transportation & Air Quality Collaborative (STAQC). 2005. *Best Practices for Universal Design.* Sacramento, Calif.: Sacramento Transportation & Air Quality Collaborative. www.sacta.org/pdf/STAQC/FinalReportII_BPUniversalDesign.pdf.

Saelens, Brian E., and Susan L. Handy. 2008. "Built environment correlates of walking: a review." *Medicine and Science in Sports and Exercise* 40, 7 Supp: S550–66.

Sallis, James F., and Karen Glanz. 2006. "The role of built environments in physical activity, eating, and obesity in childhood." *The Future of Children* 16, 1: 89–108.

Sallis, James F., Heather R. Bowles, Adrian Bauman, Barbara E. Ainsworth, Fiona C. Bull, Cora L. Craig, Michael Sjöström, I. De Bourdeaudhuij, J. Lefevre, V. Matsudo, S. Matsudo, D. Macfarlane, L. Gomez, S. Inoue, N. Murase, V. Volbekiene, G. Mclean, H. Carr, L. Heggebo, H. Tomten, and P. Bergman. 2009. "Neighborhood environments and physical activity among adults in 11 countries." *American Journal of Preventive Medicine* 36, 6: 484–490.

Samet, Jonathan M. 2010. "Urban Air Quality." In *Urban Health: Global Perspectives*, ed. David Vlahov, Jo Ivey Boufford, Clarence Pearson, and Laurie Norris. San Francisco: Wiley.

Sampson, Robert J., Stephen Raudenbush, and Felton Earls. 1997. "Neighborhoods and Violent Crime: A Multilevel Study of Collective Efficacy." *Science* 277: 918–924.

Sampson, Robert J., and Stephen W. Raudenbush. 2001. *Disorder in Urban Neighborhoods: Does it Lead to Crime?* Washington, D.C.: U.S. Department of Justice, Office of Justice Programs, National Institute of Justice. www.scholar.harvard.edu/files/sampson/files/2001_nij_raudenbush.pdf.

Saraiva, Miguel, and Paulo Pinho. 2011. "A comprehensive and accessible approach to crime prevention in the planning and design of public spaces." *Urban Design International* 16, 3: 213–226.

Schill, Michael H. 2005. "Regulations and housing development: what we know." *Cityscape* 8: 5–19.

Schneider, Richard H. and Ted Kitchen. 2007. *Crime Prevention in the Built Environment.* London: Routledge.

Scholes, Lian, D. Michael Revitt, and J. Bryan Ellis. 2008. "A systematic approach for the comparative assessment of stormwater pollutant removal potentials." *Journal of Environmental Management* 88, 3: 467–478.

Schueler, Thomas R. 2000. "Comparative pollutant removal capability of stormwater treatment practices." In *The Practice of Watershed Protection,* ed. T.R. Schueler and H.K. Holland. Elliot City, Md.: Center for Watershed Protection.

Schwab, James. 2011. *Hazard Mitigation: Integrating Best Practices into Planning.* Paper presented at Disaster Resilient Communities: A State-Level Executive Program in Resilience and Risk Management, University of New Orleans, June 24, 2011. http://scholarworks.uedu/ebr2011/1.

Schwarzenbach, Rene P., Thomas Egli, Thomas B. Hofstetter, Urs von Gunten, and Bernhard Wehrli. 2010. "Global water pollution and human health." *Annual Review of Environment and Resources* 35: 109–136.

Schweitzer, Lisa, and Zhou J. 2010. "Neighborhood air quality, respiratory health, and vulnerable populations in compact and sprawled regions." *Journal of the American Planning Association* 76: 363–371.

Scott, John. 2014. *A Dictionary of Sociology.* 4th ed. Oxford University Press. Online resource. doi: 10.1093/acref/9780199683581.001.0001.

Scott-Samuel, A., M. Birley, and K. Ardern. 2001. *The Merseyside Guidelines for Health Impact Assessment.* 2nd ed. Liverpool: International Health Impact Assessment Consortium.

Seadon, Jeffrey K. 2010. "Sustainable waste management systems." *Journal of Cleaner Production* 18, 16: 1639–1651.

Seadon, Jeffrey. 2006. "Integrated waste management–looking beyond the solid waste horizon." *Waste Management* 26, 12: 1327–1336.

Sepúlveda, Alejandra, Mathias Schluep, Fabrice G. Renaud, Martin Streicher, Ruediger Kuehr, Christian Hagelüken, and Andreas C. Gerecke. 2010. "A review of the environmental fate and effects of hazardous substances released from electrical and electronic equipments during recycling: examples from China and India." *Environmental Impact Assessment Review*k

Sharp, Joanne, Venda Pollock, and Ronan Paddison. 2005. "Just art for a just city: public art and social inclusion in urban regeneration." *Urban Studies* 42, 5–6: 1001–1023.

Shea, Katherine M., and the Committee on Environmental Health. 2007. "Global climate change and children's health." *Pediatrics* 120: e1359–e1367.

Shibata, Seiji, and Naoto Suzuki. 2002. "Effects of the foliage plant on task performance and mood." Journal of *Environmental Psychology* 22, 3: 265–272.

Shoup, Donald. 2005. *Parking Cash Out (PAS 532).* Chicago: American Planning Association.

Sirven, Nicolas, and Thierry Debrand. 2012. "Social capital and health of older Europeans: causal pathways and health inequalities." *Social Science & Medicine* 75, 7: 1288–1295.

Skiba, Isabella, and Rahel Zuger. 2009. *Barrier-Free Planning.* Basel, Switzerland: Birkhauser.

Slotterback, Carissa, Ann Forsyth, Kevin Krizek, Amanda Johnson, and Ali Pennucci. 2011. "Testing three health impact assessment tools in planning: a process evaluation." *Environmental Impact Assessment Review* 31: 144–153.

Sobal, Jeffery, and Brian Wansink. 2007. "Kitchenscapes, tablescapes, platescapes, and foodscapes: influences of microscale built environments on food intake." *Environment and Behavior* 39: 124–142.

Sovocool, Kent A., Mitchell Morgan, and Doug Bennett. 2006. "An in-depth investigation of Xeriscape as a water conservation measure." *Journal of the American Water Works Association* 98,2: 82–93.

Stanke, Carla, Virginia Murray, Richard Amlot, Jo Nurse, and Richard Williams. 2012. "The effects of flooding on mental health: outcomes and recommendations from a review of the literature." *PLoS Currents* 4. Online resource. doi: 10.1371/4f9f1fa9c3cae.

Stansfeld, Stephen, and Rosanna Crombie. 2011. "Cardio-vascular effects of environmental noise: research in the United Kingdom." *Noise and Health* 13, 52: 229–233.

Stone, Brian, Jeremy J. Hess, and Howard Frumkin. 2010. "Urban form and extreme heat events: are sprawling cities more vulnerable to climate change than compact cities?" *Environmental Health Perspectives* 118, 10: 1425–1428.

Story, Mary, Karen M. Kaphingst, Ramona Robinson O'Brien, and Karen Glanz. 2008. "Creating Healthy Food and Eating Environments: Policy and Environmental Approaches." *Annual Review of Public Health* 29: 253–72.

Subramanian, S. V., Kimberly A. Lochner, and Ichiro Kawachi. 2003. "Neighborhood differences in social capital: a compositional artifact or a contextual construct?" *Health & Place* 9,1: 33–44.

Sugiyama, Takemi, Maike Neuhaus, Rachel Cole, Billie Giles-Corti, and Neville Owen. 2012. "Destination and route attributes associated with adults' walking: a review." *Medicine & Science in Sports & Exercise* 44, 7: 1275–86.

Sun, James, and Gord Lovegrove. 2013. "Comparing the road safety of neighbourhood development patterns: traditional versus sustainable communities." *Canadian Journal of Civil Engineering* 40, 1: 35–45.

Suzuki, Hiroaki, Robert Cervero, and Kanako Iuchi. 2013. *Transforming Cities with Transit: Transit and Land Use Integration for Sustainable Urban Development.* Washington D.C.: World Bank.

Swinburn, Boyd, Gary Sacks, Kevin Hall, Klim McPherson, Diane Finegood, Marjory Moodie, and Steven Gortmaker. 2011. "The global obesity pandemic: shaped by global drivers and local environments." *Lancet* 378: 804–814.

Sykes, Andrew, Livingstone James, and Maurice Green.1967. *Cumbernauld 67: A Household Survey and Report. Occasional Paper Number 1.* Glasgow, Scotland: University of Strathclyde, Department of Sociology.

Taylor, Andrea Faber, Frances E. Kuo, and William C. Sullivan. 2001. "Coping with ADD: the surprising connection to green play settings." Environment and Behavior 33, 1: 54–77.

Taylor, Andrea Faber, and Frances E. Kuo. 2009. "Children with attention deficits concentrate better after walk in the park." Journal of Attention Disorders 12, 5: 402–09.

Taylor, B. D., and C. N. Y. Fink. 2013. "Explaining transit ridership: What has the evidence shown?" *Transportation Letters* 5, 1: 15–26.

Tchobanoglous, George, Franklin L. Burton, and H. David Stensel. 2002. *Wastewater Engineering: Treatment and Reuse.* New York: McGraw-Hill Science.

Tennessen, C.M., and B. Cimprich. 1995. "Views to nature: effects on attention." Journal of Environmental Psychology 15, 1: 77–85.

The Center for Universal Design. 1997. *The Principles of Universal Design.* Version 2.0. Raleigh: North Carolina State University.

Thompson, Hilary, and Sian Thomas. 2015. "Developing empirically supported theories of change for housing investment and health." *Social Science & Medicine* 124: 205–214.

Timperio, Anna, David Crawford, Amanda Telford, and Jo Salmon. 2004. "Perceptions about the local neighborhood and walking and cycling among children." *Preventive Medicine* 38, 1:39–47.

Timperio, Anna, Kylie Ball, Jo Salmon, Rebecca Roberts, Billie Giles-Corti, Dianne Simmons, Louise A. Baur, and David Crawford. 2006. "Personal, family, social, and environmental correlates of active commuting to school." *American Journal of Preventive Medicine* 30, 1: 45–51.

Transit Cooperative Research Program (TCRP). 1995. "An Evaluation of the Relationships Between Transit and Urban Form." *Research Results Digest 7.*Online resource. http://onlinepubs.trb.org/Onlinepubs/tcrp/tcrp_rrd_07.pdf.

Transit Cooperative Research Program (TCRP). 1998. "Continuing examination of successful transit ridership initiatives." *Research Results Digest*, 29. http://onlinepubs.trb.org/Onlinepubs/tcrp/tcrp_rrd_29.pdf.

Trost, Stewart G., Neville Owen, Adrian E. Bauman, James F. Sallis, and Wendy Brown. 2002. "Correlates of adults' participation in physical activity: review and update." *Medicine & Science in Sports & Exercise* 34,12: 1996–2001.

Tsai, Alexander C. 2015. "Home foreclosure, health, and mental health: a systematic review of individual, aggregate, and contextual associations." *PLoS One* 10,4: e0123182. Online resource. doi: 10.1371/journal.pone.0123182.

Tsunetsugu, Y., Y. Miyazaki, and H. Sato. 2005. "Visual effects of interior design in actual-size living rooms on physiological responses." *Building and Environment* 40,10: 1341–1346.

Tsunetsugu, Yuko, Yoshifumi Miyazaki, and Hiroshi Sato. 2007. "Physiological effects in humans induced by the visual stimulation of room interiors with different wood quantities." *Journal of Wood Science* 53, 1: 11–16.

Tveit, M.S., A.O. Sang, and C.M. Hägerhall. 2007. "Scenic Beauty: Visual Landscape Assessment and Human Landscape Perception." In *Environmental Psychology: An Introduction,* ed. L. Steg, A. E. van den Berg, and J. I. De Groot, 37–46. Chicester, U.K.: Wiley.

UCL Institute of Healthy Equity. 2014. *Review of Social Determinants and the Health Divide in the WHO European Region: Final Report.* Updated Reprint. Denmark: WHO Regional Office for Europe.

Ulrich, R.S. 2002. *Health Benefits of Gardens in Hospitals.* Paper for conference, Plants for People, Proceedings of the International Exhibition Floriade, Haarlemmermeer, Netherlands.

Ulrich, Roger S. 1984. "View through a window may influence recovery from surgery." *Science* 224: 420–421.

Ulrich, Roger. 1999. "Effects of gardens on health outcomes: theory and research." In *Healing Gardens: Therapeutic Benefits and Design Recommendations* ed. Clare Cooper Marcus and Marni Barnes, 27–86. New York: Wiley.

United Kingdom Ministry of Transport. 1963. *Traffic in Towns.* London: HMSO.

United Nations (UN). 2004. *World Population to 2300.* New York: United Nations Population Division. www.un.org/en/development/desa/population/publications/pdf/trends/WorldPop2300final.pdf.

United Nations Scientific Committee on the Effects of Atomic Radiation (UNSCEAR). 2008. *Sources and Effects of Ionizing Radiation. Report to the General Assembly with Scientific Annexes.* Volume 1. New York: United Nations.

United Nations, Department of Economic and Social Affairs (UNDESA), Population Division. 2013. *World Population Prospects: The 2012 Revision.* New York: United Nations. http://esa.un.org/unpd/wpp/Publications/Files/WPP2012_Volume-II-Demographic-Profiles.pdf

United Nations, Department of Economic and Social Affairs (UNDESA), Population Division. 2014. *World Urbanization Prospects: The 2014 Revision, Highlights (ST/ESA/SER.A/352).* New York: United Nations. http://esa.un.org/unpd/wup/Highlights/WUP2014-Highlights.pdf.

United Nations, Department of Economic and Social Affairs (UNDESA), 2015. Population Division. 2015. *World Urbanization Prospects: The 2015 Revision, Highlights (ST/ESA/SER.A/352).* New York: United Nations. http://esa.un.org/unpd/wpp/Publications/Files/Key_Findings_WPP_2015.pdf.

United States Centers for Disease Control and Prevention (U.S. CDC). 2009. *Physical Inactivity and People with Disabilities.* Atlanta: CDC. www.cdc.gov/ncbddd/documents/physical-inactivity-tip-sheet-_phpa_1.pdf.

United States Centers for Disease Control and Prevention (U.S. CDC). 2013. *Well-being Concepts.* www.cdc.gov/hrqol/wellbeing.htm.

United States Centers for Disease Control and Prevention (U.S. CDC). 2015a. *Health in All Policies.* www.cdc.gov/policy/hiap.

United States Centers for Disease Control and Prevention (U.S. CDC). 2015b. Assessment and planning models, frameworks, and tools. www.cdc.gov/stltpublichealth/cha/assessment.html.

United States Census Bureau. 2015. International Data Base (IDB). Online Resource. www.census.gov/population/international/data/idb/informationGateway.php.

United States Department of Health and Human Services (U.S. HHS). 1993. *Guidelines for Primary Medical Care/Dental HPSA Designation.* (Codified 42 CFR Chapter 1, Part 5). Online resource. http://bhpr.hrsa.gov/shortage/hpsas/designationcriteria/medicaldentalhpsaguidelines.html.

United States Environmental Protection Agency (U.S. EPA). 2002. *Solid Waste Management: A Local Challenge with Global Impacts.* www.epa.gov/osw/nonhaz/municipal/pubs/ghg/f02026.pdf.

United States Environmental Protection Agency (U.S. EPA). 2013. *A Review of Health Impact Assessments in the U.S.: Current State-of-Science, Best Practices, and Areas for Improvement.* www2.epa.gov/sites/production/files/2015-03/documents/review-hia.pdf.

United States Nuclear Regulatory Commission (U.S. NRC). 2014. Regulation 100.11. *Determination of exclusion area, low population zone, and population center distance.* Online resource. www.nrc.gov/reading-rm/doc-collections/cfr/part100/ part100-0011.html.

University of Kansas. 2013. Section 4, Community Tool Box. *Ensuring Access for People with Disabilities.* Online resource. Work Group for Community Health and Development. http://ctb.ku.edu/en/table-of-contents/implement/phsical-social-environment/housing-accessibility-disabilities/main.

University of Kansas. 2015a. *Toolkit 2: Assessing Community Needs and Resources.* Box. Online resource. Work Group for Community Health and Development. http://ctb.ku.edu/en/assessing-community-needs-and-resources.

University of Kansas. 2015b. Toolkit 12: *Evaluating the Initiative.* In The Community Tool Box. Online resource. Work Group for Community Health and Development. http://ctb.ku.edu/en/evaluating-initiative.

Urban Land Institute (ULI). 2015. *Building Healthy Places Toolkit: Strategies for Enhancing Health in the Built Environment.* Washington, D.C.: Urban Land Institute.

Uscher-Pines, Lori. 2009. "Health effects of relocation following disaster: a systematic review of the literature." *Disasters* 33, 1: 1–22.

Van Cauwenberg, Jelle, Ilse De Bourdeaudhuij, Femke De Meester, Delfien Van Dyck, Jo Salmon, Peter Clarys, and Benedicte Deforche. 2011. "Relationship between the physical environment and physical activity in older adults: a systematic review." *Health & Place* 17, 2: 458–469.

Van den Berg, Agnes E., Terry Hartig, and Henk Staats. 2007. "Preference for Nature in urbanized societies: stress, restoration, and the pursuit of sustainability." *Journal of Social Issues* 63, 1: 79–96.

Van Holle, Veerle, Benedicte Deforche, Jelle Van Cauwenberg, Liesbet Goubert, Lea Maes, Nico Van de Weghe, and Ilse De Bourdeaudhuij. 2012. "Relationship between the physical environment and different domains of physical activity in European adults: a systematic review." *BMC Public Health* 12, 1: 807. Online resource. doi: 10.1186/1471-2458-12-807.

van Kamp, Irene, and Hugh Davies. 2013. "Noise and health in vulnerable groups: a review." *Noise & Health* 15, 64: 153–159.

van Kempen, Elise E.M.M., Hanneke Kruize, Hendriek C. Boshuizen, Caroline B. Ameling, Brigit A.M. Staatsen, and Augustinus E.M. de Hollander. 2002. "The association between noise exposure and blood pressure and ischemic heart disease: a meta -analysis." *Environmental Health Perspectives* 110, 3: 307–317.

van Stralen, Maartje M., Hein De Vries, Aart N. Mudde, Catherine Bolman, and Lilian Lechner. 2009. "Determinants of initiation and maintenance of physical activity among older adults: a literature review." *Health Psychology Reviews* 3, 2: 147–207.

Visser, Johan, Toshinori Nemoto, and Michael Browne. 2014. "Home delivery and the impacts on urban freight transport: a review." *Procedia-Social and Behavioral Sciences* 125: 15–27.

Vogt, W. Paul. 1993. *Dictionary of Statistics and Methodology.* Newbury Park, Calif.: Sage.

Vuchic, Vukan R. 2007. *Urban Transit Systems and Technology.* Hoboken, N.J.: John Wiley & Sons.

Wamsler, Christine. 2014. *Cities, Disaster Risk and Adaptation.* London: Routledge.

Wang, Xiaochang C. 2015. *Water Cycle Management: A New Paradigm of Wastewater Reuse and Safety Control.* Berlin: Springer.

Wanner, Miriam, Thomas Götschi, Eva Martin-Diener, Sonja Kahlmeier, and Brian W. Martin. 2012. "Active transport, physical activity, and body weight in adults: a systematic review." *American Journal of Preventive Medicine* 42, 5: 493–502.

Wei, Vicky Feng, and Gord Lovegrove. 2012. "Sustainable road safety: A new (?) neighbourhood road pattern that saves VRU lives."*Accident Analysis & Prevention* 44, 1: 140–148.

Wells, Nancy, and Kimberly Rollings. 2012. "The natural environment: Influences on human health and function." In *The Handbook on Environmental and Conservation Psychology*, ed. S. Clayton. New York: Oxford University Press.

Wells, Nancy M. 2000. "At home with nature: effects of greenness on children's cognitive functioning." *Environment and Behavior* 32, 6: 775–795.

Wells, Nancy M., Susan P. Ashdown, Elizabeth HS Davies, F. D. Cowett, and Yizhao Yang. 2007. "Environment, design, and obesity: opportunities for interdisciplinary collaborative research." *Environment and Behavior* 39, 1, 6–33.

Welsh, Brandon C. and David P. Farrington. 2008. "Effects of improved street lighting on crime." *Campbell Systematic Review*s 13:1–46. www.crim.cam.ac.uk/people/academic_research/david_farrington/light.pdf.

Wendel-Vos, W., M. Droomers, S. Kremers, J. Brug, and F. van Lenthe. 2007. "Potential environmental determinants of physical activity in adults: a systematic review." *Obesity Reviews* 8: 425–440.

Whiston-Spirn, Ann. 1986. *Air Quality at Street-Level: Strategies for Urban Design*. Prepared for Boston Redevelopment Authority. www.annewhistonspirn.com/pdf/Air-Quality_1986.pdf.

White, Daniel K., Alan M. Jette, David T. Felson, White, Daniel K., Alan M. Jette, David T. Felson, Michael P. LaValley, Cora E. Lewis, James C. Torner, Michael C. Nevitt, and Julie J. Keysor. 2010. "Are features of the neighborhood environment associated with disability in older adults?" *Disability and Rehabilitation* 32, 8: 639–645.

Williamson, Thad. 2010. *Sprawl, Justice, and Citizenship: The Civic Costs of the American Way of Life*. Oxford, U.K.: Oxford University Press.

Wilson, E.O. 1984. *Biophilia: The Human Bond with Other Species*. Cambridge, Mass.: Harvard University Press.

Wisetjindawat, Wisinee. 2010. "Review of good practices in urban freight transportation." In *Transport and Communications Bulletin for Asia and the Pacific,* ed.United Nations Economic and Social Commission for Asia and the Pacific (ESCAP), 44–60. Bangkok: United Nations ESCAP. www.nttfc.org/reports/intl/Sustainable%20Urban%20Freight%20Transport%20b80_fulltext.pdf#page=53.

Wisner, Ben, Piers Blaikie, Terry Cannon, and Ian Davis. 2004. *At Risk: Natural Hazards, People's Vulnerability and Disasters*. London: Routledge.

World Bank. 2015. *Overview: Social Capital*. Online resource http://go.worldbank.org/C0QTRW4QF0.

World Health Organization (WHO). 1999. *Community Noise Guidelines*. Geneva: World Health Organization.

World Health Organization. 2001. *Community Health Needs Assessment*. Copenhagen: World Health Organization. www.euro.who.int/__data/assets/pdf_file/0018/102249/E73494.pdf.

World Health Organization (WHO). 2006, orig 1946. *Constitution of the World Health Organization*. 45th ed. Online resource. www.who.int/governance/eb/who_constitution_en.pdf.

World Health Organization (WHO). 2007. *Global Age-Friendly Cities: A Guide*. Geneva: World Health Organization. www.who.int/ageing/publications/Global_age_friendly_cities_Guide_English.pdf.

World Health Organization. (WHO). 2008. *Speed Management: a Road Safety Manual for Decision-makers and Practitioners*. Geneva: Global Road Safety Partnership.

World Health Organization (WHO). 2011. *Burden of Disease from Environmental Noise*. Copenhagen: World Health Organisation. www.euro.who.int/__data/assets/pdf_file/0008/136466/e94888.pdf.

World Health Organization (WHO). 2012. *Burden of Disease from Household Air Pollution for 2012*. Geneva: World Health Organization. www.who.int/phe/health_topics/outdoorair/databases/HAP_BoD_results_March2014.pdf?ua=1.

World Health Organization (WHO). 2013a. *Disability and Health*. Fact sheet N°352. Geneva: World Health Organization. www.who.int/mediacentre/factsheets/fs352/e.

World Health Organization. (WHO). 2013b. *Global Status Report on Road Traffic Safety 2013: Supporting a Decade of Action*. Geneva: World Health Organization. www.who.int/violence_injury_prevention/road_safety_status/2013/e/.

World Health Organization. (WHO). 2014. *Ambient (Outdoor) Air quality and Health*. Fact sheet N°313.

Geneva: World Health Organization. www.who.int/
mediacentre/factsheets/fs311/e/.

World Health Organization (WHO). 2015a. *Road safety*.
Geneva: World Health Organization.www.who.int/
gho/road_safety/en.

World Health Organization (WHO). 2015b. *Health and
Environment Linkages Initiative - Priority Environment
and Health Risks*. Geneva: World Health Organization.
Online resource. www.who.int/heli/risks/en.

World Health Organization. 2016. *Social Determinants of
Health*. Geneva: World Health Organization. www.
who.int/social_determinants/en.

World Meteorological Organization. 2015. DRR Definitions. Online resource. //www.wmo.int/pages/prog/
drr/resourceDrrDefinitions_en.html.

Yang, Lin, Shannon Sahlqvist, Alison McMinn, Simon
J. Griffin, and David Ogilvie. 2010. "Interventions
to promote cycling: systematic review." *BMJ: British
Medical Journal* 341: 870.

Zavestoski, Stephen, and Julian Agyeman, eds.
2014. *Incomplete Streets: Processes, Practices, and
Possibilities*. New York: Routledge.

Zhang, Junfeng, Denise L. Mauzerall, Tong Zhu, Song
Liang, Majid Ezzati, and Justin V. Remais. 2010.
"Environmental health in China: progress towards
clean air and safe water." *The Lancet* 375, 9720:
1110–1119.

Zhou, Ying, and Jonathan I. Levy. 2007. "Factors influencing the spatial extent of mobile source air pollution
impacts: a meta-analysis." *BMC Public Health* 7:89.
Online resource. doi: 10.1186/1471-2458-7-89.

Zube, Erwin H., and David G. Pitt. 1981. "Cross-cul-
tural perception of scenic and heritage landscapes."
Landscape Planning 8: 69–81.

Index